50 TOPICS ON BRITISH SOCIETY AND CULTURE

英汉对照读本

英文看客
知性英语 · 精致阅读

英国原来是这样
——英国社会与文化50主题

Martin Boyle 著

鄞玲玲 译

外文出版社
FOREIGN LANGUAGES PRESS

图书在版编目（CIP）数据

英国原来是这样/（英）博伊尔（Boyle, M.）著；鄞玲玲译.
—北京：外文出版社，2009
ISBN 978－7－119－05600－5

Ⅰ. 英… Ⅱ.①博… ②鄞… Ⅲ.①英语-汉语-对照读物 ②英
国-概况 Ⅳ. H319.4：K

中国版本图书馆 CIP 数据核字（2008）第 214257 号

责任编辑　李　溲
装帧设计　奇文云海
印刷监制　冯　浩

英国原来是这样

作　　者　Martin Boyle（英国）
翻　　译　鄞玲玲
摄　　影　邵　东　王　欢
ⓒ 外文出版社
出版发行　外文出版社
地　　址　中国北京西城区百万庄大街24 号　　邮政编码　100037
网　　址　http://www.flp.com.cn
电　　话　（010）68995883/68995964（编辑室）
　　　　　（010）68320579/68996067（总编室）
　　　　　（010）68995844/68995852（发行部/门市邮购）
　　　　　（010）68327750/68996164（版权部）
制　　版　贵艺图文设计中心
印　　制　北京信彩瑞禾印刷厂
经　　销　新华书店／外文书店
开　　本　小 16 开　　　　　印　　张　15.125
装　　别　平　　　　　　　　字　　数　200 千
版　　次　2012 年第 1 版第 3 次印刷
书　　号　ISBN 978－7－119－05600－5
定　　价　29.00 元　　　　　上架建议：英语阅读　出国留学

What Is Culture?

什么是文化?

There is a BBC radio programme called *Desert Island Discs* in which famous people are interviewed and asked what books and music they would take if they had to live on a desert island; in addition to their choices they automatically receive the Collected Works of Shakespeare and the King James version of the Bible. Why is this? Because received wisdom says that these texts epitomise English culture in the form of literature, and that no educated person should be without them. Other nations and groups around the world have classical texts which perform the same function.

When we use the word culture, we may think of high culture like art, literature, music and so on. We might think of classical culture and tradition — the arts, language and literature, clothing, cuisine, society, history and religion of a group of people. We might think of the 5000 year history of China with its distinctive calligraphy, Confucian philosophy and Taoist temples, or the long classical culture of Europe with its Greek philosophy and Roman literature. People who use the word culture in this way tend to see culture and civilization as being linked, and some people being more civilized and cultured than others. They use phrases like, "she's a very cultured person," "he likes cultural things" or " those people have no culture." On the other hand, other people may talk about "street culture" or "popular culture". They might say that the novels of *Wang Shuo* or the rock music of *Tang Dynasty* represent a different kind of culture to Beijing Opera or the poetry of *Lu Xun*. When they do so, they are distinguishing them from "high culture" or "classical culture", but these things are all recognisably part of Chinese culture. However, these examples do not help us very much if we are looking for an overall definition of the word culture.

According to the Modern Dictionary of Sociology, culture is the accepted values, norms and artifacts of a particular group of people which distinguish them from another group of people.[1] The United Nations defines culture as the "set of distinctive spiritual, material, intellectual and emotional features of society or a social group and that it encompasses, in addition to art and literature, lifestyles, ways of living together, value systems, traditions and beliefs".[2] It is something which expresses our individual and group identity, places us within groups and in relation to other groups and helps us to interpret and explain the world. In Business Studies, culture is commonly defined as "the collective programming of the human mind that distinguishes the members of one human group from those of another."[3] Biologists grow cultures in dishes in the laboratory, and evolutionary biologist Richard Dawkins has coined the term *memes* (things imitated by the mind + genes), or "theoretical building blocks of cultural evolution which spread through humans within cultural groups."[4] A biological culture in this sense becomes a system of collectively held values. When a group of people are to exist together, they need a set of rules that helps everyone know what to do in various circumstances, from arguing with one another to dealing with outsiders. These rules help to spread shared meaning and help people make sense of what is happening and what is done.

When different groups which do not share the same culture come into contact, we get what are known as culture bumps. Perhaps one of the most famous Chinese – British culture bumps occurred when Lord Macartney led Britain's first diplomatic and trade mission to the Chinese Empire in 1793. He notoriously refused to *kow tow* to the emperor *Qianlong* and referred to a gift of jade as a "worthless lump of rock," while *Qianlong* referred to the British as "barbarians" in a strongly-worded letter to King George, and ordered the king to "tremblingly obey and show no negligence!"[5] More recently, we have seen culture clashes and misunderstandings over Western press reports about China; Westerners think that China is fascinating and exotic but some Chinese think that the West is trying to hold it down.

In the 1950s the poet, T. S. Eliot (who was actually American but desperately wanted to be English), said that culture included 'all the characteristic activities and interests of a people'. He said that for England this should include 'Derby Day, the Henley Regatta, Cowes, the twelfth of August, a cup final, the dog races, the pin table, the dart board, Wensleydale cheese, boiled cabbage cut into sections, beetroot in vinegar, nineteenth-century Gothic churches, and the music of Elgar.' In 2008, few British people would agree with Eliot's list. There are some unifying patriotic events like the last Night of the Proms, Armistice Day and the FA Cup final, but British culture in this sense is mostly media based these days, and those

1. Theodorson, G. , A Modern Dictionary of Sociology, Ty Crowell Co, 1969.

2. UNESCO, http://www. unesco. org/education/imld_ 2002/unversal_ decla. shtml, 2002.

3. Hofstede, G. , Cultures and Organizations, McGraw – Hill, 1991.

4. Dawkins, R. , The Selfish Gene, OUP, 1976.

5. Qianlong's letter to King George III, 1793, in F. Schurmann et al. , (eds.), Imperial China, Random House, 1967, http://web. jjay. cuny. edu/ ~ jobrien/reference/ob41

arts which are not fuelled by the internet are dependent on television and radio for their transmission — the National Lottery and Big Brother for example, or celebrity culture based on people like David and Victoria Beckham, Naomi Campbell and Amy Winehouse.

This book, therefore, aims to give you an overview of different aspects of British culture and situations in which you as a Chinese student might find yourself in cross-cultural conflict with British people, or where misunderstandings might occur. Language will be presented through a series of background introductions followed by a dialogue in which Chinese students interact with a British host family. This will be followed by a language study section which will highlight certain aspects of grammar and vocabulary.

■ ■ ■ ■ ■ ■ ■ ■ ■ ■ ■ ■ ■ ■ ■

英国广播电台 BBC 有个节目叫"放逐荒岛时的必备专辑"。在这个节目中，主持人会问一些知名人士，当他们被放逐荒岛时会带哪些书籍及音乐。除了那些书籍与音乐之外，他们还会获得莎士比亚全集和詹姆斯王钦定本的圣经。为什么要附赠莎士比亚全集和詹姆斯王钦定本的圣经呢？因为大家公认这些作品在文学方面代表着英国文化，而且任何受过教育的人都应该阅读这些作品。其它国家及民族也有类似的古典文学作品可以提供相同功能。

当我们谈到"文化"时，我们所想的也许是高雅文化，如艺术、文学、音乐等等。我们也有可能想到一个族群的古典文化与传统，包含艺术、语言、文学、服饰、饮食、社会、历史及宗教。我们也有可能想到中国五千多年的历史，独特的书法、儒家哲学及道家的寺庙，或是希腊哲学及罗马文学所代表的历史悠久的欧洲古典文化。这种对文化的诠释方式更能将文化与文明连结在一起，而且你会发现有些人比另一些人更加文明。这些人的习惯用语是"她是一个有文化的人"，"他喜欢有文化气质的事物"或是"那些人一点文化也没有"。从另一方面来说，有些人会谈论"街头文化"或"通俗文化"。也许有人会说王朔的小说、唐朝乐队的摇滚乐与京剧或鲁迅的作品代表着不同的文化。当他们这么说时，是将文化分为古典文化和通俗文化，这些都是中国文化的一部分。可是这些例子都无法给我们的文化下一个完整定义。

根据现代社会学字典的定义，文化是某一人类群体的共享成果，这些共有产物包括价值观、规范及实体对象，但又与其它族群有所区别。[1]联合国的定义则是："文化是特定的群体或社会所持有的在精神、物质、知识及情感方面的态度，这包含了艺术、文学、生活方式、群居方式、价值观、传统及信仰。"[2]文化能表现出个人及族群的特点，将自己的族群与其它族群区分，并帮助我们理解这个世界。在商业研究里，文化通常被定义为"人类心灵的共同设定，可以将一个族群的成员同其它族群的成员区分出来。"[3]生物学家则将文化放在实验室的培养皿内，生物进化学家理查德·道金斯创造出"谜米"这个字，意思是被心智及基因仿效的事物，或者"文化进化在人类不同文化人群中传播的基本单元"。[4]生物学角度的文化成了共同的价值观。当一个族群的人们要共同相处时，他们需要一套通行的规范，帮助每个人了解在不同的环境中如何与他人相处，从如何与他人争吵到如何与不同族群的人接触。这些规范协助传播共有的意识，并且帮助人们了解发生了什么事，该如何处理。

不同文化族群的人接触时会产生我们所知的文化冲击。也许最出名的中英文化冲击发生在 1793 年马戛尔尼勋爵率领第一批英国外交及商业使团到访中国时。勋爵拒绝向乾隆皇帝磕头并将乾隆赐给他的玉称为"不值钱的破石头"，而乾隆则在给英王乔治三世的国书中严厉谴责英国为"野蛮民族"，命令英王"尔国王当仰体朕心，永远遵奉。"[5]近代的文化冲突及误解可由西方媒体对中国的报导中看出，西方人认为中国引人入胜，充满了异国情趣，有些中国人却认为西方想抑制中国发展。

诗人艾略特（他实际上是美国人却拼命想成为英国人）于上世纪 50 年代曾说，文化包含了一个民族所有特殊的行为和兴趣。对英国人来说这包括了"德比赛马会、亨利赛船会、考斯赛船周、猎禽活动、足协杯决赛、赛狗、弹珠台、飞镖、温斯利代的干酪、切段的水煮包心菜、泡醋的甜菜根、十九世纪的哥特式教堂及埃尔加的音乐。"在 2008 年，仅有少部分的人会同意艾略特的清单。在英国有一些充满爱国情操的集体活动存在，例如逍遥音乐节的最后一晚、停战日及英超决赛。近来英国文化在这一点来说几乎都是以传媒为载体的文化，那些尚未借助互联网的部分也会依靠电视及电台来传播，例如乐透转播及电视节目"老大哥，当然还有名人文化，比如大卫·贝克汉姆和他的妻子维多利亚·贝克汉姆，名模纳奥米·坎贝尔及歌手艾米·怀恩豪斯。

本书主旨是向你展示英国文化中的方方面面，以及身为一个中国学生可能会遇到的各种文化冲突或误解的情景。文体的呈现以一系列背景介绍为主，然后是一段会话，以中国学生与英国住宿家庭之间的互动为情节。附录中有每一课的语言学习段落，包括语法和单词练习。

---

1. 乔治·西尔德森，《现代社会学辞典》，克罗韦尔公司，1969 年。

2. 联合国教科文组织，http://www.unesco.org/education/imld_2002/unversal_decla.shtml，2002 年。

3. 豪夫斯帝德，《文化与组织》，麦格罗-希尔国际出版公司，1991 年。

4. 理查德·道金斯，《自私的基因》，牛津大学出版社，1976 年。

5. 乾隆给英王乔治三世的敕谕，1793 年，舒尔曼等编译，《中国帝国》，兰登书屋，1967 年，http://web.jjay.cuny.edu/~jobrien/reference/ob41

Contents

目　录

50 TOPICS ON

BRITISH

SOCIETY AND

CULTURE

英汉对照读本

英文看客
知性英语·精致阅读

英国原来
是这样

——英国社会与文化50主题

Chapter 1

Stereotypical Views of the British

英 国 人 的 刻 板 印 象

What do you think of when you think of Britain? Do you think of tradition and history, extremely polite gentlemen in bowler hats trudging through the fog and the rain in London with umbrellas? Do you think of tweed-clad aristocrats, hunting on their country estates or the Queen and Prince Charles and the Mother of Parliaments at Westminster? Do you think of Grenadier Guards in bearskin hats at Buckingham Palace, or the Household Cavalry on their horses in Whitehall? Do you think of William Shakespeare and Charles Dickens and Sherlock Holmes? Do you think of fish and chips, afternoon tea and full English breakfasts? What about historical costume dramas like *Pride and Prejudice*, or Hugh Grant films, or James Bond or the BBC World Service or Tony Blair? What about lovely old country churches and cottages, warm beer and cricket matches on the village green on lazy Sunday afternoons?

There is, however, another image of British identity which the New Labour government of Tony Blair liked to promote; that of a hip, young modern European country which is at ease with itself and the rest of the world — the Britain of the English language, of the best rock and pop music in the world, of exciting art and cinema, of David Beckham and the Premier League — Chelsea, Manchester United and Arsenal. It promotes the Mini, the Rolls Royce and London buses and taxis while at the same time stressing the vibrant multicultural identity of modern Britain — a Britain of many ethnic groups and races, of a dynamic financial and service sector, of liberty of democracy and of freedom — but which avoids the excesses, dangers and extremes of America. Even this is a construct, though — the reality is even more confusing and, perhaps after reading this book, you will have a different understanding of the people in that tiny, complex group of islands off the North-West coast of Europe who have had such an impact on recent world history.

In reality, there are huge differences in the ways that people behave and interact with each other in different parts of the British Isles. Try telling a Scotsman that he is English, and you will get short shrift. Even within the individual nations of the UK there are differences of behaviour based on class, outlook, education and language, and some British people themselves revert to pejorative stereotypes to describe people from different parts of the islands — "soft" Southerners, "down-to-earth" Northerners, "mean" Scots, "drunken" Irish and so on. These stereotypes serve a purpose, but like all stereotypes they are only partly true and need to be used with care.

■ ■ ■ ■ ■ ■ ■ ■ ■ ■ ■ ■ ■ ■ ■

　　当提到英国时你会想到什么呢？是英国的传统和历史，还是英国绅士们头戴圆顶硬礼帽、手持雨伞穿梭在伦敦的雨雾中？是身穿猎装的贵族们在乡下的庄园内打猎，还是女王和查尔斯王子，抑或是"议会之母"在威斯敏斯特的英国国会？是白金汉宫戴着熊皮帽的近卫步兵团，还是在白厅的王家禁卫骑兵旅？是大文豪莎士比亚、狄更斯，还是名侦探福尔摩斯？是炸鱼薯条、下午茶，还是英式早餐？是历史古装剧《傲慢与偏见》，还是休·格兰特的电影，或是詹姆斯·邦德、BBC和前首相托尼·布莱尔？是美丽的乡村教堂和农舍、温啤酒，还是慵懒的星期天下午在村庄草坪上的板球赛？

　　还有另一种英国形象是新工党政府托尼·布莱尔所倡导的，一个年轻、摩登，走在潮流尖端的欧洲国家，自得其乐并且与世界各国和平相处，拥有国际共通的英语、世界上最棒的摇滚乐和流行音乐、令人兴奋的艺术和电影、大卫·贝克汉姆、英超联赛——切尔西、曼联和阿森纳。英国推广着迷你汽车、劳斯莱斯、伦敦巴士及黑色出租车，还强调它生气勃勃的多元文化——拥有不同种民族、高效的金融服务产业、自由民主的权力，却没有美国的暴力、危险及极端行为。这种说法也只是抽象概念，英国的真实情况要复杂得多。也许在阅读本书之后，你会对那些居住在欧洲西北海岸外一小列复杂的群岛上，给世界近代史留下深远影响的居民，有一些与以往不同的了解。

　　事实上，英国各地人们的行为举止也不尽相同。试着对苏格兰人说他们是英格兰人，你肯定会得到冷漠的对待。即使是同一个国家的人也会因为等级、见解、教育及语言的差异而有不同的行为举止，有些英国人也会恢复旧习，以轻蔑的刻板印象来形容从不同地方来的人，例如温和的南方人，务实的北方人，斤斤计较的苏格兰人以及醉醺醺的爱尔兰人等等。这些刻板印象有其用处，但和所有的刻板印象一样，其中只有部分是真实的，所以使用时一定要小心。

I'm a Northerner

Gang: Greg, you're from the North of England, aren't you?

Greg: Aye, and I'm proud of it.

Gang: So, does that mean that you drink and fight a lot, and are more down-to-earth and straight forward than they are in the South?

Marie: Hahaha; well he likes to think he is!

Greg: Come on; you know that's just the stereotype. I mean, people are people — we're all individuals, you know. Within the

North there are huge differences in culture and behaviour based on class, education, age — all sorts of things.

Gang: What do you mean?

Greg: Well, I mean, I come from Durham. Now, people from Newcastle, which is only twelve miles away, would say that people from Durham are posher and more refined — some of them even say, "Durham is a Southern city stuck in the North!" because of the ancient University and the Cathedral. But, if you look at it, that's not completely true.

Marie: Oh, come on Greg! You do talk more posh than other Geordies. Listen to yourself!

Greg: Yes, but it's not like a posh Southern accent — it's distinctly Northern and, anyway, I behave like a Northerner.

Gang: What do you mean by that?

Greg: Well, we Northerners are more honest and friendly; we are more likely to say hello to people in the street, we know our neighbours and we look after our own. In the South, people are less friendly and more distant, you can't leave your door unlocked there and most people don't know their neighbours. The South is more middle-class and people are constantly struggling to keep up with the Joneses. In the North, on the other hand, there's a more working-class culture — people are happy with what they've got and they watch out for each other. You can see that in the way they talk and the way they treat each other!

Marie: Rubbish! I'm from Portsmouth — you can't get more Southern than that, and we are all of the things you've just said!

Greg: I don't mean big cities like Portsmouth. I mean middle-class places like the Home Counties, Tunbridge Wells, Bath... places like that. Most Southerners don't understand anything about the rest of the country. I mean, they think civilization ends at Watford!

Marie: Well, I went to university in Liverpool for four years, and I have loads of Northern friends. I've stayed with them in Sheffield and Nottingham!

Greg: Well, there you go! That just proves my point! We wouldn't even call Sheffield and Nottingham the North, and Liverpool is an Irish city in England full of whining, self-pitying Scousers!

Gang: Gosh! It looks like you like relying on stereotypes too.

我是北方人

王刚：格雷，你是从英格兰北边来的，对吗？

格雷：对，而且我引以为荣。

王刚：这么说你很能喝酒，很爱打架，而且比南方人更脚踏实地、更直率喽？

玛丽：呵呵呵；他喜欢被人看作那种人。

格雷：别这么说嘛，你知道那只是对北方人的刻板印象。我是说人就是人，我们都是独立的个体。北方人因阶级、教育程度、年纪等的不同，还是有很大差别的。

王刚：什么意思？

格雷：噢，我是说，我是从达累姆来的。12英里之外的纽卡斯尔人会说达累姆人比较时髦高尚，有些人甚至还因为达累姆拥有古老大学及教堂而说"达累姆是困在北方的南方城市"。但是如果你仔细研究，就会发现这不全对。

玛丽：哦，别这么说嘛格雷。你讲话真的比一些纽卡斯尔人来得时髦。听听你自己的口音。

格雷：对啦，但是我的口音一点都不像时髦的南方音，我的口音是非常独特的北方音，而且我的行为举止也是纯正的北方人。

王刚：你那样说是什么意思？

格雷：噢，我们北方人比较诚实友善；我们在街上爱和别人打招呼，我们认识自己的邻居，会照顾自己人。在南方，人们不怎么友善，喜欢保持距离，住在哪里都必须锁门，而且大多数人不认识自己的邻居。在南方有较多的中产阶级，人们经常与邻居们互相攀比。在北方则有较多的工人阶级，人们知足常乐，相互照应。你可以从他们说话及对待别人的方式看得出来。

玛丽：胡扯！我是从朴次茅斯来的，你找不到比那里更南方的地方了，但是我们跟你所形容的北方人是一样的。

格雷：我不是指像朴次茅斯那样的大城市。我指的是一些中产阶级地区像是大伦敦地区、唐桥泉、巴斯等地方。大多数的南方人对南方以外的事都不了解。我是说他们认为文明世界止于沃特福德！

玛丽：噢，我在利物浦上了4年大学，我有很多的北方朋友。我曾经跟他们在谢菲尔德及诺丁汉待过。

格雷：噢，你看吧！这证明了我的想法！我们不把谢菲尔德及诺丁汉当作北方，我们认为利物浦是在英国的爱尔兰城市，那里充满了爱发牢骚、自怨自艾的人。

王刚：天啊，这样看来你对很多事的判断也都是倚赖刻板印象。

Chapter 2

Class

社 会 等 级

British society is often said to be "class-ridden", with a particularly complex and confusing class system. Despite what many people say about equality of opportunity, British society is shot through with class anxiety. The simple upper, middle and lower class relationship is satirised in a famous British TV sketch in which three men look either up to or down at each other according to their class,[1] and the middle class in Britain can be divided into even smaller segments. George Orwell, the famous writer who wrote *1984* and *Animal Farm*, ironically referred to his own family as "lower-upper-middle class".[2] He was educated at Eton, an elite private school, and was dependent on the tight class structure of the British Empire for his position, yet his family were poorer than many people in supposedly lower classes. The relationship is a complex one based on ownership of business, inheritance, education, connections and accent, and George Bernard Shaw once famously said that an Englishman only needs to open his mouth to make another Englishman hate him.[3]

In the 1980s the former prime minister, Margaret Thatcher, famously claimed to have created an "enterprise culture" in which the working classes could become anything they wanted to be through sheer hard work and wise investment in newly-privatised industries. Certain regional accents became markers of style and fashion rather than class, and people who had previously spoken in the clipped tones of The Queen's English started speaking in modified regional accents. Regional accents became badges of status and can be heard more and more on the BBC. In the 1990s, Tony Blair confidently asserted, "we're all middle-class now." Traditional class barriers were supposed to be coming down and the upper classes were becoming more like other people in their accents while working class were aspiring to better things.

However, social researchers have shown that this idealised view is a myth. The wealthy families who run the City of London remain at the core of the British upper

---

1. The Frost Report, 1966, http://www. youtube. com/watch? v = zIfzDyVBG_ M
2. Orwell, G. , The Road to Wigan Pier, Penguin, 2001.
3. Shaw, G. B. , Pygmalion, 1912.

class, alongside the aristocracy, the BBC, Oxford and Cambridge universities, elite schools and the Church of England. They pass on wealth from generation to generation and enjoy a dominant position in society. Athough there is also a more globalised financial elite ranging from Russian oil tycoons to the "City fat cats" who benefited from economic reforms in the 1980s, this is a tiny, self-selecting elite.

The UK Office of National Statistics is possibly the best indicator of what class people belong to. It divides social classes in the UK not according to income or interests or education, but on employment. Classes are given letters and numbers, with A (judges, medical consultants, heads of government departments) being the highest, and E (unskilled and unemployed) being the lowest.

■ ■ ■ ■ ■ ■ ■ ■ ■ ■ ■ ■ ■ ■ ■

英国经常会被形容成一个被等级差别所支配的社会，有一套特别复杂且令人疑惑的等级制度。尽管有不少人大讲机会均等，还是有很多人对于阶级感到忧心忡忡。在一部著名的英国电视剧中，这种上、中、下阶级间彼此那种向上卑躬屈膝，对下趾高气昂的关系通过3个男主人公被表现得淋漓尽致。[1]英国的中产阶级则更是被细分成更多的等级。撰写《1984》及《动物农庄》的著名作家乔治·奥威尔讽刺他的家族是"较低的中上阶级"。[2]奥威尔受教于贵族学校伊顿公学，他的家族虽然凭借大英帝国的等级制度而享有地位，但是他们比很多阶级更低的人还穷。这种复杂的等级制度是建立在财富、世袭、教育、人际关系及口音上。文学家萧伯纳曾说过一句名言："一个英国人只需要开口就可以让另一个英国人恨他。"[3]

在20世纪80年代，英国前首相撒切尔夫人曾声称创造了一种新的"创业文化"，即工人阶级只要辛勤工作，或者明智地投资于刚刚私有化的企业，就可以实现他们的目标。一些区域性口音成为新的流行指标，而不是等级差别的象征；从前那些满口女王口音的人也开始改口使用改良的区域性口音。区域性口音成为新的身份象征，在BBC的节目里可听到这些口音的机会也越来越多了。到了90年代，当时的首相布莱尔非常自信地断言"我们都是中产阶级了。"人们认为传统的阶级藩篱就会被拆除，上流社会的人将融入一般人民的口音，而工人阶级将会追求更美好的事物。

然而，社会学者认为，这个理想化的想法是个神话。事实上，英国上流社会还是以那些控制着伦敦金融中心的富有家族为核心，还包括贵族、BBC、牛津和剑桥等名校，以及英国国教。他们将财富代代相传，并且享有特殊的社会地位。当然，也有一小群通过上世纪80年代的经济改革脱颖而出的全球化财富精英，从俄罗斯石油大亨到金融巨富。

英国全国资料统计处提供了最佳的等级指标。他们依据职业来划分社会阶级，而不是以收入、兴趣或教育程度来分类。他们以字母及数字来代表各种等级，A等（法官、医疗顾问，政府官员）代表最高等级，E等（无技能及失业者）代表最低等级。

---

1. 《弗罗斯特报告》，1966，http://www.youtube.com/watch?v=zlfzDyVBG_M
2. 乔治·奥威尔，《到威根码头之路》，企鹅出版社，2001年。
3. 萧伯纳，《卖花女》，1912年。

She's So Middle Class!

Greg: God! I was round at Julie's house this morning to drop Marie off for her coffee morning, and they were all being so middle class.

Gang: What do you mean? It's good to be middle class, isn't it?

Greg: Well, yes and no. I mean, it's all right to aspire to do well in life I think, but the word "middle class" has connotations of hypocrisy and pretentiousness in Britain. You know... social climbing and thinking that you're better than others when you aren't really.

Marie: That's just so English, Greg. You've got a chip on your shoulder. It's like, "don't get above yourself."

Greg: Well, you know what I mean, Marie. They all sit round comparing house prices, moaning about getting their kids into a good school and then sending them to private music lessons on top of that, and then driving them there in a four-by-four that they don't need.

Marie: It's not like that at all, Greg. My friends all went to uni. They are all intelligent girls. They read the *Guardian* and serious books, and they know what's going on in the world.

Greg: I'm not saying they aren't. It's just that they live in nice houses in the suburbs, are married to nice guys who do boring managerial jobs and are trapped in them by the pension. They go shopping for organic food and compete over how they are going to get the house of their dreams in the Mediterranean. It's all a bit like *Desperate Housewives* on the telly!

Gang: Well, surely it's good to want to have these things. I mean, years ago my parents in China had nothing. My dad was a manager in a state-owned factory, and my mother was an accountant, but they weren't well-off. Everyone was officially working class. They got their house and food from their work unit. Then after the four modernsation my father got a chance to be involved in a management buyout. He and my mother worked hard and they built up the factory as a private firm. Now they are well-off.

Greg: So, do your parents consider themselves middle class, then?

Gang: It's hard to say. They were brought up for so long with the belief that everyone was the same class. I think people in China these days talk more about "having money" and "not having money".

Marie: You know, Greg, there are as many definitions of middle-class as there are middle-class people. It covers a whole range of people with different interests and aspirations. I mean look at us, for example... what are we? We have strong local accents, but we aren't working class.

Greg: Well, my dad was a miner until Thatcher closed the coal mines, so my background is working class.

Marie: Yes, but we live in a different world now. That heavy industry is gone now. Class is much more fluid than it was. I mean, you work in IT, and your boss is a woman! Your dad would never have accepted that.

她太中产阶级了！

格雷：我的天啊，我今天早上送玛丽到茱莉家去参加他们的咖啡聚会时，他们都表现得非常中产阶级。

王刚：你是什么意思？中产阶级不是很好吗？

格雷：噢，可以说是也可以说不是。我是说，我认为渴望在生活上更进一步是好事，但是中产阶级在英国有虚伪及矫揉造作的意思。你知道，像是要跻身上流社会，还有自以为高人一等，但又不是那么回事。

玛丽：格雷，英国人就这样。你有点愤世嫉俗了。这个说法就好像要别人不要逾越自己的阶级。

格雷：玛丽，你知道我的意思。他们就知道坐在那里比较房价，抱怨他们如何辛苦地把小孩送进好学校，还得在放学后送小孩去上音乐课，然后毫无必要地在市区内开着四轮驱动的越野车到处跑。

玛丽：格雷，不是那样的。我的朋友们都上过大学，她们都很有智慧。她们都看《卫报》，读正经书，也知道世界上发生了什么事。

格雷：我不是说她们不好。只是她们住郊区的好房子，嫁给不错的男人。她们的丈夫却为了退休金而被乏味的管理工作绑得动弹不得。她们只买有机食品，互相攀比看谁能得到梦寐以求的地中海房子。这就像是《绝望的主妇》里的剧情。

王刚：噢，想要这些应该是一件好事。以前我父母在中国什么也没有，我父亲在国营工厂当经理，母亲是一名会计。他们并不富裕。所有的人都是工人阶级，他们从工作单位得到房子及食物。实现四个现代化后，我父亲得到一个机会参与资方买断。我的父母努力经营，让这家私有化厂子兴旺起来。现在他们富有了。

格雷：那么你的父母认为他们是中产阶级吗？

王刚：这很难说，他们从小就被灌输大家都是同一阶级的观念。我想现在的中国人会按照有钱和没钱来划分人群。

玛丽：格雷，你要知道，中产阶级的定义跟中产阶级人数一样多。中产阶级涵盖了一群拥有不同嗜好及抱负的人。就拿我们来说吧，我们算是什么？我们有很重的地方口音，但我们并不是工人阶级。

格雷：我父亲直到撒切尔夫人关闭煤矿前都是矿工，所以我应该算是工人阶级。

玛丽：对啊，但是我们现在生活在不同的世界了。那些重工业已经消失。阶级的区分比以前更灵活也更模糊。就像你在 IT 业工作，而你有个女主管，你的父亲恐怕永远也无法接受这事。

Chapter 3

Ways of Connecting

与 人 接 触

The stereotype of the "English gentleman" is well known throughout the world. However, these days, this is nothing more than a stereotype — a hangover from Victorian times when etiquette and codes of behaviour were highly formalised, as in Imperial China. These days, many cultural commentators are highly worried about more unsavoury character types in Britain — the "lager lout", "the hoodie" and the "football hooligan" are perhaps equally as representative of Britain these days as the traditional gentleman in a bowler hat carrying an umbrella. Indeed, a recent edition of *Time* magazine called British youth, "angry, disaffected and dangerous", and British newspapers are full of articles and features complaining about a "lack of respect" in society. The latest edition of the *Rough Guide to Britain* claims that British people are insular, self-important, stuck up and irritating, as well as being obsessed with celebrities. The author of this guide even goes so far as to accuse British people of being "beer-swilling, overweight telly addicts". This image of the British is as much of a caricature as the picture of animal-loving, tea-drinking, class-obsessed ladies and gentlemen.

The stereotypical British characteristics of politeness, good manners, reserve in behaviour and dress, patience and tolerance, punctuality, self-deprecation, ironic humour and formality are often misunderstood by people from outside the British Isles. For instance, many people think that British people greet each other by shaking hands and saying, "How do you do?" all the time. This is not actually the case. As has already been pointed out, many British people are acutely embarrassed and ill-at-ease in social situations, and do not know whether to shake hands, kiss or hug. Do not be too worried, therefore, if you find yourself in a situation where you are a bit confused.

There are, however, certain rules that you should bear in mind which are fail-safe, and which you should always follow. For instance, you should always say 'sorry' if you bump into people, you should always say 'please' and 'thank you', you should never jump a queue, you should never ask prying personal questions, you should never spit, burp or make hacking noises in public.

Many people see traditional rules of behaviour as essential social lubricants which keep society running smoothly and prevent misunderstandings and offence, while others see them as stuffy relics of a stricter time in the past when Debrett's was the arbiter of polite behaviour, books like *Manners for Men* were best sellers. Increased individuality and freedom generate a disrespect for traditional class-based codes of behaviour, and it is certainly true that manners are becoming more fluid these days.

Having said that, however, there are certain aspects of social behaviour and conventional norms which, although not universal in multicultural Britain, are seen as guides to polite behaviour.

■■■■■■■■■■■■■■■

"英国绅士"这个形象是全球闻名的。但是，在这个年代这只不过是维多利亚时期遗留下来的刻板印象。当时人们对礼仪及行为举止都非常郑重其事，就像中国古代一样。现今，许多文化评论家相当担忧英国人令人不快的行为举止，比如喝酒闹事的人、小混混及足球流氓等，这些人与戴高帽手持雨伞的传统绅士同样代表着英国给人的印象。事实上，最近一期的《时代周刊》形容英国的年轻人是"充满怒气、不满及危险的一代"，而英国报纸也有大量文章批评年轻一代对人缺乏尊重。最新一期的《英国简介》里也说英国人偏狭、自负、骄傲自大，令人生厌，并且对名人过分崇拜。这篇简介的作者甚至形容英国人是"狂饮啤酒、超重的电视迷"。这种印象与那种爱护动物、爱喝茶并对等级痴迷的英国绅士淑女一样，都成了英国人的漫画形象。

人们常常认为英国人还是像刻板印象中那样非常有教养，行为及衣着保守、有耐性、准时、幽默并拘谨。例如，很多人认为英国人现在碰面时还是会握手并问候对方："你好吗？"事实上并非如此，许多英国人非常害羞，在社交场所时会手足无措，不知道该握手、亲脸颊还是拥抱。所以当你遇到一些场合觉得有点混乱，不必太担心。

当然，有一些规则是可以帮你避免出错。例如，如果你撞到别人一定要道歉，常说"请"和"谢谢"，还有不要插队，不要探问别人的隐私，不要随地吐痰，不要在公共场所打嗝或干咳。

许多人将传统的行为规范视为必要的社会润滑剂，可以让社会运作顺畅，并可避免误会及无礼行为的发生，但是也有些人认为传统的行为规范太过迂腐，还停留在德布雷特[1]的时代，当时的畅销书是像《男人的礼仪》这类的书。在强调自我及自由的年代，人们不再尊重传统的等级行为规范，而现代的礼仪也变得更为强调自然。

话虽如此，还是有一些行为和传统的规范，虽然在多元化的英国不完全被接受，但仍被视为礼貌行为。

---

1. 德布雷特（John Debrett, 1750—1822），英国著名出版家。

When Do I Shake Hands?

Gang: Marie, this dinner party we're going to tonight. I'm really worried that I don't know how to behave politely. I mean, what if I mess up?

Marie: Don't worry about making a *faux pas* Gang. Everyone knows that you are not from here and, anyway, people don't worry too much about etiquette these days.

Greg: Yeah. Just make sure you don't kiss the men when you meet them. Ha ha.

Gang: Well that's what worries me. I mean, when do I shake hands and when do I kiss?

Greg: It's funny you should say that; on *Breakfast News* this morning they were talking about how most people don't know when to kiss and when to shake hands.

They were saying that, as a general rule, you should shake hands when you meet a person for the first time. A firm handshake — not one like a wet fish, mind. A firm handshake shows that you are honest and trustworthy.

Marie: Yeah, but that's really in Business or formal situations, isn't it? I mean, most British people don't actually shake hands when they meet for the first time. That's a myth. As for kissing, well I was always told that two women can kiss on the cheek, or a man and a woman can kiss on the cheek if they know each other or if they are saying goodbye and the woman offers her cheek.

Greg: Yes, but that can be embarrassing. I mean, do you give one kiss on each cheek? And what happens if you glide from one cheek to the other and accidentally brush lips or bump noses or foreheads. I mean, that can be really embarrassing.

Marie: I know. And there's nothing worse than air kisses — you know, mwaah! I think that the person with the higher status or the host needs to take the lead in offering a hand or a cheek.

Gang: What about saying hello? I mean, are there any polite forms? Should I call people by their title or 'Mr' or just 'hello'?

Greg: Well, that's not as hard in English because we only have one pronoun to address people — 'you'. In other languages like French they have a familiar pronoun and a polite one — 'tu' and 'vous'.

Gang: That's like Chinese, we say 'ni' normally, and 'nin' if we want to be really polite.

Marie: Yeah, well... obviously if the person has a much higher social status, like if he's a professor or if he's very old you should call him by his title, 'Professor Smith' or 'Mr Baker'. But among friends, you can just use the first name. Even professors will sometimes say, 'just call me John'. You don't need to call people 'sir' or 'madam'.

Gang: What about 'mate'?

Greg: Well that's a difficult one; we call our friends 'mate' in informal situations, or out in the street if we bump into someone we say "sorry, mate". The thing is that if you use it people might think you're being funny.

我该什么时候握手?

王刚：玛丽，我有点担心今天晚上参加的晚宴。我实在不知道该怎么做，很怕我会搞砸。

玛丽：王刚，别担心你会失态。每个人都知道你是外国人，而且现在人们也不那么在乎礼仪了。

格雷：对啊。你只要保证见到男人不要去亲他们就行了。哈哈。

王刚：噢，这个就是我担心的。我是说我该什么时候亲脸颊，什么时候握手?

格雷：说起这个，有趣的是今天早上的早间新闻才谈到大多数的人不清楚该亲脸颊还是握手。他们说，一般的规则是，第一次碰面时你应该握手。强而有力的握手，而不是那种柔软无力的握手。强而有力的握手，代表你是个诚实可靠的人。

玛丽：但那是在正式或商业上的场合吧。我是说大部分的英国人第一次见面时并不会握手。这是个凭空而来的说法。至于亲脸颊，我常被告知，两个女人可以亲脸颊，或是熟识的男女可以亲脸颊，还有当道别时如果女方自动伸出她的脸颊时也可以。

格雷：是啊，可是那也可能很尴尬。我是说，你是一边亲一下吗? 万一你从一边脸颊滑过另一边时不小心碰到嘴唇，或撞了鼻子或额头，你不觉得会很不好意思吗?

玛丽：我明白你的意思。而且没有比飞吻更糟的了。我觉得主人或是身分较高的人应该主动伸手或是伸出脸颊。

王刚：还有该怎么打招呼? 我是说有什么比较礼貌的方式吗? 我应该用职位称呼别人，还是某某先生或是只要说你好就可以了?

格雷：噢，在英文里我们只有"你"这个字，所以不会很难。其他的语言，比如法语里他们有一个普通的代名词还有一个敬称。

王刚：那很像中文，我们有一个普通的代名词"你"，还有一个敬称"您"。

玛丽：对。如果一个人有较高的地位，像是教授，或是他年纪很大，你就称呼他某某教授或某某先生。但是朋友间你可以直呼名字。即使是教授，他们有时候也会让你称呼他们的名字，"叫我约翰好了。"你不必称呼别人先生或夫人。

王刚：那"哥们儿"呢?

格雷：噢，那是个难题。我们在非正式的场合称呼朋友"哥们儿"，或在街上撞到别人时会说，"哥们儿，对不起"，但如果一个外国人用的话，别人可能觉得你在故意卖弄。

Chapter 4

British Humour

英 式 幽 默

Have you ever found yourself in a situation where you are simply lost in a conversation in English even though you understand all the vocabulary and grammar? This is because all British communication — not just jokes and comedy — employs particular form of self-deprecating, understatement and irony. Even when you want to insult someone, it is often done with razor-sharp wit and humour. This humour pervades all conversation, is common to all classes, and is almost like a coded language designed to exclude foreigners. Even Americans who some say are our closest cousins (perhaps because they are so naive and lacking in irony) are constantly frustrated by this *Alice Through the Looking Glass* language in which everything is back to front. Foreigners are never quite sure whether we are being serious or not.

This ironic teasing, banter, understatement, self-deprecation and mockery is the cultural default mode for the British. It exists partly because we dislike gushing emotions and mistrust people who are too pompous or who "wear their hearts on their sleeves", and also because British people value negative politeness — the idea that one must not give too much away and people's privacy must be respected.

"An ability to laugh at oneself" and "not taking oneself too seriously" are characteristics which are highly valued. For instance, the way that American politicians talk in shamelessly cliched platitudes and the way that Hollywood actors cry and say they love their directors when they get an Oscar leaves us cringing with embarrassment or smugly amused. Sentimental and over-the-top earnestness on the part of public figures can be detected very quickly by our linguistic radar and quickly shot down. If a politician or public figure wants to create a bond with people in Britain, she needs to show that she does not boast or take herself too seriously. A strong sense of justice, the desire to work together while being stubbornly individualistic and a deep cynicism seem to show that the British prefer satire to revolutions.

Some foreigners find British humour subtle, restrained and refined, but others find this trait totally bewildering and infuriating; they say, "I don't get it", and cannot understand why we do not laugh if it is supposed to be funny. "Why can't they just say what they mean?" is a constant complaint. However, if you want to understand the British, you need to be constantly on the lookout for this kind of humour. Dry, deadpan indifference and understatement are a convoluted game of bluff that are a way of life in Britain .

· · · · · · · · · · · · · ·

你是否曾经有过虽然对每个单词和语法都了解，但是却完全听不懂别人的英语对话？那是因为所有的英式沟通中，人们都使用独特的方式，不仅有笑话和幽默，还有自嘲和反讽。即使想要侮辱一个人，也会运用极富智慧、幽默犀利的言辞。这种英式幽默充斥于言谈中，普及于任何阶级，几乎像是一种语言密码，故意让外国人听不懂。即使是所谓英国人近亲的美国人（也许是美国人比较天真，缺乏讽刺的天性），也常常因为这种如《爱丽丝镜中奇遇记》般前后颠倒的语言而感到沮丧。

外国人常常搞不清楚，英国人到底是认真的，还是在开玩笑。

这种反讽的戏弄、取笑、轻描淡写、自嘲和挖苦的修辞方法对英国人来说是文化上的先天设定。英式幽默的存在一部分是因为英国人不喜欢过分热情的表现，不信任那些太傲慢或是夸大流露情感的人。同时英国人也较看重消极的礼貌，即一个人不应该过于外露，而且个人的隐私是必须被尊重的。

英国人对自嘲的能力及谦虚的人格特性看得很重。例如，当美国政治人物发表厚颜无耻的陈腔滥调时，当好莱坞演员获得奥斯卡金像奖哭着说热爱他们的导演时，英国人都会觉得难为情或很可笑。公众人物多愁善感的表现及过分的热情会很快地被英国人的语言雷达侦测出来，然后加以排斥。如果一个政治家或公众人物希望被英国民众接受，她必须要让人们觉得她不会自吹自擂，自视过高。强烈的正直感、希望与别人同心协力但又固执地想保有自己的特色，强烈的愤世嫉俗感，都显现出英国人喜欢讽刺远超过剧烈变革。

有些外国人觉得英式幽默微妙、严谨、优雅，但也有些人认为这种幽默让人不知所措，令人生气。那些人会说，"我不明白你在说什么"，而且也不明白如果是在说笑话为什么英国人都不笑。外国人经常会抱怨为什么英国人不直接把想说的话说出来。但是如果你想了解英国人，你就必须时时注意英国人的言外之意。英国人的生活方式就是用冷漠、无表情、不在乎的态度来虚张声势。

Morning Coffee

Jane: Hi Marie, I'm here. Oh, hi Lei Lei. This is Karen.

Lei Lei: Hi Jane. Hi Karen. Marie, Jane and Karen are here.

Marie: Oh, hello Jane. How's things?

Jane: Mustn't grumble. How's Greg?

Marie: Oh, you know. He's his usual kind, caring, loving, attentive self.

Jane: Oh, it's like that, is it? So when are you getting divorced, then?

Marie: The sooner the better if I have anything to do with it.

Jane: Let me introduce Karen. Karen, Marie.

Marie: Hi Karen. Sorry, you've caught me in such a foul mood.

Karen: That's all right. I think marriage is overrated anyway.

Marie: Well, I'm really pissed off with Greg. You know what happened the other day? We went to this restaurant. The service was absolutely awful. The waiter was rude, he brought the wrong dishes, the meat was overcooked and leathery, the vegetables were soggy and the soup was cold. Greg just wouldn't complain... I had to go on and on at him. It was awful. He just paid up and we crept out quietly like it was our fault. God! I wish he wasn't so British!

Karen: So... you wouldn't recommend this restaurant, then?

Marie: Well, it wasn't very pleasant. Anyway, let's have a coffee.

Lei Lei: Do you work near here Karen?

Karen: Yes; I'm a barrister. I work at the Crown Court.

Lei Lei: Gosh, that's amazing. You must be really bright.

Karen: Oh, god, I'm not brainy at all. It's just that I've always been a horrible little swot, and I'm nosey and it's a good excuse for asking people intensely personal questions. Actually, being a barrister is not as hard as you think. The only qualifications are that you need to be able to read and write and be a total workaholic with no friends or social life.

Lei Lei: I don't believe you. You seem really smart.

Karen: Yes, but there's a difference between being smart and looking smart. Ha ha.

Marie: Shall we have that coffee?

Jane: Oh! Fairtrade coffee?! Saving poor farmers in the Third World are we?

Marie: God, I have such a social conscience, don't I? It's no better than normal instant coffee, but I'm so guilt-ridden I always go for it... and we usually eat tinned food and take aways. We only serve organic food when we have visitors.

16

早晨咖啡

珍：嗨，玛丽，我来了。嗨，蕾蕾，这是凯伦。

蕾蕾：嗨，珍，嗨，凯伦。玛丽，珍和凯伦在这儿。

玛丽：哦，你好，珍。最近好吗？

珍：还过得去。格雷好吗？

玛丽：哦，你是知道的。他还是一副老样子，非常"亲切、有爱心、体贴"。

珍：哦，真是毫无进步，对吧？那你们什么时候办离婚？

玛丽：如果由我决定的话，就越快越好。

珍：让我介绍凯伦给你认识。凯伦，这是玛丽。

玛丽：嗨，凯伦。对不起，让你看到我心情不好的样子。

凯伦：没关系。我想大家对婚姻都要求过高。

玛丽：噢，我真的被格雷气死了。你知道前几天发生了什么事？我们到这家餐厅吃饭，他们的服务真是糟透了。服务生态度恶劣，上错菜，我们点的肉又老又硬，蔬菜煮糊了，汤端上来是冷的。真的很糟糕，我一直唠叨，格雷就是不肯向餐厅投诉。他就那样付了钱，然后偷偷地离开餐厅，好像一切都是我们的错。天啊，我真希望他的行事作风不要这么英式。

凯伦：嗯，所以你不推荐这家餐厅啰？

玛丽：噢，感觉很不好。不讲了，我们还是喝咖啡吧。

蕾蕾：凯伦，你在附近工作吗？

凯伦：是的。我是律师，我在刑事法院工作。

蕾蕾：天啊，那真有意思。你一定很聪明！

凯伦：哦，我一点也不聪明。我一直以来都是临时抱佛脚，而且我很喜欢探人隐私，这个工作让我有很好的借口追问一些私人问题。事实上，当律师不如你想象中那么难。唯一的要求是你要会读会写，而且要是个没有朋友及社交生活的工作狂。

蕾蕾：我不相信你说的。你看起来很聪明。

凯伦：哦，看起来很聪明跟实际上很聪明是有很大差异的，哈哈。

玛丽：我们可以喝咖啡了吗？

珍：哦！公平贸易咖啡？！我们在拯救第三世界的贫穷农民吗？

玛丽：天啊，我真的很有社会良知，不是吗？这虽然和普通的速溶咖啡没什么两样，但是我还是会出于内疚而购买这种咖啡。我们平常都是吃罐头食物和外卖，只有在有客人时才会用有机食品。

Chapter 5

Weather Talk

谈 论 天 气

There is a radio programme on the BBC called *The Shipping Forecast*. It lasts for fifteen minutes and consists of a man reciting what sounds like a sonorous religious mantra in soothing tones, "Dover Straits, Channel, Irish Sea. Westerly or southwesterly three or four, increasing to five later. Good, becoming moderate. Rain later," and so on, in the calm, measured, voice of an English gentleman. This programme is phenomenally popular and it expresses perfectly how the British want to be told about their weather in a way which provides a sense of safety, security and continuity.

The thing about the weather in the British Isles is that 'there isn't much of it.' It is annoying and unpredictable. You never know when you go out dressed for rain in the morning whether it will become warm and sunny later. However, the comforting thing about the weather here is that, despite Global Warming and the Greenhouse Effect, there are few extremes; there are no hurricanes, cyclones and blizzards, no earthquakes or droughts. British weather is boring.

When it comes to talking about the weather, many foreigners think that the British are absolutely obsessed with it. They think that our desire to talk about it reflects some kind of mad eccentricity. But, get this — before travelling to Taiwan in 1993, I bought a teach-yourself Mandarin book to read on the plane. Lesson one consisted of the following dialogue:

A: Zǎo a! /B: Zǎo! Tiānqi zhēn hǎo. /A: Zhēn hǎo, bù lěng bú rè.

* * *

A: Hǎo a! /B: Nǐ hǎo! / A: Tiānqi zhēn lěng! /B: Zhēn lěng! Zuótiān zhēn rè! /A: Rè?! /B: Nǐ bú rè a? /A: Wǒ bú rè! /B: Zhēn bú rè ma? /A: Zhēn bú rè!

Sounds like the Chinese are just as obsessed with the weather as the British! In fact, talking about the weather is just a way of striking up a conversation or greeting someone. It's just a way of saying, "Hi. I want to talk to you" or "let's keep chatting," and consists of ritual, choreographed exchanges which reflect what is important in the local culture. In Britain, these cultural norms are social distance, politeness, humour, subtlety, understatement, moderation and restraint — and also that great British capacity for moaning or complaining politely and ironically. You will almost never find British people contradicting each other forcefully over the weather to the degree that the speakers in the Chinese example above do. George Mikes, the Hungarian immigrant who wrote about British habits back in the 1950s said, "you must never contradict anybody when discussing the weather, and if you are a foreigner you should never criticize British weather." He is right; the only contradictions or complaints you will hear in weather talk are self-deprecating and apologetic ones like, "Mr Wang, I'm so sorry about the weather!"

■ ■ ■ ■ ■ ■ ■ ■ ■ ■ ■ ■ ■ ■ ■

　　BBC有一个节目叫"海运气象播报"。在15分钟长的节目里，有一位男性以诵经般冷静谨慎的英国绅士声音响亮地列举各地气象，"多佛海峡、英吉利海峡爱尔兰海，西风或西南风强度3或4级，晚点增强至5级。天气由晴好转为多云，稍后会下雨。"等等。这个节目非常受欢迎，它以英国人希望的方式将气象播报出来，提供了一种安稳及持续的感觉。

　　英国的天气可以说是"令人乏味"，即讨厌又无法预测。你永远无法知道当你白天出门因下雨所做的装扮，到了下午会不会因为出太阳，天气变得太热而感到不适。但好处是，虽然因全球变暖及温室效应导致各地的气候产生很大的变化，在英国却很少有气候问题，英国没有台风、旋风、暴风雪或干旱。英国的天气真是非常无趣。

　　当谈论到天气时，很多外国人认为英国人对天气非常痴迷。他们认为英国人讨论天气的欲望是一种非常疯狂的怪癖。但是，在1993年我到台湾之前，买了一本中文的自修书想在飞机上自学，书里的第一章包含了以下对话。

　　甲：早啊！／乙：早！天气真好。／甲：真好，不冷不热。

　　＊　＊　＊

　　甲：好啊！／乙：你好！／甲：天气真冷！／乙：真冷！昨天真热！／甲：热?！／乙：你不热啊？／甲：我不热！／乙：真不热吗？／甲：真不热！

　　听起来中国人和英国人一样对天气非常热衷。事实上，谈论天气是打开话匣子或跟人问候的很好方法。那就像是在向对方说"我想跟你聊天"或"我们来聊天吧"。这就像一个经过设计的仪式，反映出当地文化的重要方面。在英国，这些文化规范就是社会距离、礼仪、幽默、沉稳、不夸大、中庸之道及严谨，还有英国人在委婉的抱怨或冷言冷语方面的非凡能力。所以你几乎看不到英国人像上述中文对话里那样对天气互相反驳。匈牙利移民乔治·迈克在1950年写的关于英

国人习惯的文章中提到，"你绝对不可以在讨论天气时反驳对方，而且如果你是外国人，你绝对不可以批评英国的天气。"他说的对，在讨论天气时你唯一可以听到的反驳或抱怨是来自英国人的自贬及道歉，像是"王先生，真抱歉，天气这么差。"

Awful Weather, Isn't It?

Postman: Morning! Registered letter for Mr Wang Gang.

Gang: That's me.

Postman: Just sign here, please... brrr... cold, isn't it?!

Gang: Really? Do you think so? You know, I don't tend to notice the cold much — this feels quite warm to me. You should go to Harbin in China. Now, that's really cold! I think it's quite warm here. It is a bit wet and miserable though.

I find the rain really miserable...

Postman: Really? Well it feels cold to me. But I tend to feel the cold. I probably need to wear more clothes.

Lei Lei: Hello there. Oh, I know what you mean. I feel the cold as well, but I tend to find cold weather quite invigorating. It really gets me going in the morning.

Postman: Mmm. Yes, well at least it's not raining.

Lei Lei: Yes. I find the rain really miserable.

* * *

Shopkeeper: Phew! It's a bit hot, isn't it? It must be over 30 degrees C.

Customer: Just a bit.

Lei Lei: It's not as hot as where I'm from.

Shopkeeper: Where's that, then?

Lei Lei: Guangzhou, in China. It's really hot and humid there Really sticky. It get's up to 40 degrees C.

Shopkeeper: God! I don't think I could stand that. I'd melt!

Lei Lei: Yes, we need air con there.

Shopkeeper: I think we need it in here, actually. This global warming is getting ridiculous. They say the sea levels are going to rise because the ice caps are melting. We're all going to end up flooded here.

Customer: Gosh. Yes. Isn't it terrible.

Shopkeeper: Still, mustn't grumble. Now, what was it you wanted?

天气很坏，对吧？

邮差：早！王刚先生的挂号信。

王刚：是我的。

邮差：麻烦在这里签名。嗯，天气很冷，对吧？

王刚：真的吗？你觉得很冷吗？我不怎么怕冷，对我来说还挺暖和的。你应该去中国的哈尔滨，喂，那里真的很冷！我觉得这里算是很温暖的，只是有点潮湿，让人有点沮丧。

邮差：真的吗？我觉得有点冷。我比较怕冷，我也许该多穿点衣服。

蕾蕾：噢，你好。我想我知道你的意思。我也觉得有点冷，可是我总觉得冷一点可以提神，让我可以开始面对早晨。

邮差：嗯，对啊，至少没有下雨。

蕾蕾：对啊，我觉得下雨总让人觉得沮丧。

* * *

店员：啊！有点热，不是吗？一定超过30度了。

顾客：是有点热。

蕾蕾：这里不像我的家乡那么热。

店员：你的家乡在哪里？

蕾蕾：在中国的广州。那里非常的湿热，到处粘粘的，最高气温会到40度。

店员：天啊！我觉得我肯定无法忍受那里的温度，我会融化的！

蕾蕾：对啊，我们那里需要冷气。

店员：我觉得我们这里也需要冷气。全球暖化变得越来越离谱。他们说南极的冰山融化会导致海水水位上涨，我们这里到最后会被水淹没的。

顾客：天啊，那不是很糟吗。

店员：嗯，不要抱怨了。你刚刚想买什么呢？

Chapter 6

Fair Play

公 平 竞 争

A traditional English criticism of unsportsmanlike or unethical behaviour is, "it's not cricket". This is because the game of cricket is supposed to epitomise everything that is moral and upstanding in an English gentleman's behaviour. The notion of fair play pervades British notions of acceptable and ethical behaviour; to cheat or to act in bad faith is one of the worst things you can be accused of. This is, perhaps, best exemplified by British attitudes to queuing. To cut or push into a queue is possibly the worst social crime you can commit in Britain, and it is almost impossible to describe just how serious an offence it is. People who do this are considered completely beyond the bounds of civilized society.

The British are typically believed to behave fairly and in a sportsmanlike way in football and other sports. They do not cheat or resort to ungentlemanly behaviour. Generally, fair play in a social context consists of: commitment to cooperation, acknowledgement of mistakes, respect for rules, respect for social conventions, respect for your colleagues and opponents and not showing a poor attitude.

Attitudes to queue-jumping run deep, and can also be seen in British attitudes to immigration, provision of health, welfare and social services. For instance, there is a general consensus in Britain that health care should be available to those who need it, but that it should not be abused. There is also general agreement that council housing should be available to poor families who need it, but that when people jump the queue to get a house ahead of a family which is already on the waiting list this is deeply offensive to notions of fair play.

The British like to think that the notion of fair play extends to the worlds of international politics and business as well. Therefore, to cheat or act dishonestly in business is considered demeaning, as is underhand political behaviour, and people who display this behaviour are deemed to be of bad character. Any suggestion that British politics and business are entirely clean, however, would be laughable; recent news reports are full of reports of corruption and dodgy deals with foreign governments, and some foreign critics see British attitudes in this respect as mere dishonesty and hypocricy.

对于没有运动家精神或不道德的行为，英国人传统的评语是"这不是板球。"这是因为英国绅士的道德及正直的行为在板球比赛中表现无遗。公平竞争的精神影响了英国人的道德观念，作弊或不诚实是对人最严重的批评，而最好的例子是英国人对排队的态度。在英国，最糟的社交犯罪就是插队，而且无法用言语来形容它的严重性。插队的人会被认为是文明社会之外的人。

英国人一向被认为在足球或任何体育竞赛中最守法，最有体育精神。他们不会作弊或使用非绅士的手段。一般说来社会的公平竞争包含了承诺合作、承认错误、遵守规则、遵守社会习俗、尊敬你的同事及对手、不展现任何不好的态度。

英国人将插队这件事看得很严重，这种态度同时可以在英国人对移民、医疗、福利、社会服务的态度上看出来。例如，英国人一致认为医疗资源应该提供给需要的人，但却不应该被滥用。还有，英国人也认为廉租房应该提供给较穷苦的家庭，而那些在等待廉租房的名单中插队的家庭，则严重违反了公平竞争的精神。

英国人倾向于相信公平竞争的精神延伸至国际政治及商业行为。因此，在商业活动中有欺骗及不诚实的行为时会被认为贬低了自己的人品，而在政治上如有台面下的小动作也会被认为人品不良。但是，如果因此就认为英国的政治及商业是完全光明正大的，那也是个笑话。最近的新闻报导充斥着贪污舞弊及与外国政府见不得人的交易。在外国的评论家看来，所谓的英式观念在这个时候简直就是欺骗和伪善。

At the Ticket Office

[*Man pushes in*]

Gang: Oi! I was next. What do you think you are doing?

Man: Sorry, my friend. I am hurry. I am miss my train if I am not get my ticket now.

Woman: "My friend?" Young man, you're clearly not from here, but you should know that in this country we queue in an orderly manner.

Man: But I need to get my ticket now!

Gang: Well, you should have come earlier, then! We are all in a hurry!

Woman: This is outrageous! Don't they have queues in your country? You aren't the only foreigner here, you know. Everyone else knows to queue!

Girl: Yeah, get to the back of the queue! Who do you think you are!

Man: [to clerk] Please. One ticket for Cambridge.

Woman: [to clerk] Don't you dare sell that man a ticket! He's just jumped the queue!

Ticket clerk: Sir. Get to the back of the queue.

Man: Huh! You English! Why you are so strict?

Woman: What a rude man!

At Home

Gang: You'll never believe what happened at the station this morning. This guy... I think he was foreign... tried to cut the queue. I thought it was going to kick off.

Marie: Yeah. You'd be surprised how angry that makes people here. It's as if our entire inner being has been violated when somebody jumps the queue in front of us. It goes against all notions of fair play and that.

Gang: I know. I mean, even I felt really angry and people in China do it all the time.

Greg: Yeah. When people jump the queue in front of me it's like a shudder goes right through me and I tense up and get ready for a fight. I get like that when people smoke in no-smoking areas as well, or when they use mobile phones in restaurants. It's so selfish and inconsiderate. I take it as a personal insult, and it really creates a bad atmosphere.

Marie: I think the only place I've seen where people started jumping the queue **en masse** was when they introduced the new airport security checks and it was clear that people were going to miss their flights. Everyone started jumping the queue and fights broke out everywhere.

Greg: Haha. I guess that's what the terrorists need to do to destroy British society. Subvert the queuing system and you can bring the whole country down. That would totally mess with people's heads!

在售票柜台

有人插队。

王刚：喂！我排下一个。你以为你在干什么？

男人：对不起，朋友。我在赶时间。我现在要是买不到票，就会错过我的火车。

女人："朋友？"年轻人，你一定不是英国人，在英国我们一向按顺序排队买票。

男人：可是我现在一定要买到票！

王刚：那你应该早一点来买！大家都赶时间！

女人：这真是太过分了！你们国家的人都不排队吗？你不是唯一的外国人。大家都知道要排队！

女孩：对啊，去后面排队！你以为你是谁啊！

男人：[对着售票员]请给我一张票到剑桥。

女人：[对着售票员]你敢卖票给他，试试看！他刚插队！

售票员：先生，请到后面排队。

男人：哼！你们英国人！怎么那么死脑筋？

女人：这人真没礼貌！

在家中

王刚：你绝对不会相信今天早上在车站发生了什么事。有个家伙，我想他是外国人，想要插队。我以为要打起来了。

玛丽：对啊。你会很诧异插队这件事会让我们这么生气。有人插队会让我们怒火中烧，这完全违反了公平竞争的精神。

王刚：我知道。我是说，即使在中国常常有插队的现象，我还是会觉得很生气。

格雷：对啊。当有人在我前面插队时，我会全身打颤，神经紧绷，准备好要打一架。我每次看到有人在非吸烟区吸烟，或是在餐厅里打电话，都会有同样的感觉。这些人都非常自私，不会为别人着想。我把这些当作是对我的污辱，他们也把气氛搞得很糟。

玛丽：我想我唯一看过的插队场面是机场开始推行新的安检时，很多人都快错过他们的班机了，所以就开始插队，然后大家大打出手。

格雷：呵呵。我猜那些恐怖分子只要那么做就可以摧毁英国社会，只要颠覆排队制度，就可以把整个国家推翻了。插队可以让英国人发疯！

Chapter 7

Extracting Information

收 集 信 息

In Jane Austen's novel, *Pride and Prejudice*, Elizabeth says to Mr Darcy, "one must speak a little, you know. It would look odd to be entirely silent." Strangers might stick to the weather at a social function. This is the only topic that is entirely 'safe'. If you are foreign, however, you may be asked about your country and what you think of Britain, and some people are naturally more gifted at sliding this into social chit-chat than others. It's a good idea to be able to chat about famous celebrities or favourite football teams, but try to be more imaginative than Manchester United and Chelsea.

Unlike the vulgar Americans who tell you about their divorce and their therapy all within five minutes of meeting you, the British are famously restrained and private. British people will not tell you about their job, their family or their private life until they know you quite well. Prying or being nosey is bad manners in Britain; you cannot ask people straight out how many children they have, and asking people how much money they earn is a gross violation of one of the greatest taboos — the money taboo. Nor do people generally like to talk about religion or politics if they do not already know you quite well. People do not talk about physical appearance or features. It is acceptable to make ironic jokes in order to extract information, but it is rude to be direct.

Because of the privacy rule and the taboo on prying, it is often difficult to find out what people do for a living sometimes, so there are ways of asking. You should also not ask directly about marital status. This information can be got from clue-dropping and so on. Don't say kinds of "I admire you." It's too direct. If you do praise someone in public — or even in private — he will feel honour-bound to deflect the compliment in a jokey way by downplaying it. If you praise someone's job or car, he will generally downplay it — either by making a joke or by saying that it is not as good as it looks.

It is often necessary to play things by ear, to test the water before jumping into a conversation about controversial issues. If you listen to what other people are talking about, you can generally take their cue from them. Generally safe topics are food, fashion, music and films, the lives of celebrities, football and, of course, the weather.

■ ■ ■ ■ ■ ■ ■ ■ ■ ■ ■ ■ ■ ■ ■ ■ ■

在简·奥斯汀的小说《傲慢与偏见》里，女主角伊丽莎白对达西先生说："一个人总得说点什么，完全沉默不语，看起来会很奇怪。"在社交场合，陌生人最好只谈论天气，因为只有这个话题是最安全的。如果你是外国人，可能会被问到关于你的祖国的问题，或是你对英国的看法。有些人会很自然巧妙地将谈话转向闲聊。聊一聊知名人士或受欢迎的足球队是很好的主意，但是要有点想象力，不要老说曼联和切尔西。

不像一般美国人会在认识你 5 分钟内告诉你有关他们离婚及看心理医生的事，英国人比较内向、注重隐私。他们不会一开始就告诉你有关他们的工作、家庭或私生活的事，他们会等到跟你很熟时才会提起这些。在英国，探听别人的隐私被视为没有礼貌。你不可以直接问对方有几个小孩，赚多少钱，这会侵犯最严重的禁忌之一——金钱。而且，对不熟的人他们也不喜欢谈论宗教及政治。人们也不喜欢讨论长相或相貌特征。以开玩笑的方式获得信息是可以被接受的，但是直接的询问会被认为不礼貌。

因为对隐私的重视和对窥探的禁忌，人们通常很难知道别人是靠什么维生的，所以有很多问话的技巧，可以帮你打听出你想要的信息。还有，你也不可以直接询问别人的婚姻状况，只能从一些小地方找线索。不要直接说出像"我很崇拜你"这样的话，对英国人而言太直接了。如果你在公开场合或甚至私下里称赞英国人，用戏谑的似贬实褒的方式会让他们倍感荣幸。如果你称赞别人的工作或车子，对方通常会开玩笑说他的工作或车子不像看起来那么好。

所以，在加入讨论一些争议性的话题前，通常要先听听别人怎么说，先测试一下"水温"。如果你仔细倾听别人的谈话，你可以从中找到一些暗示。一般而言，食物、流行信息、音乐、电影、知名人士的生活、足球是安全的话题。当然，还有天气。

Really? How Fascinating!

Gang: So, have you come far?

Jane: Not far, but the traffic was a nightmare. It took me an hour to get here from St Mary's.

Gang: St Mary's?

Jane: Yes, the hospital. I work there.

Gang: Oh, the hospital. So you're a doctor, then?

Jane: Well, actually, I'm a GP. I just had to go to the hospital today for a meeting.

Gang: Oh really? How fascinating! You must be really dedicated and hard working.

Jane: Not really. You just need to turn up to work and be there and you'll get promoted in the NHS. Being a doctor just shows how unimaginative and boring I am. Haha.

Gang: So, do you live nearby, then?

Jane: Yes, actually. I live just round the corner. I have known Greg and Marie since we were at school together. I was bridesmaid at their wedding.

Gang: Wow. That's interesting. What do they say? "Three times a bridesmaid, never a bride?"

Jane: Haha. Well, that doesn't apply to me. I got married six months ago. In fact, my husband, Jim, should be here in a moment.

Marie: Hi Jane. You look great! When's the baby due?

Jane: Oh, not for another six months yet.

* * *

Gang: Greg! Hi. I thought Jane was a little bit fat, but I didn't want to say. Good job I didn't — she's pregnant.

Greg: Yes, you have to watch out sometimes.

* * *

Jim: Smart new car you've got there, Greg. It must have cost a pretty penny.

Greg: Not really, mate. It's second hand. I could never afford a new one. I think I still might have to get rid of it, though. It's costing me a fortune to run.

Jim: Get away! Pull the other one!

真的吗？太有趣了！

王刚：你是从很远的地方来的吗？

珍：不远，可是交通一塌糊涂。我从圣玛莉到这里花了一个小时。

王刚：圣玛莉？

珍：对，圣玛莉医院，我在那里上班。

王刚：噢，圣玛莉医院。这么说你是个医生啰？

珍：噢，事实上，我是个全科医生。我今天只是到医院开会。

王刚：哦，真的吗？多有趣啊！你一定很认真负责，工作非常辛苦。

珍：还好啦。你只要每天都去上班就可以在医序系统升官。当医生只是说明我是个多么没有想象力，多么无趣的人吧，哈哈。

王刚：所以，你住在附近啰？

珍：对啊，我就住在街角。我在学校就认识格雷和玛丽了。我是他们的伴娘。

王刚：哇，真有趣。那话是怎么说的？"当过三次伴娘，永远别作新娘？"

珍：呵呵。这在我身上不适用，我六个月前就结婚了。事实上，我先生吉姆待会儿就会过来。

玛丽：嗨，珍。你看起来气色不错！你什么时候生？

珍：哦，还有六个月呢。

* * *

王刚：嗨，格雷。我觉得珍有一点胖，但是我没敢跟她说。还好我没说，原来她怀孕了。

格雷：对啊，你得小心点。

* * *

吉姆：格雷，你买了一部漂亮的新车，一定花了很多钱。

格雷：其实没花多少，老兄。这是二手车。我可养不起一辆新车。我想我可能得把它卖掉，我快养不起这辆车了。

吉姆：去你的！别想蒙我！

Chapter 8

Complaining Politely

斯 文 地 抱 怨

The British — and especially the English — are notoriously bad at complaining. Because of British politeness rules which dictate that confrontation should be avoided, people either just do not complain and then moan to each other afterwards, or sometimes they bottle it up and then explode in an inappropriate outpouring of aggressive complaints. In fact, there is a *Candid Camera* style TV programme which shows people in typical situations where they would be perfectly justified in complaining, but they don't. In one scene, a woman reads a newspaper over people's shoulders and the people say nothing or look embarrassed.

The British are also notorious for putting up with bad service everywhere from restaurants to airports and railway stations because the standard rules of behaviour say that it is bad to draw attention to yourself. This is why, when you travel on the Tube in London and there is yet another delay, the passengers will look at each other, sigh, smile wearily and raise their eyes to heaven. They might even say, "huh! Typical!" in a resigned tone of voice that says that there's nothing that can be done about it. When complaints are made, they are made in a self-deprecating apologetic or a humorous tone of voice. In France, on the other hand, irate passengers might riot and burn down the Metro station if they had to put up with the poor service that the London Underground provides.

Americans and other Europeans, who are much more direct and in-your-face than the British, often wonder why British people always say 'sorry' or 'excuse me' when they complain. 'It's like they're apologizing for something that isn't their fault,' they say. They are missing the point. British people are not really sorry — it is because the word 'sorry' actually works as a distancing mechanism. This is crucial in terms of negative politeness and not drawing attention to yourself. If you do not say 'sorry' or use other distancing words like 'could', 'would', 'might' 'possibly' and so on, you will be seen as rude.

英国人，尤其是英格兰人不会抱怨是出了名的。因为英国的礼仪规范要求他们要尽量避免冲突，所以英国人要么就什么都不抱怨，只是事后互相吐吐苦水，要么就会将憋在心里的怨气猛地爆发出来而不可收拾。事实上，有一个偷拍视频的节目就播出一些应该可以抱怨但人们却忍耐着的情况。有一幕是一个人在看报纸，旁边的女人把头伸过来一起看，看报纸的那个人看起来很尴尬，却一言不发。

英国人还出了名地能忍受恶劣的服务，从餐厅到机场、火车站，因为他们所受的教育告诉他们不要引人注目。这就是为什么，当伦敦地铁再三延误时，所有的乘客会相互对视，叹口气，疲倦的一笑，然后仰天长望。他们也许会用一种怨恨的口气说："哼！老这样！"表达无可奈何的心情。当有人抱怨时也会带着自贬或幽默的口气。不同的是，在法国，如果乘客也要忍受像伦敦地铁一样的服务，激动的乘客很可能会发起暴动或烧了地铁站。

美国人或其他欧洲人都比英国人直接，他们会有话就说，所以他们经常搞不懂英国人为什么抱怨时总是加句抱歉或对不起，就好像英国人是在为不是他们的错道歉。他们忽略了重点，英国人不是真的为了别人的错来道歉，sorry 这个词其实起到了"保持距离"的作用，有助于维护自己的谦逊态度并且避免吸引别人的注意力。如果不用 sorry 或其他有助于保持距离的字眼，比如 could、would、might、possibly 等，会被认为非常不礼貌。

In the Restaurant

Greg: Oh, no. The waitress has given me boiled potatoes, and I asked for roast potatoes. Oh well. It doesn't matter, I suppose.

Marie: No, Greg. Tell her that's not what you ordered.

Greg: No, it's all right. Really. I don't want to create a scene. I quite like boiled potatoes, actually. Really, it's OK.

Marie: Greg! For god's sake, we're paying enough for it!

Greg: All right... erm... uh... excuse me; I'm terribly sorry to be such a pain, but I think I ordered roast potatoes, and you've given me boiled potatoes.

Waitress: Oh! I'm sorry, sir. Let me take your plate and I'll tell the cook. He must have made a mistake.

Greg: Thank you, I'm awfully sorry.

Marie: See! Easy, wasn't it?

Waitress: Here you are, sir. Roast potatoes, with the compliments of the house.

Greg: Oh... er... thank you... sorry.

Noisy Neighbours

Gang: Excuse me. I'm really sorry to bother you, but do you think you could turn the music down? It's one in the morning and I have to get up early tomorrow.

Teenager: Uh! Sorry mate... urm... hang on a minute. Oi! Paul! Turn that music down, will you? You're keeping the neighbours up!

Gang: Thanks. I'm so sorry to be a pain. It's just that I have an exam tomorrow.

Teenager: All right. See you.

[*Half an hour later*]

Gang: Look, I'm sorry. I've already complained about the noise, and you've turned the music up again. I can't stand this. If you don't turn it down, I'll have to call the police.

Teenager: Uh... oh... look mate, why don't you come in and join the party? Have a beer and relax. Don't be so boring.

在餐厅

格雷：啊，错了。服务员给我的是水煮马铃薯，可是我点的是烤马铃薯。嗯，不过也没什么大不了的。

玛丽：别这样，格雷，跟服务员说那不是你点的东西。

格雷：不用了，没关系。真的，我不想闹出动静来。我也挺喜欢煮马铃薯的。真的，没关系。

玛丽：格雷！看在上帝的分上，我们是付了钱的！

格雷：好吧。嗯……对不起，很抱歉给你找麻烦，可是我点的是烤马铃薯，你给我的是煮马铃薯。

服务员：哦！先生，很抱歉。我这就端走，我会跟厨师说的。他一定是弄错了。

格雷：谢谢你，真的很抱歉。

玛丽：你看！很简单不是吗？

服务员：先生，您的烤马铃薯，本店免费赠送。

格雷：嗯，谢谢你，真是不好意思。

吵闹的邻居

王刚：对不起，很抱歉打扰你，可不可以请你把音乐关小声一点？已经是凌晨一点钟了，我明天还要早起。

青少年：嗯！对不起，哥们……嗯……等一下。喂！保罗！把音乐关小声一点，你吵得邻居没法睡觉了。

王刚：谢谢。很抱歉麻烦你，因为我明天要考试。

青少年：没关系，再见。

半个小时后

王刚：喂，我很抱歉，可是我已经抱怨过你们太吵，你们又把音乐开得更大声了。我实在无法忍受了，如果你们不把音乐关小一点，我就要去报警了。

青少年：哦，哥们儿，你为什么不进来加入我们的聚会呢？喝点儿啤酒，放松一下，不要这么扫兴嘛。

Chapter 9

Dining Etiquette

餐桌礼仪

Nineteenth century etiquette manuals like *Manners for Men* and *Debrett's* (which is still published today) laid down precise and fussy rules over where cutlery should be placed on a dining table, which fork should be used first and in which direction a soup bowl should be tilted to get the last of the soup from it. Some people still worry about whether the tea or the milk should be poured into a teacup first, claiming that you could tell a person's social class from this. There were also intricate class-based rules on whether a meal should be called 'dinner', 'tea', or 'supper'. Thankfully, these rules are becoming less and less important, and dining etiquette now concentrates on ensuring that people eat in a way which does not offend others or make them feel queasy.

Generally speaking, you should learn how you use a knife and fork properly, eat with you mouth closed, not speak with your mouth full and not make a lot of noise when you are eating. Meat on the bone should be eaten with a knife and fork, or picked up if it is a chop or a leg, but spitting meat bones onto the plate is not good manners. Generally, parents tell their children not to put their elbows on the table and not to slurp their soup or drinks.

Interestingly, despite the perceived differences, traditional Chinese etiquette manuals also emphasise consideration for others, serving guests first and watching your table manners. Indeed, the former Chinese Foreign Minister, Zhou Enlai, was famous for his good manners at state banquets — always making sure that he had a bowl of noodles in the kitchen with the cooks beforehand so that he could attend to his guests. Ironically, he could pass for a stereotypical English gentleman.

If you are invited to dinner, it is good manners to arrive to time, or up to five minutes late. In some cultures it is all right to arrive hours late, but not in Britain. Also, you should take some flowers for the hostess and maybe a small gift or a bottle of wine (remember, wine in English is NOT *jiu* in Chinese).

19世纪的礼仪手册如《男人的礼仪》及《德布雷特的礼仪手册》（这本书至今仍在发行）列出了精确繁琐的规矩，比如餐具该如何摆放于餐桌上，哪一把叉子该先用，汤碗该如何倾斜才可以喝到最后一口汤。有些人到现在还为应该先把茶还是牛奶倒进茶杯中而犯愁，因为从倒茶的先后顺序可以看出这个人的社会等级。关于餐点该称为 dinner，tea 还是 supper 还有更错综复杂的等级规矩。令人欣慰的是，这些规矩已经越来越不重要了。现在的餐桌礼仪只是要确保人们在进餐时不要冒犯到别人，或让人觉得不愉快。

一般来说，你必须学习如何正确使用刀叉，吃东西时嘴要闭上，嘴里有东西时不要说话，还有咀嚼时不要发出声音。带骨的肉要用刀叉来进食，如果是腿肉可以用手拿起来啃，但是把骨头吐到盘子上是非常不礼貌的行为。一般而言，父母会告诉小孩不要把手肘靠在桌上，也不要咕噜咕噜地喝汤或饮料。

有趣的是，虽然东西方文化不同，传统的中国礼仪也强调要考虑别人的感受，还有先服务客人并注重餐桌礼仪。事实上，周总理就以他在国宴上的礼仪闻名。他通常会在厨房和厨师们一起先吃一碗面条，这样他就能在国宴上专心款待贵宾了。他完全比得上一名标准的英国绅士。

如果你被邀请去参加晚宴，准时到达或是晚个5分钟都是有礼貌的表现。在有些文化里晚上几小时都可以接受，但在英国不行。还有，你应该准备一束花送给女主人，或许再带一份小礼物或是一瓶酒（请记住，英文的酒指的是葡萄酒，不是中国的白酒）。

Which knife and Fork Should I Use?

Gang: What about eating, Greg? I mean, which knife and fork should I use?

Greg: Well, generally in Britain we hold the knife in the right hand and cut food with our index finger on top — not like a pen — and the fork in the left hand. Then we transfer the food to our mouths with the fork. In America, it's different — there, they put the knife down and transfer the fork to the right hand before putting the food in their mouths.

Gang: It sounds complicated.

Marie: Actually, Gang, it doesn't matter too much. As long as you don't slurp, or eat noisily or speak with your mouth full of food. These are things which will really turn people's stomachs. And you should always try to finish what is on your plate before you take any more food — that shows that you are not greedy. Just watch what other people do, and follow them.

Greg: Do you have rules like this in China?

Gang: Well, they aren't very strict. I mean, of course it is good manners to serve your guests first and not to take the last piece of food from the serving dish. The thing is, though, that we all share from common dishes in the middle of the table and we dip our chopsticks into the same dishes.

Greg: I heard that there were some quite elaborate rules around drinking in China. Like, you have to go "bottoms up" around the table and if you are the honoured guest, everyone will drink a shot with you in turn to get you drunk.

Gang: That's not really true. There is only one quite important rule — if you are drinking alcohol at a meal, you should raise your glass and propose a toast before drinking. You really shouldn't drink without others drinking too. The thing about "bottoms up" is just for macho business dinners. And if you don't want to drink like that, you just say "drink slowly".

Marie: Are there any rules for chopsticks?

Gang: Well, we say that the further up the chopsticks you hold them, the more generous you are, and the further down you hold them, the more mean you are.

Greg: Actually, here in Britain some people are worried that children don't know how to use knives and forks properly any more because they are eating hamburgers, chips, pizza and sandwiches all the time!

Marie: By the way, Gang. Remember to switch your mobile off when you sit down to dinner.

Gang: Why?

Greg: Well, letting your phone ring is bad enough, but answering your mobile in a situation like that is a real *faux pas*. It's considered really impolite to have a conversation on a mobile when you're in company. Doing this in a restaurant is the height of bad manners.

我该用哪副刀叉?

王刚: 格雷, 吃东西时该怎么办? 我是指我该用哪一副刀叉?

格雷: 噢, 在英国通常我们会右手持刀,
食指放在刀柄上切食物, 不要把刀像笔
一样用, 然后左手持叉。切好食物后再
用叉子送进嘴里。在美国, 刀叉的用法
不同, 他们把食物切好后, 会把刀子放
下, 把叉子换到右手, 再用右手持叉把
食物送到口中。

王刚: 听起来真复杂。

玛丽: 王刚, 事实上, 不用担心那么多。
只要你不咕噜咕噜地喝水, 或发出声音,
或一边吃东西一边讲话, 就没问题了。
那些真的会令人作呕。而且你应该把盘
子里的食物先吃完, 再去盛更多的食物,
让人家觉得你不是很贪心。你只要注意
看别人怎么做, 然后跟着做就行了。

格雷: 你们在中国有这样的饮食礼仪吗?

王刚: 噢, 我们的饮食礼仪不像这里的规矩那么严格。我的意思是说, 当然礼貌上
要让客人先动筷子, 还有不要拿走盘子里最后剩下的食物。可是我们都是从桌上的
盘子里取菜, 大家都用自己的筷子从盘里夹菜。

格雷: 我听说在中国你们喝酒有很多详细的规矩。像是, 你得跟整桌的人干杯, 而
且, 如果你是重要的客人, 每个人会轮流跟你干杯直到你喝醉。

王刚: 那不是真的。只有一个重要的规矩, 如果你用餐时喝酒, 你应该在喝酒之前
举起酒杯敬酒。你不应该只闷头喝酒, 应该敬别人酒才对。干杯的情况通常发生在
商业餐会上, 是有胆量的象征。而且, 如果你不想喝那么多, 你只要说 "慢慢喝",
就可以了。

玛丽: 使用筷子有什么该注意的吗?

王刚: 噢, 我们说筷子握的越高说明你越大方, 握的越低说明你越小气。

格雷: 事实上, 有些英国人担心他们的小孩不知道该怎么用刀叉, 因为现在的小孩
几乎只吃汉堡、炸薯条、比萨饼和三明治。

玛丽: 对了, 王刚。吃晚餐时, 不要忘了把你的手机关掉。

王刚: 为什么?

格雷: 噢, 因为让你的手机在餐桌上响已经很糟了, 如果在餐桌上接电话那就真的
很没礼貌。在和别人聊天时接电话是很不礼貌的, 如果在餐厅里接电话可以
算是极为失礼的事了。

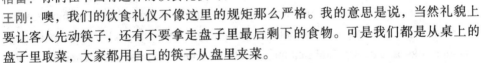

Chapter 10

Gossiping

说 长 道 短

Gossip is a universal human trait and seems to have evolved in order to facilitate communication and permit bonding. Part of the attraction is the element of risk involved, and the understanding that it is naughty or forbidden.

Research shows that both sexes devote the same amount of time — about 65% — to social topics such as personal relationships, only that men seem to dress this up as more serious, analytical and highbrow. Some research shows that men do indeed devote more time to serious matters like politics or cultural matters or solving the world's problems while the women are in the kitchen discussing gossiping. Other research shows that what women call 'gossip', men call 'exchanging information'.

There is a difference in the way that men and women talk when they gossip. For women, the gossip tone should be generally high and quick, or even a stage whisper, like a naughty child making something sound surprising or scandalous. For some it might even be sly and vindictive — an accusing tone. Women tend to speculate more on why someone did something, or embellish a story more, and become emotional. Men tend to pretend they are talking about serious subjects like cars or football, and their tone of voice will be generally serious and might not show that they are gossiping. This is, in fact, what they are doing though. It will just be dressed up as analysis or observation. British males can express three emotions, provided they do it in a macho way accompanied by swear words: surprise, anger and elation.

When women are bonding they tend to use complements and counter-complements, praise each other's hair, looks, clothes and to issue self-deprecating denials, witty self-critical remarks — so much so that they vie with each other to see who can put themselves down the most — there are important social points to be scored here. Complements should never be accepted straight away — that would be considered impolite or arrogant. You should NEVER say to people that they look very fat or thin, or make direct neutral comments on the colour of their skin or their eyes.

Men, on the other hand, indulge in humorous putting each other down —
usually on topics like cars, political party, choice of beer, wet shaving versus dry
shaving. All of this is just ritual and is to do with establishing the required degree of
mock seriousness and irony in a conversation. You should never show too much
emotion or be too earnest. It would not be considered manly.

说长道短是人类的特性，而且似乎是促
进沟通及保持关系的最好方式。说长道短吸
引人的一部分原因是其冒险的成分，还有明
知不妥而故犯的快感。

研究显示两性投入一样多的时间（约
65%）在诸如私人关系的社交话题上，但是
男性把饶舌包装得更严肃、更有学问。有些
研究显示男性的确投入更多的时间谈论政治、
文化或是世界问题，女性则花较多的时间在
说闲话上。其它研究也显示女性所谓的"说
闲话"，男性则称之为"交换意见"。

男性与女性说长道短的方式不太一样。女性在饶舌时音调通常较高且说话较快，
甚至是交头接耳，像是顽皮的小孩把事情讲得很离奇、夸张，有时甚至有狡诈的、
恶狠狠的控拆式言语出现。女性倾向于推测什么人为什么做某事或添油加醋，变得
比较情绪化。男性则倾向于装作在讨论严肃的话题，像是汽车或足球，而且他们的
音调也很正经，可能听不出他们正在闲聊。这就是男性在饶舌时做的，把饶舌装饰
得像是在做分析或观察。英国男性可以显现出三种情绪：惊讶、生气和兴高采烈，
只要他们做的很男性化，再夹带着一些脏话就行了。

女人们扎堆时喜欢互相恭维或反恭维，她们称赞彼此的头发、长相、衣服，同
时用俏皮的自我批评自贬身价，甚至比赛着看谁能把自己贬得最低，这些方法都可
以获得很好的社交评价。永远不能直接接受别人的赞美，那会被认为没礼貌或是骄
傲。绝不可以说别人看上去很胖或很瘦，或评论别人的皮肤或眼睛的颜色。

在另一方面，男人喜欢以开玩笑的方式相互打趣，通常的话题是车子、政
党、啤酒、胡子干刮还是湿刮等等。这些都只是一些仪式，用来营造假正经的、
戏谑的谈话氛围。绝对不要表现得太情绪化或是太认真，不然会被认为不够
男人。

K

Go on! Tell me!

Marie: Oh, Jane, I like your new hairstyle. It looks great. I wish I had hair like yours. Mine's so boring and mousy.

Jane: Oh no! My hair's so frizzy. That's why I got it done like this. I just can't control it. I wish I could have my hair like yours but I just don't have the right cheekbones. You've got such good bone structure.

Marie: Oh, thanks, but my skin's so bad. I had really bad acne as a teenager and you can still see the pock marks. I love your shoes as well... they're lovely.

Jane: Oh, I just got them down the market. I'm going to have to stop buying so many shoes. Jim says I've just got no self control. Anyway. Wait till I tell you... guess what?

Marie: Go on, tell me!

Jane: You know what I heard? You know Sarah, my neighbour from number 42?

Marie: What? Tell me, tell me!

Jane: Well you have to promise not to tell anyone, but she's having an affair.

Marie: No! Really?! Oh my god?! Who with?

Jane: Dr Jones.

* * *

Greg: Is that your car outside, Jim? It's all right, isn't it?

Jim: Yeah I think I'm going to have to get rid of it, though. It's costing me an arm and a leg to run. I think the newer model does more miles to the gallon.

Greg: The doctor down at the Health Centre's got one of the new X-Types. Saw it yesterday.

Jim: Oh yeah? He must be trying to impress someone.

Greg: What do you mean?

Jim: Well, I hear that Sarah from number 42 likes X-Types. Know what I mean?

快说！快说！

玛丽：哦，珍，我喜欢你的新发型。真的很好看。我希望我的头发像你的一样。我的发型太无趣又缺乏活力。

珍：哦，才不会，我的头发很鬈，所以我才会把它剪成这样。我的头发真的很难梳。我希望我可以剪你那样的发型，可是我的颧骨不好看。你的脸型真的很美。

玛丽：哦，谢谢，可是我的皮肤很不好。我在青春期时长过很多粉刺，你现在还可以看到以前留下来的疤痕。我很喜欢你的鞋子，漂亮极了。

珍：哦，我在市场上买的。我得停止买鞋子了。吉姆说我一点自制力也没有。对了，听我说……你猜怎么着？

玛丽：赶快说！

珍：你知道我听到什么了？你认识我的邻居莎拉吧，住在42号的那个？

玛丽：怎么了？快说，快说！

珍：噢，你得保证你不会跟别人说，莎拉有外遇了。

玛丽：不会吧！真的吗？我的天啊！跟谁？

珍：琼斯医生。

* * *

格雷：吉姆，在外面的那辆车是你的吗？很棒，不是吗？

吉姆：对，可我得把它卖掉，养这车太费钱了。我想新车型用一加仑汽油可以跑得更远。

格雷：我昨天看到健康中心的那个医生买了一辆新的 X 型汽车。

吉姆：是吗？他一定是想让某人印象深刻。

格雷：什么意思？

吉姆：噢，我听说住在42号的莎拉喜欢 X 型的车。你明白我的意思了吗？

Chapter 11

The British Constitution

英 国 宪 政

Britain is often described as a "constitutional monarchy". That means that, although the Queen is the Head of State, she has no political power. The country is run by the Prime Minister, who is the head of the political party that wins the most votes in democratic General Election which is held every four years. The main political parties in Britain are Labour, Conservative, Liberal Democrats, the SNP and Plaid Cymru. There are also many minor parties.

Members of Parliament sit in the House of Commons, which is the main law-making body for the United Kingdom. The House of Lords is a higher chamber of parliament which is made up of appointed and hereditary peers. There is a vigorous constitutional debate over their role. Scotland, Wales and Northern Ireland have their own parliaments, and pass laws which affect their own states. Some people think that Scotland will become independent of the rest of the UK one day and that Northern Ireland will join the Republic of Ireland.

The constitutional settlement refers to the agreement between monarchy and parliament over who runs the country, and originally dates from 1688, although the system was not originally democratic. Some other Europeans accuse the British of being hypocritical; they are certainly ironic. Britain is almost unique in the world in having no written constitution of Bill of Rights, yet the Queen is called a "constitutional monarch", and certain politicians like using the word "constitutional" to describe things that are legal or right in terms of the law.

■ ■ ■ ■ ■ ■ ■ ■ ■ ■ ■ ■ ■

　英国的宪法体制经常被形容成君主立宪制，这表示虽然女王是国家元首，但是她没有政治实权。整个国家是由首相管理，首相这个位置是由每四年大选中获胜的政党领袖来担任。英国目前主要的政党为工党、保守党、自由民主党、苏格兰民主党及威尔士民主党。英国除了主要的政党外，还有一些其他小党。

　英国的下议院设立在国会大厦，是英国的主要立法机构。上议院则由指派及世袭贵族构成。关于上议院的职责，一直存在强烈的争议。苏格兰、威尔士及北爱尔兰都有自己的国会，也可制订效力局限于自己区域的法律。有些人认为苏格兰有一天会从英国中独立出来，而北爱尔兰则会加入爱尔兰共和国。

　　"宪政协议"指的是王室与国会间的合同，内容订立出由谁来掌管国家。此协议起源于 1688 年，虽然是协议但却以非民主的方式产生，因此有些欧洲国家批评英国虚伪。在世界上，英国算是非常独特的国家，英国没有成文的宪法，但是英国女王却被称为宪政君主，而一些政客喜欢以"符合宪法的"这个词来形容所有合法的权力。

That's Not Democratic, Is it?

Gang: Greg. There's something I don't understand about the government in Britain. It's a democracy, right?

Greg: Yeah. So they say!

Gang: Well, how come you have a queen? I mean, that's not democratic, is it? She's a hereditary monarch.

Greg: Well that happens in other countries too. I mean, look at the ex-president of the United States. Ha ha... I'm only kidding, but you know what I mean. The thing is that the Queen is a constitutional monarch. That means that she doesn't have any political power.

Marie: Ooh, that's not true, Greg. She's part of the Establishment, and they are the ones who really run things — despite all this talk of democracy.

Greg: Yes, I know, but look. There is a constitutional settlement in Britain which means that, although the Queen is Head of State, the country is actually run by the political party that wins the general election, and the Prime Minister is the leader of that party. So, although the Queen does ceremonial things like opening parliament, signing laws and appointing prime ministers, she has no political power. It's the same in the Netherlands and in Scandanavia.

Gang: So, is the Queen a citizen like everyone else? I mean, does she vote?

Marie: Well, monarchists always say that the Queen is above politics. She is certainly very rich and privileged. Her name is Elizabeth, and her family name is Windsor, but her ancestors were all German; she is descended from the family of Saxe-Coburg Gotha, and they had to change their name during the First World War. In fact, all of the European royal families are related. The Queen's husband, Prince Phillip, is actually from the Greek royal family.

Gang: Why is he not called King Phillip?

Marie: Because the succession passes to the eldest son of the previous monarch. If the monarch has no sons, the eldest daughter succeeds to the throne. The Queen's father, George VI, had no sons. The Queen does have three sons, though, and the eldest, Charles, will become King when Elizabeth dies. Charles' eldest son, William, will become King in turn. The thing is, though, that the monarchy is less popular now than it used to be, so it might end up being abolished.

Gang: We had an emperor in China at one time. That all ended in 1912 though, when the Nationalist government overthrew the Qing Dynasty. We were trying to become a modern, republic even then, but it looks like you British are stuck in the past!

Greg: Well, I think we do have a bit of an obsession with traditions and history.

那就不民主了，对吗？

王刚：格雷，我对英国政治并不是很清楚。英国是民主政治，对吧？

格雷：是啊，他们是这样说的。

王刚：噢，那你们为什么有女王呢？如果是这样，那就不民主了。女王是个世袭的君主。

格雷：噢，这在其他国家也是有的，看看美国的前总统。哈哈，我只是开玩笑，你懂吧。英国是君主立宪制，所以女王并没有实权。

玛丽：哦，那不对，格雷。女王是整个体制的一部分，而这个体制是真的在治理国家，虽然大家都在谈论民主政治。

格雷：是啊，我知道，但是在英国我们有"宪政协议"，虽然女王是国家元首，但是国家实际上是由赢得大选的政党来治理，而首相的职位就是由这政党的领袖来担任。所以说女王虽然执行一些形式上的仪式，像是国会的开会仪式、签订法案及首相任命等，但却无实权。这跟荷兰和斯堪的纳维亚半岛的挪威、瑞典是一样的。

王刚：所以，女王跟其他人一样是公民吗？我是说，她投票吗？

玛丽：噢，保王派的人总是说女王是高于政治的。她非常富有，并享有特权。她的名字是伊丽莎白，姓温莎，但她的祖先都是德国人，她是萨克森-科堡-哥达王朝的后裔。在第一次世界大战中，为了撇清与德国的关系他们被迫改姓。事实上，所有的欧洲王室都有亲戚关系，英国女王的丈夫，菲利浦亲王，是希腊王室成员。

王刚：为什么不叫他菲利浦国王呢？

玛丽：因为王位的继承是传给前一任君主最年长的儿子，如果前一任君主没有儿子则传给最年长的女儿。现任女王的父亲乔治六世没有儿子。现任女王有3个儿子，最长的儿子查尔斯将于女王过世后继承王位。查尔斯的长子威廉则会继查尔斯之后成为国王。但是君主制不像以前那么受欢迎了，所以很有可能会被废除。

王刚：我们以前也有皇帝。但是当民族主义政府于1912年推翻了清朝后，一切就结束了。我们在那时候就想要成为现代化的共和国，看来你们英国人还沉缅于过去。

格雷：噢，我想我们对传统和历史有点执着。

Chapter 12

Political Parties

政　党

The British like to think that they gave democracy to the world and that they have the 'Mother of Parliaments' at Westminster. This is broadly true. The English king, Charles I was defeated by the Parliamentary army during the Civil War in 1640, and the 1688 Settlement ensured that the monarch would be subservient to Parliament. The Great Reform Act of 1832 gave the vote to most men who owned property, but the system did not become fully democratic until 1919, when women were given the vote. Now, every person over the age of 18 can vote for the party of his or her choice. Britain is divided into 603 constituencies. The party which wins the most constituencies (not the most votes) in the country forms the government, and the leader becomes the prime Minister and forms a cabinet. The party that comes second forms the Opposition and its leader forms the Shadow Cabinet. The other parties have MPs at Westminster if they win a constituency, so smaller parties like the Liberal Democrats, the Scottish Nationalists and Welsh Nationalists have representatives in the House of Commons. Sometimes, by combining with the Opposition and rebels from the ruling party they can defeat government Bills, or proposed laws.

The three main parties are the Labour Party, which is broadly left wing, the Conservative Party, which is broadly right wing and the Liberal Democrats, who say they are middle-of-the-road. As with everything in Britain, class rules. Despite the fact that Margaret Thatcher was supposed to have broken down old class divisions and Tony Blair said that everyone was middle class in modern Britain, old class allegiances still influence the way people vote. Labour is traditionally working class and strong in the North and industrial areas, and also has support among intellectuals and public-sector managers and professionals. The Conservative Party, on the other hand, is traditionally strong among the middle and upper classes in the South and rural areas. Both Margaret Thatcher and Tony Blair claimed to have overturned these traditional support bases by making people vote against their tribal allegiances.

The Labour Party is traditionally a Socialist party which supports more government control and intervention in the economy, and more government provision of health, welfare and education. Since the 1990s, though, it has moved to the right and follows more Capitalist policies. The Conservative Party is traditionally Capitalist and friendly to business, and supports free markets and enterprise with minimal government intervention. Conservative policies emphasise low taxes, cuts in public spending and private provision of health and education, although all Conservative governments have kept the NHS and a minimum level of welfare. The Liberal Democrats see themselves as a moderate and sensible alternative to Labour and the Conservatives. Their support is traditionally rural and among some intellectuals and professionals who think they have a social conscience. The word "Liberal" in Britain is very different in meaning to its meaning in both the US and in other languages. The original British Liberals believed in free markets, but gradually came to believe in government intervention in the economy and social issues. Now, in Britain, the word "liberal" means *socially liberal* — slightly left of centre and soft with a social conscience, while in the rest of Europe it means *economically liberal* with a harder Capitalist edge.

■ ■ ■ ■ ■ ■ ■ ■ ■ ■ ■ ■ ■ ■ ■ ■

　　英国人认为是他们将民主传给了全世界，而且他们在西敏寺拥有世界议会之母。广义地说这是正确的。1640 年查理一世的军队在内战中被议会的军队打败，而 1688 年的合约又确保了王室必须服从议会。1832 年产生的《改革法案》，将投票权授于大部分有产者，但是直到 1919 年妇女获得投票权英国才算真正实施了民主政治。目前，18 岁以上的人可以投票给他们所选择的党派。英国分为 603 个选区，哪个党派赢得最多的选区（不是获得最多的选票），则可获得执政权，而政党的领袖则成为首相并由其组织内阁。获得第二多选区的政党成为反对党，其领袖组建"影子内阁"。其他的政党如果赢得一个选区便在下议院拥有一席，所以像自由民主党、苏格兰民主党及威尔士民主党都有代表在下议院。他们有时还和反对党及执政党中的"叛变者"联合，否决政府议案或法律。

　　英国 3 个主要的政党为，被归为左派的工党、右派的保守党及自称中间派的自由民主党。和英国所有的事一样，政治也被阶级所支配。尽管撒切尔夫人宣称等级差别已被打破，托尼·布莱尔也声称在现代化的英国每个人都是中产阶级，但是对等级的忠诚度还是会影响人民的投票行为。工党的选民以工人阶级为主，在英国北部及工业区获得较多的选票，他们同时也得到知识分子及政府机关管理者的支持。保守党则得到中产及上流阶级的支持，主要的得票区域为南部及乡村。撒切尔夫人及布莱尔均宣称已打破了传统的忠诚度，让选民叛离他们传统支持的政党，转而投票给敌对党。

　　工党传统上是社会主义政党，主张政府应更多地干预并介入经济，并提供更充分的费用在保健、社会福利及教育上。自上世纪 90 年代开始，工党的政策方向已由左偏向右，渐渐向资本主义政策靠拢。保守党传统上都是资本主义者，重视商业，支持自由经济和尽可能少的政府干预。保守党政策主张降低税率，紧缩公共支出、私人投资健康和教育事业。然而所有的保守党政府并未将全民保健及社会福利废除，只是将支出保持在最低。自由民主党则自认为比工党及保守党更稳健、更理性。他们的支持者多来自乡下，还有知识分子及专业人士，这些人自认较具社会良知。"自由"这个词的含义在英国与在美国或在其它语言中的含义是大不相同的。传统的自由民主党主张市场自由，但是他们的主张渐渐转向政府应介入经济并提供社会福利。现在"自由"在英国指的是"社会的自由"——中偏左的政治主张和宽松的道德感。在欧洲其它国家，这个词则是指"经济的自由"，具有自由资本主义的含义。

The Day of the Local Elections

Marie: Hi Jane, did you go and vote at the polling station on your way here?

Jane: Naah! They're all the same, aren't they? You can't trust politicians.

Marie: Of course they aren't! You should always fulfil your democratic duties, you know. You know, we're very lucky to be living in a democracy here, and people like you can't even be bothered to vote. I think it should be compulsory, like in Brazil or Australia. That's-the only way you can protect the democratic process. Do you know, in the last mayoral election only 40% of the electorate turned out and the media thought it was great, and less than half of the electorate voted!

Jane: Oh, come off it, Marie! Look, when that lot came to power last time they said that everything was going to be different. They said that they were going to make a break with the past. All those promises they made about nursery provision, the NHS, tackling immigration, gun and knife crime, public transport, inflation, the cost of living and all of that, and what's happened? I have to wait a week for a doctor's appointment because there are fifty asylum seekers who can't speak English in the queue before me, three teenage boys have been stabbed to death on the council estate up the road so far this year, the trains cost a fortune and never run on time and now that interest rates have gone up again I have to pay £100 a month more on my mortgage on the same wages. And you know what? I now have to pay for the privilege of parking my car outside my front door!

Marie: Well, of course there are going to be problems, but these things go up and down with the economy. I mean, the inflation and interest rates are all to do with a knock-on effect from the US mortgage market, aren't they? And the crime and problems with public spending will be sorted out if people demand action and vote for a party that promises to deliver. Anyway, unless you vote you have no right to criticise what the government is doing.

Jane: Oh yeah? Well maybe if nobody voted at all it would send a message to the politicians that they are out-of-touch with what the public want. Then they'd have to do something.

Marie: Of course they wouldn't! Politicians thrive on public apathy. It just means that they can do what they want and there's no comeback. If they really had to fight for their seats, they would deliver on their promises. I think we get the politicians we deserve.

Gang: Gosh. Does everybody get this worked up here on polling day?

Greg: Only people like Marie. I mean, most people are pretty laid back about it. What's it like in China? I mean do you vote?

Gang: Well we vote for local representatives. Provincial representatives vote for deputies to the National People's Congress, who vote on proposed laws and vote for the Chairman, the Premier and others leaders as well.

Greg: I suppose they all call each other 'comrade', instead of 'the honourable gentleman' like they do in the House of Commons.

政　党

Gang: Well，yes，they do．But you have to be careful these days with the word "comrade"，… ha ha.

Greg: Why's that? Because China is becoming more Capitalist?

Gang: No… not that. I'll tell you later.

地方选举日

玛丽：嗨，珍，你在过来的路上去投票处投票了吗？

珍：没有。那些人不是一丘之貉吗？政客都是不能信任的。

玛丽：当然了！但你应该履行你的民主义务去投票。我们很幸运可以住在民主的国家，但是你连投票都懒得去。我觉得应该把投票改为强制性的，像巴西跟澳大利亚一样，这是保护民主过程的唯一方式。你知道吗？上一次的市长选举只有 40% 的选民投票，新闻媒体认为是相当好的投票率，才不到一半的投票率啊！

珍：哦，玛丽，别扯了。之前那一票人当选前说一切都会改变，说他们会有新的表现。他们保证解决育婴福利、全民保健、移民、枪械犯罪、大众交通、通货膨胀、生活成本等等问题，可结果呢？我得等一个星期才能约到医生，因为前面排了 50 个连英文都不会说的政治难民；今年到目前为止有 3 个青少年在前面的廉租屋被杀；火车票非常昂贵而且火车从不准时；利率又升高了，我每个月得用同样的薪水多付 100 镑的贷款。还有呢，我还得付停车费才能把车停在我家门口。

玛丽：噢，当然会有些问题，但是这些都跟经济有关，会时好时坏的啊。我的意思是，通货膨胀及利率问题都跟美国抵押市场的连锁效应有关，不是吗？还有，如果人们执意要求，并投票给保证执行的政党，那犯罪及公共支出的问题就可以解决了。无论如何，除非你投票，否则你没有权利批评政府的施政。

珍：是吗？也许如果没有人投票，就可以让所有的政客意识到他们不了解人民的需求。到时候他们就会去做些事。

玛丽：他们当然不会！政客们是靠着人民的冷漠而获益。人民的冷漠只会让政客们为所欲为。如果他们必须靠争取才能获得席次，他们就会去做他们保证的事。我想我们会得到应得的政客。

王刚：天啊。大家在选举日都这么冲动吗？

格雷：只有像玛丽一样的人才会。大部分人都不太积极。在中国怎么样？你们会投票吗？

王刚：噢，我们投票选举地方人大代表。省人大代表中会选举出全国人大代表。全国人大代表会投票制定法律，选举国家主席、国务院总理和其他领导人。

格雷：我想他们称呼对方为"同志"，不像在下议院，他们称呼对方为"可敬的绅士们"。

王刚：噢，对啊。但是现在你称呼别人"同志"时得小心一点儿，哈哈。

格雷：为什么？因为中国变得更贴近资本主义吗？

王刚：不是因为这个，我以后再跟你说。

Chapter 13

The British Commonwealth

英 联 邦

What do Canada, Australia, Nigeria, Singapore, Jamaica, South Africa, Cyprus, India, Kenya, Trinidad, Fiji, Malaysia and New Zealand have in common? They are all members of the British Commonwealth, or the Commonwealth of Nations.

The Commonwealth of Nations is an international organisation which was set up in 1931, and is a community of 53 sovereign states — former British colonies and member states of the British Empire. The only exceptions are the UK itself and the former Portuguese colony of Mozambique. It is often divided into the ' old Commonwealth', represented by countries like Canada, Australia and New Zealand, which achieved independence from the UK early, and the ' new Commonwealth', which is made up of former colonies like India, Bangladesh, Ghana and Kenya, which became independent after the Second World War. According to the Singapore Declaration, the aims of The Commonwealth are the promotion of democracy, individual liberty, the rule of law, human rights, good governance, free trade, multilateralism, egalitarianism and world peace.

Queen Elizabeth II is the head of The Commonwealth, but she does not lead the organisation in any political capacity, being more a symbolic figurehead. As well as being the sovereign of the UK, she is official Head of State of sixteen Commonwealth member states; in this capacity, though, she is merely a figurehead. The United Kingdom is not the head state and, as the organisation is not a political union, so the UK cannot exercise any political control over other member states. Like the United Nations, The Commonwealth has a secretary general; in 2008 this was Kamalesh Sharma of India, who took over from Don McKinnon of New Zealand.

The Commonwealth is often criticised for being either a hangover from the British Empire or nothing more than a ' talking shop', which can have no real influence on world events. This is unfair, though. The Commonwealth is seen by its own members and other states as a prestigious organisation, and it has proven its political independence from the UK by criticizing UK foreign policy and expelling

South Africa during the Apartheid era against the wishes of the British government. The Commonwealth has also recently suspended Pakistan.

The organisation provides scholarships for students from member states to study in other member states, and many high-ranking world leaders are former Commonwealth scholars. The Commonwealth Games — held every four years — is the second biggest sporting event in the world after the Olympics.

■ ■ ■ ■ ■ ■ ■ ■ ■ ■ ■ ■ ■ ■ ■ ■

加拿大、澳大利亚、尼日利亚、新加坡、牙买加、南非、塞浦路斯、印度、肯尼亚、特立尼达、斐济、马来西亚及新西兰有什么共同点吗？他们都是英联邦的成员或英联邦成员国。

英联邦成立于1931年，是个国际性的组织，由53个独立自主的国家组成。这些成员均为前英国殖民地或是大英帝国的附属国，唯一的例外是英国本身及葡萄牙的前殖民地莫桑比克。英联邦常被区分为老联邦，包括加拿大、澳大利亚及新西兰这些较早从英国独立的国家，以及新联邦，包括二战后独立的国家，像印度、孟买、加纳及肯尼亚。根据《新加坡声明》，联邦的主要目的是为了促进民主、个人自由、法制、人权、善治、自由贸易、多边主义、平等主义及世界和平。

英国女王伊丽莎白二世是英联邦的名义元首，但她没有政治上的实权，仅为名义上的领导人。作为英国国王，她还是16个联邦附属国名义上的国家元首。不过，这个职位也是有名无实。英国并非英联邦的主宰，英联邦也不是一个政治组织，所以英国对其他联邦国没有政治约束力。如同联合国，英联邦设有一位秘书长。2008年，秘书长一职由前任、新西兰的唐纳德·麦金移交至印度的卡马莱什·夏尔马。

英联邦经常被批评为大英帝国的遗物或是一个"空谈会"，对任何世界大事都无影响力。其实这是非常不公平的评语。英联邦被其会员国及其他国家视为一个有威信的组织。英联邦也因其批评英国的外交政策，并违背英国政府的意愿于南非执行种族隔离政策时开除南非会籍而展现出政治独立的能力。英联邦也于最近中止了巴基斯坦的成员资格。

英联邦提供奖学金让成员国的学生到其他成员国进修，许多世界领袖就曾是英联邦留学生。英联邦运动会每4年举行一次，是仅次于奥运会的世界第二大运动会。

It Depends On Who You're Talking To

Gang: Marie. What do British people think of the Commonwealth?

Marie: Well, it depends on who you're talking to. It's a very prestigious organisation, but it's also very controversial. Britain seems to have a love-hate relationship with the Commonwealth, I think.

Greg: Yeah. I think some people think it's just a talking shop or a hangover from the British Empire.

Marie: Yes, but it does do lots of good. I mean, it promotes cultural and educational contacts between member states, and it's outgrown its links to Britain in many ways.

Gang: So, is it controlled by Britain? Back home, you know, we look at Hong Kong and we think, "oh yes, that used to be a British colony, but it's come back to the motherland now."

Greg: Well it's not really like that. The Commonwealth isn't controlled by Britain — it's an independent grouping.

Gang: But English is the official language, isn't it? So, it's controlled through the language.

Marie: English is the official language in the United States, Gang, and you wouldn't say that Britain controls the US! No — I mean, look at India — you have loads of different languages there like Hindi and Gujarati and Bengali, and they're all in conflict, so the Indian government made English the official language because it was seen as neutral and international as well.

Gang: I suppose you're right. You could say the same about Singapore too. Do ordinary British people have much contact with the Commonwealth?

Greg: Well, many British families have emigrated to countries like Australia, Canada and New Zealand over the years. I mean, we have cousins in Melbourne and Toronto.

Marie: Yes, and my friend Jasmin's family is from Jamaica. There are communities here in the UK with very close ties to countries like Jamaica, Pakistan and Bangladesh.

Gang: Well, I have cousins in Vancouver in Canada... that's like a completely Chinese city now.

这个因人而异

王刚：玛丽。英国人怎么看英联邦？

玛丽：噢，这个因人而异。英联邦是个有威信的组织，但也非常具有争议性。我想，英国对英联邦是爱恨交加。

格雷：对啊，我想有些人认为英联邦只是一个"空谈会"或大英帝国的遗物。

玛丽：是这样，可是英联邦做了很多好事。我是说，它促进了联邦成员国之间的文化及教育交流，而且它在很多方面都突破了对英国的依附。

王刚：那它还由英国控制吗？在我的祖国，我们认为香港曾经是英属殖民地，现在回归到祖国的怀抱。

格雷：噢，英联邦并不像你想的那样。它并非由英国控制，而是一个独立的组织。

王刚：但英语是英联邦的官方语言，不是吗？所以说它是通过语言被控制的。

玛丽：英语也是美国的官方语言，王刚，可你不会认为英国也统治美国吧？就拿印度来说吧，印度境内有许多的方言，像印地语、古吉拉特语及孟加拉语等，他们互不通用，所以印度政府把英语定为官方语言，因为他们认为英语是中立的，也是国际通用的。

王刚：我想你说的对。新加坡也是这样。普通英国人和英联邦有关系吗？

格雷：噢，多年来有很多英国人移民到英联邦国家，像澳大利亚、加拿大及新西兰。我家也有亲戚在墨尔本和多伦多。

玛丽：对啊，我的朋友茉莉全家是从牙买加来的。在英国，有些社区跟英联邦成员国，像牙买加、巴基斯坦及孟加拉有很密切的联系。

王刚：对了，我也有亲戚在加拿大温哥华，那里简直就像是一个中国城市了。

Chapter 14

The National Health Service

国 家 医 疗 服 务

Overseas visitors in Britain are often surprised to find that when they have an accident in the UK or they need to visit the hospital in an emergency, they do not need to pay for their treatment. The National Health Service is the publicly-funded healthcare system in the UK, and provides free healthcare to all residents. It started operating in 1948, and came about as a result of the reforms introduced by the Labour government of Clement Atlee, which came into power at the end of the Second World War in 1945 promising a "peace dividend" which would include "cradle to grave" welfare services. Before then, health care had been private or charitable and almost impossible for ordinary people to afford, and people wanted it because they wanted a complete change from the unequal and unfair society which had existed before the war.

Each British resident is registered with a GP, or local family practitioner, who is the first port of call when the case is not an emergency. If the matter is serious and cannot wait, people should go directly to the A&E department and be seen to there.

Ever since the NHS was set up, certain sections of British society, notably the Establishment, represented by right-wing newspapers, have persistently attacked it. They criticise it for being bureaucratic, wasteful, inefficient and expensive. They say that it is prey to spongers and malingerers and 'welfare tourists' from other countries, and say that a privatized system would be more efficient and provide better service. Most governments have tinkered with the original idea behind it, and charges have been introduced for things like prescriptions, glasses and dental care, and at every election the different parties vie with each other to see who can be toughest on NHS spending while still promising that "the NHS is safe in our hands". What is clear from public opinion is that any attempt to privatise healthcare in the UK would be deeply unpopular with most British people.

The NHS is divided up throughout the UK into regional primary healthcare trusts, and employs millions of people. One recurring complaint is that there are great variations in the standard of care and cleanliness of hospitals, and that there is a 'post-code lottery' which means that in some areas patients get access to certain treatments that patients in other areas do not. Some people also claim that the NHS is under extreme pressure because of increased immigration. The fact is, though, that many of the doctors, nurses and ancillary staff in the NHS are from Commonwealth or other countries, and that the NHS would grind to a halt without them.

Interestingly, the NHS is the world's fourth largest employer — and it is said to be the closest thing the British have to a national religion.

■ ■ ■ ■ ■ ■ ■ ■ ■ ■ ■ ■ ■ ■ ■

到英国的外国访客常会很惊讶地发现，当他们在英国发生意外或因生病需要去医院急救时，他们无须负担任何费用。英国的国家医疗服务是由公费承担的医疗体系，政府为所有的居民提供免费医疗。这项服务始于1948年，由前工党首相克莱门特·艾德礼所推行的改革而来，艾德礼于1945年二战结束后上任，他所许诺的"和平红利"包括"从摇篮到坟墓"的社会福利。在此之前，医疗保健是自费或由慈善机构提供，对一般人而言是无法负担的。人们想要公费医疗，因为他们希望能改变战前那个不平等、不公平的社会。

每个英国居民需到全科医生或家医处注册。除了急诊，如果出现任何健康方面的问题都先到这里治疗。如果问题较严重或是急诊，则可直接到医院的急诊室就诊。

自从国家医疗保健体系建立后，英国社会的部分群体，尤其是以右派报社为代表的权力机构，便不断对之进行攻击。他们批评这个体制太官僚、太浪费、工作效率低而成本高，是好吃懒做者、装病者及外来"医疗游客"的牺牲品，而一个私有化的体制能提供更有效率、更好的服务。多数历任政府都对原有设计进行了修补，并推行了一些自费项目，如领药、配眼镜及看牙。每次选举中，不同的党派会相互竞争看哪个可以更有效地控制体制的花费，而且保证"体制在我们手里会很安全"。民意很明确地反映出，任何想将国家医疗保健体制私有化的尝试都是极其不受欢迎的。

国家医疗保健体系在英国被划分成遍布全国的社区医疗中心，雇用了上百万员工。受大众所诟病的是，不同的医院有不同的服务及卫生水平，"邮政编码乐透"的说法应运而生，这是指有些地区的患者可以获得的治疗是其他地区的患者无法得到的。有些人也声称国家医疗保健体系因移民的增加而面临极度的压力。事实上，国家医疗保健体系内有很多医生、护士及医疗助手来自英联邦或其他国家，没有这些医疗人员，英国的医疗保健体系将无法运作。

有趣的是，英国的医疗保健体系是世界第四大雇主。有人还说这个体系是英国最接近国教的东西。

At Home

Gang: Uugh... Greg. I'm ill. I feel terrible. I think I have flu. I have a fever and a sore throat, and I feel weak. Maybe I should go to hospital.

Greg: What?

Gang: Yes. This is serious. I need to go and get some antibiotics from the doctor at the hospital. I'm dying.

Marie: Come on, Gang. It can't be that bad. You just have a cold. And, anyway, what good will antibiotics do if you have a cold or flu? They're viruses.

Gang: That's what we always do in China. If we have flu, we need to get antibiotics or get put on an IV drip.

Marie: That's mad! What a bunch of hypochondriacs! The hospitals must be full of people with colds lying there with drips in their arms!

Greg: Well, my friend worked in China and he said that he saw people threatening the doctors and telling them to give their relatives a drip for a cold.

Gang: Well what am I supposed to do?

Greg: Well if you have a cold, just drink plenty of liquids and stay at home. And if it's flu, we have a saying, "flu lasts for a week with treatment, and seven days without". But if you really want to go to the doctor's, we can try and make an appointment. I doubt they'll see you today though.

Marie: I'll call the surgery... they said you can go along to the walk-in centre this morning, and they'll see you there. You'll need to wait though.

At the Walk-in Centre

Nurse: OK, open your mouth and let me see inside... say "aaah."

Gang: Aaah.

Nurse: Right, I need to take your temperature... pop this in your mouth. Hmmm. Right... roll your sleeve up and I'll just pop this round your arm. Now, let me listen to your chest... take your shirt off... hmmm... ok... right.

Gang: Is it serious?

Nurse: No. You have a cold. How long have you been here?

Gang: Not long.

Nurse: Well these things happen when you move to a new environment. It takes time for your body build up resistance. You know, Mr Gang, there's no cure for the common cold. All you can do is drink plenty of fluids and stay at home. If your headache is bad, just take some asprin or paracetemol. You know, healthcare is free at the point of delivery here — that's why we don't abuse it.

在 家

王刚：啊，格雷。我生病了，难受极了。我想我感冒了，有点发烧，喉咙痛，觉得很虚弱。也许应该去医院。

格雷：为什么？

王刚：当然了，病很严重。我得到医院去拿消炎药，我快死了。

玛丽：得了，王刚，没那么糟吧。你只是感冒而已。而且消炎药对着凉或感冒有什么帮助？感冒是病毒感染。

王刚：我们在中国都这样，感冒就吃消炎药或打点滴。

玛丽：这太疯狂了！大家都得了疑病症吗？医院里一定躺满了感冒患者在打吊瓶吧？

格雷：噢，我的朋友在中国工作，他说他看到有人威胁医生，要医生帮他们患感冒的亲戚打点滴。

王刚：噢，那我该怎么办呢？

格雷：如果你着凉的话就多喝水，待在家里。如果是感冒的话，我们常说："感冒治得一周，不治也得7天"。如果你真想要去看医生，我们可以试着预约。不过我怀疑你今天根本约不上。

玛丽：我来打电话给诊所……他们说你今天上午可以去门诊中心，不过你到那儿可得等。

在门诊中心

护士：嘴巴张开让我看一下，说"啊"。

王刚：啊。

护士：好，我得量一下你的体温，把这个放进你的嘴里。噢，把你的袖子卷起来，我要把这个围在你的手臂上。让我听一下你的胸腔，把你的衬衫解开，噢，好了。

王刚：很严重吗？

护士：没有，你着凉了。你来这儿多久了？

王刚：才来不久。

护士：噢，你刚换环境，这种事常会发生。你身上产生抵抗力会花点时间。王刚，普通着凉是没有药治的，能做的就是多喝水，待在家里不要出去。如果你头很痛，就吃一点阿司匹林或镇痛剂。你知道医疗保健是免费的，所以我们不能滥用。

Chapter 15

The British Broadcasting Corporation

BBC（英 国 广 播 公 司）

    The BBC was set up by Royal Charter in 1927 and is the largest, most professional and most respected broadcasting organisation in the world. It produces programmes and information worldwide on television, radio and the Internet.

    The organisation holds a curious legal position; it is a quasi-autonomous public corporation which exists on the basis of a 'royal charter'. This gives it a similar legal status to a university. So it is neither fully state-owned nor a private organisation. It is controlled by the BBC Trust and headed by a Director General. It is 'free from both commercial and political influence and answers only to its viewers and listeners.' Because of this, there is no advertising on the BBC; it is funded mainly through the television licence fee, which everyone who has a TV must pay. Having said that, the BBC does run commercial operations abroad, such as *BBC World* and *BBC America*, and the *World Service* on BBC radio which broadcasts in many foreign languages.

    Because the BBC does not answer to the government, it has often been the target of politically-motivated criticism. Right-wing politicians accuse it of being a nest of socialists and subversives while many on the left say that it represents the right-wing conservative Establishment.

    At one time the standard 'educated' accent of British English was referred to as 'BBC English' because that was the accent spoken by newscasters on the BBC. Times are changing though, and the BBC is leading the way in accepting regional accents. One of the top reporters on the highbrow *Newsnight* programme who reported recently from China has a very marked Lancashire accent while one of he most popular newscasters on the 10 0'Clock News has a marked Welsh accent. The BBC's mission is 'to inform, educate and entertain', and that is the motto which has ensured that it has kept producing high-quality programmes since its inception, despite mischievous accusations of "dumbing down".

    One of the best ways of practising your English is to visit *BBC English*, a BBC website where you will find magazine programmes and other items of interest. The BBC also has a news site in Chinese.

BBC（英国广播公司），依据英国王室颁发的"皇家特许证"于1927成立，是世界上最大、最专业、口碑最好的传播机构。BBC通过电视台、电台及互联网播放节目和信息。

BBC拥有一个很奇妙的法律地位，它是一个准自治的民营机构，但却是基于"皇家特许证"而存在的。它的法律地位类似于一所大学，所以既不算国营机构也不算民营企业。BBC由BBC信托委员会管理，最高主管是行政总裁。"BBC不受商业或政治势力的影响，只对观众或听众负责。"也正因如此，BBC是没有广告的，其资金来源主要是电视执照费，任何拥有电视的人必须付费。话虽如此，BBC在国外确有商业化的经营，像BBC世界台、BBC美洲台、BBC全球服务等，用不同的语言对全球进行节目播放。

因为BBC不用对政府负责，所以经常成为政治批评的目标。右派政治家们经常谴责BBC为社会主义颠覆分子的老巢，而左派政治家则批评它代表了右派的保守势力。

曾经有一段时间，标准的、"有教养的"英国口音被称为"BBC英语"，因为BBC的播报员都以相同的口音播报新闻。时过境迁，BBC正带头采用不同区域的口音。最近，在"高端"节目《新闻之夜》的一则发自中国的报道中，一位优秀的记者露出一口兰开夏郡口音，而另一位知名的新闻播报员在晚间10点的新闻里说着一口威尔士口音。BBC的使命是"通告、教育和娱乐"。他们自成立起便以此座右铭来确保公司制作高品质的节目，尽管如此，还是有人恶意指控他们的节目"肤浅"。

练习英语的最好方式之一就是登录BBC英语网站，在那里你可以找到杂志或其他有趣的文章。BBC也有中文的新闻网页。

In Front of the Telly

Greg: Hello love. Back from the shops? Where do you fancy going tonight? Pub? Cinema?

Marie: God, no! I'm absolutely knackered. I can't face going out again. Why don't we just crash out in front of the telly with a take-away and a bottle of wine?

Greg: OK. Gang, do you fancy that? Why don't you call Lei Lei and we can all have a Saturday night in front of the telly?

Just crash out in front of the telly ...

Gang: OK. Sounds good. What's on?

Marie: Dunno. Let's have a look. Right ... BBC 1, at 7.00, there's *Strictly Come Dancing*... then at 8.20 there's *Casualty*. That's a drama about a hospital. Then at 9.00 there's the *National Lottery Draws*. Did you buy a lottery ticket, Greg?

Greg: Yes.

Marie: Good. If you win, half of it is mine, all right? Now, at 10 o'clock there's the news, and after that there's *Match of the Day* — Portsmouth versus Aston Villa. Oh, I listened to the match on Radio 5 Live in the car — Portsmouth won... they're going through to the FA Cup Final.

Greg: Why did you tell me that, Marie? I wanted to watch the match on the telly tonight. You've spoiled it now!

Gang: Ha ha... we'll just have to watch the other side then.

Greg: What ITV?

Gang: No. BBC 2. There's a very interesting programme about the Terracotta Warriors exhibition at the British Museum at 10.30.

Marie: Hmmm... let's see what else is on. Look at this — *Stars In Their Eyes* on ITV at 7.30. Let's watch that.

Greg: Naah... that's too girly, that. Is there anything good on any of the digital channels?

Marie: Let's see... ooh look. Film Four at 9 o'clock, *Love Actually*, with Hugh Grant and Colin Firth and a host of other stars.

Greg: Oh no... I think I'm going to be sick. Give me a look at that paper... right, let's see, BBC 2 at 10 o'clock... *Later With Jools Holland*... 'Jools introduces some groovy sounds from Snow Patrol, Van Morrison and Estelle.' Groovy[1]? Do you think they're being ironic?

Marie: Are we going to make up our minds, then?

Greg: All right, all right. Keep your hair on. Let's sort out the take away first. Gang, are you going to give Lei Lei a call?

电视机前

格雷：嗨，亲爱的，刚逛街回来吗？你今天晚上想去哪儿？酒吧还是电影院？

玛丽：天啊，不要！我快累死了。我不想再出去了。我们为什么不叫个外卖，再开一瓶酒，然后躺那儿看电视呢？

格雷：好啊。王刚，你喜欢这样吗？你打电话给蕾蕾叫她过来，我们待在家里看星期六的晚间电视好吗？

王刚：好啊，听起来不错。晚上有什么节目呢？

玛丽：不知道，我们来看一下。BBC1台，7点有国际标准舞比赛，8:20有《受伤者》，是个有关医院的连续剧。然后9点时有乐透抽奖。格雷，你买过乐透奖券吗？

格雷：买过。

玛丽：很好，如果你中奖，一半的奖金是我的哦。10点有新闻，之后有今天的足球比赛转播，朴次茅斯对阿斯顿维拉。我在车上听了5点钟的球赛实况，朴次茅斯赢了，他们进入决赛了。

格雷：玛丽，你为什么要跟我说比赛结果？我晚上想自己看今天的比赛，你破坏我的兴致了！

王刚：呵呵，我们只好看其他台的节目了。

格雷：看什么？独立台？

王刚：不，是BBC2台。10:30有个关于兵马俑在大英博物馆展出的节目，很有趣。

玛丽：噢，看看还有哪些节目。7:30在独立台有星光大道，我们看这个节目好了。

格雷：不要，那是女孩看的节目，数字频道有什么好看的吗？

玛丽：我来看看，噢，第4电影台9点钟有"真爱至上"，是休·格兰特、柯林·菲尔斯和其他一些明星主演的。

格雷：哦，不要，我想我会烦的。让我看一下节目表，噢，BBC2台10点钟有霍兰德秀。霍兰德会介绍一些老流行音乐，像是雪警合唱团、范·莫里森，还有艾丝特尔。老流行音乐？你觉得他们是在讲反话吗？

玛丽：好了，我们到底要看什么呢？

格雷：好啦，好啦，你冷静一点。我们先点外卖。王刚，你要不要先打电话给蕾蕾？

---

1. Groovy: 指上世纪60年代的流行事物。

Chapter 16

Newspapers and Magazines

报 纸 和 杂 志

Even in these days of the Internet, Britain is still a nation of newspaper readers. Sit on the bus, the train or the London Underground during the morning rush hour and you'll see everyone with their faces stuck behind one of the national daily papers or a free morning one like *Metro*. In the evening, you'll see them doing the same thing with a local evening paper. This helps British to indulge in their habit of avoiding conversations with others on public transport.

As with everything else in Britain, class and political opinion influences the newspaper people take. Broadsheet, or 'quality' newspapers like *The Times*, *the Guardian* and *The Daily Telegraph*, are usually read by educated middle and upper classes, while tabloids, or 'red tops', like *The Sun* and *The Daily Mirror* are usually read by the working class. There is an in-between group of newspapers like *The Daily Mail* and *The Daily Express*, which is aimed at less educated middle class readers. All British newspapers, even the so-called *Independent*, have a political stance which is reflected in the tone of the articles and the message in the editorial. Apart from *The Guardian* and *The Daily Mirror*, the press in Britain is broadly right-wing and Conservative, and has a lot of influence over the political scene in Britain. Indeed, The *Sun* famously proclaimed, "It's The Sun Wot Won It!" when the Conservatives won the General Election in 1992, and the London *Evening Standard* boasted that it had helped Boris Johnson to win the London mayoral election in 2008.

Sunday newspapers are a national passion. *The Observer*, *The Sunday Times*, *The Independent on Sunday* and *The Sunday Telegraph* all have colour supplements and glossy magazines which contain features on travel, family issues, sport, money and finance, arts and literature and social issues which people spend all day reading. All the other newspapers have their own supplements and magazines. It is a traditional weekend pastime to laze about and read through the Sunday papers.

Apart from daily and weekly newspapers, there are thousands of magazines and periodicals dealing with any kind of hobby or interest you can imagine from model railways to train spotting and computer games, and from fishing and pig rearing to bird watching. In fact — anything you care to think of. There are also numerous political and current affairs magazines and, of course, women's magazines like *Cosmopolitan* and *Elle*. There are, in fact, also men's versions of these women's magazines — *GQ* and *FHM* — also known as '**lads**' **mags**'. Magazines like *Hello* and Heat deal with celebrity gossip.

■■■■■■■■■■■■■■■■

　　尽管现在是互联网时代，英国还是一个拥有广大报纸读者的国家。每天早高峰时段，在公车、火车或是伦敦地铁上，你会看到每个人都埋头于报纸里，有发行全国的日报，或免费早报，如《地铁报》。傍晚，你会发现和早上一样，大家也会埋首于地方晚报里。这个举动帮助英国人满足他们不跟其他人在大众交通工具上聊天的习惯。

　　和英国所有的事一样，等级和政治理念影响着人们对报纸的选择。宽页，或称"高品质"的报纸，像是《泰晤士报》、《卫报》、《每日电讯》，通常是受过高等教育的中上阶级在阅读。而一些八卦小报，或称"红报头"，比如《太阳报》、《镜报》等，通常是工人阶级的读物。还有一些介于这两者之间的报纸，像《每日邮报》和《每日快讯》等针对受较少教育的中产阶级。所有的英国报纸，即使是著名的《独立报》都有自己的政治立场，这从文章及社论的内容反映出来。在英国，除了《卫报》及《镜报》外，其余的报纸大多为保守的右派，并对英国的政治拥有相当的影响力。确实，当保守党于1992年赢得大选，《太阳报》曾宣称"《太阳报》赢了！"2008年，《标准晚报》也吹嘘它帮助鲍里斯·约翰逊赢得伦敦市长选举。

　　英国人热爱星期天报纸。《观察家报》、《星期天泰晤士报》、《星期天独立报》，《星期天电报》都有彩色加页及杂志，内容包含旅游版、家庭版、体育版、财务版、艺术与文学版及社会版，能读上一整天。其他报纸也提供不同的加页及杂志。英国人传统的周末就在慵懒地阅读星期天报纸中度过。

　　除了日报及周报，英国还有成千的杂志及期刊提供给任何可想象得到的嗜好及兴趣，例如火车模型、搜集列车号码、计算机游戏、钓鱼、养猪及赏鸟等，任何你愿意去想的事物，都有相关的杂志或期刊。当然也有不少的政治和新闻性杂志，以及女性杂志，像是《大都会》和《Elle》等。相对于这些女性杂志，也有提供男士们阅读的时尚杂志，像是《GQ》及《FHM》，又称为小伙子杂志。此外还有专门讨论名人绯闻的杂志，如《Hello!》及《热力》。

What's the News?

Gang: Greg. My lecturers all read *The Guardian*; is it a good newspaper?

Greg: Well, it is probably one of the best in terms of the quality of the reporting; in fact, it regularly wins prizes for its journalism. Some people think it's a bit wishy-washy liberal, though... you know, soft-left and anti-business. It's concerned about progressive issues like climate change, social justice and such like. However, it generally supports the Labour Party, even though it is critical of the government.

Gang: So, is it popular?

Greg: Well it's not the most popular one. *The Sun* is the most popular paper in the country; in fact it's a national institution. It's the stereotypical builder's newspaper. The chattering classes hate it because it's crude and in-your-face; it shows pictures of semi-naked girls and doesn't carry any real analytical news reports — just gossip and opinion which is often simplistic, tacky and trivial. It's written in a cheeky, irreverent style, using a lot of slang and puns and double entendres that is very hard for foreigners to understand.

Gang: So, why is it so popular?

Greg: Well, *The Sun* claims that it's just giving people what they want in their own language, and that it really reflects the way that ordinary people feel about the bread-and-butter issues. Of course, its critics say that it is pushing a rabidly nationalistic agenda which brainwashes people into voting for the politicians that it supports.

Gang: Do you think that's true?

Greg: Well, that's the kind of debate that they devote whole Media Studies courses to... ha ha. It's interesting, though, that the *The Sun* is published by *News International*, which is owned by Rupert Murdoch.

Gang: Oh yes. I've heard of him. He's an Australian media magnate with a much younger Chinese wife. He owns Star TV, which broadcasts in China.

Greg: Yes. He also owns *The Times*, one of the big British quality newspapers, and the *New York Post*. Both Tony Blair and Margaret Thatcher courted him when they were in power; so you see how influential newspapers are to the political life of the country. They can make or break a government. I suppose Chinese newspapers all support the Chinese government, do they?

Gang: Well there are literally thousands of newspapers in China, and they are all more-or-less run by the Government. However, they are free to publish their own opinion and editorial. The only thing is that on sensitive issues which could reflect badly on China, they have to be responsible.

Greg: So you mean, they censor themselves?

Gang: Well, if you want to call it that. Ha ha. I think it's better than having the media controlled by a few barons who all have a similar agenda.

Greg: Well, some papers are quite progressive; there's *The Guardian*, *The Daily Mirror*, *The Independent* and, maybe, *The Financial Times*, which are different. Actually, we have a joke in Britain about who reads which newspapers; Because we have a Labour government, *The Guardian* is read by the people who run the country, *The Times* is read by the people who think they should be running the country, *The Daily Telegraph* is read by the people who used to run the country fifty years ago, *The Daily Mail* is read by the wives of the people who think they should run the country, and *The Sun* is read by people who don't care who runs the country as long as she is young, pretty and sexy! That's because of the page three girl.

Gang: Come on! *Sun* readers can't be that *shallow*!

Greg: Wanna bet?

有什么新闻？

王刚：格雷，我的老师们都看《卫报》，那报纸好吗？

格雷：嗯，它大概是新闻报导品质最好的报纸。事实上，他们的新闻常常得奖。有些人认为他们是软弱的自由派，稍微偏左并反对商业化。他们关心新的议题，比如气候变化、社会正义等。虽然常常可看到批评政府的报导，是他们还是支持工党的。

王刚：所以说，《卫报》是很受欢迎的了？

格雷：嗯，不是最受欢迎的。《太阳报》在英国发行量最大，甚至可以说是国家机构。大家普遍认为它是建筑工人的报纸。知识分子讨厌《太阳报》，认为它非常粗俗直接，刊有半裸的女子照片，但却没有真正的新闻分析。通篇都是八卦及简单、粗俗、浅薄的观念。里面文章的写法无耻且无礼，使用相当多的俚语、俏皮话及双关语，所以对外国人而言非常难以理解。

王刚：喔，那它为什么这么受欢迎呢？

格雷：嗯，《太阳报》声称它在用老百姓的语言写老百姓想看的事，它也的确反映了一般人对日常生活所需的看法。当然，其反对者批评它推广狂热的民族主义议题，被它洗脑的人民就会投票给它支持的政党。

王刚：你觉得那是真的吗？

格雷：嗯，这个争论是媒体学投入整堂课来讨论的内容……哈哈。有趣的是，《太阳报》隶属于国际新闻社，大老板是鲁伯特·默多克。

王刚：哦，我听说过他。他是澳大利亚的媒体大亨，有一位很年轻的中国太太。他拥有星空卫视，在中国收得到。

格雷：对，他还拥有高品质的英国报纸《泰晤士报》及《纽约邮报》。前首相布莱尔及撒切尔夫人在位时都奉他为座上宾，所以可想而知报纸对政治生活的影响有多大。他们能捧起一个政府，也能搞垮一个政府。中国报纸呢？他们都拥护政府吗？

王刚：在中国有上千的报纸，他们可以自由地发表意见及社论。但是对于敏感的或是有损国家形象的负面消息，他们需要负起责任。

格雷：你的意思是他们会自我监督？

王刚：噢，随你怎么想，呵呵。我觉得这比让少数富商来控制媒体要好得多。

格雷：有些报纸是能够保持走在时代尖端的，像《卫报》、《镜报》、《独立报》及《金融时报》，这些是不一样的。实际上，英国有个笑话，是关于什么人看什么报，因为我们的政府是工党，所以《卫报》是掌管国家的人看的，《泰晤士报》是那些自认为应该由他们掌管国家的人看的，《每日电报》是50年前掌权的人看的，《每日邮报》是那些自认为应该成为官太太的人看的，而《太阳报》是那些认为国家应该由年轻美丽性感的人来掌管的人看的，因为那些人喜欢看登在第3页的裸体女郎。

王刚：别这么说嘛！《太阳报》的读者不会那么肤浅吧！

格雷：敢打赌吗？

Chapter 17

Different Kinds of School

不 同 的 学 校

There is a problem which is peculiar to British English, and that is the meaning of the word 'public school'. A public school in Britain is not public at all — it is a very exclusive private school. What other countries call public schools, the British call state schools, and what other countries call private schools, the British call public schools. So far so clear? Some people say that this use of the word 'public' is a typical example of British hypocrisy, but this is not so. Pubic schools got their names because when they were set up they did not belong to the Church and reserved a certain number of places for poor boys. These days, of course, top public schools like Eton and Harrow provide a very expensive elite education to the richest and most powerful sections of society and send a disproportionate number of students to Oxford and Cambridge universities — about 47% of Oxbridge students are from public schools even though non-State schools actually educate only 7% of children. Former public-school pupils are also disproportionately represented in the professions, in government and in the civil service, where the old school tie network acts as a guarantee of a good job. Friends made in prep schools, which prepare boys for public school from the age of seven, carry on through university and professional life. 56% of Conservative MPs were privately educated and even many Labour MPs also went to private schools. The supporters of these "independent" schools claim that they provide an excellent education without overbearing interference from government and national tests, and that the pupil-teacher ratio allows teachers to give more one-to-one attention to pupils. Critics, however, say that these schools are bastions of privilege which perpetuate an unfair class system. The independent school sector in Britain takes many students from overseas and has even set up schools in other countries, including China.

The 1944 Education Act guaranteed free State education through secondary level and is a typical example of British fudge and muddle. There is no coordinated national standard of state education. State education is a mixture of local government and voluntary-aided schools, where the State and religious groups share costs, and the systems in England, Wales and Scotland are very different. Most schools are now comprehensive, and take pupils regardless of their academic level, but there are also grammar schools which can select their students. In addition to this there are also city academies and so-called faith schools which are run by different religions and are partially supported by the government. Government policy is to allow parents a choice over which school they send their children to; this means that schools with good exam results are over-subscribed, and house prices near these schools rise as middle-class parents move into their catchment areas. Poor children from council estates end up going to schools with poor exam results and a vicious circle ensues.

Kindergarten and nursery education is sporadic in Britain. Here is no automatic right to free nursery education. Again, some Local Education Authorities provide better and more comprehensive education than others.

■ ■ ■ ■ ■ ■ ■ ■ ■ ■ ■ ■ ■ ■ ■

　　在英式英语里有个特有的问题就是"公学"这个词。在英国，公学并不是指公立学校，而是指非常高级的私立学校。其他国家所谓的公立学校，在英国称为国立学校，而其它国家所谓的私立学校，在英国称之为公学。这样解释清楚吗？有些人认为"公学"这个词是英式虚伪的典型代表，但事实并非如此。公学名称的由来是这些学校成立时并不属于教会，而且保留了一些名额给穷学生。现在，顶尖的私立学校，像伊顿公学及哈罗公学，向非常富有及最有权势的社会阶层提供了非常昂贵的精英教育，而有相当多的从这些私立学校毕业的学生进入牛津或剑桥大学就读。约有47%的牛津及剑桥大学学生来自这些私立学校，与国立学校之间的比例相当不平衡，因为私立学校的学生仅占全部学生总数7%。私立学校毕业的学生也在专业领域、政府部门及市政机构里占有不均衡的比例。在这些机构里，老校友关系网就是好工作的保障。从七岁进入预科学校所建立的朋友关系可以持续到大学及工作生活中。约有56%的保守党议员受过私立教育，甚至许多工党的议员也上过私立学校。这些"独立"学校的支持者认为，私立学校提供了不受政府及国家考试过度干扰的优质教育，而且较低师生比例也可保证对学生一对一的关照。但是反对者却认为这些学校是特权的大本营，延续了不公平的驾级制度。在英国，这些独立学校也接收外国学生，有些甚至会到包括中国在内的其他国家设立分校。

　　《1944年教育法》保证免费的国立中学教育，但这是典型的英国式模棱两可的做法。在英国，国立学校并没有相同的标准。国立教育是由地方政府与自愿捐助的学校组成的，由国家及宗教团体共同负担费用，而且教育体制在英格兰、威尔士及苏格兰有相当大的差异。大部分学校是综合学校，不论学生的学习水平如何一律接收，但是还有一些初级中学可以依程度接收学生。另外还有城市学院，或称为信仰学校，由不同的宗教团体经营，由政府提供部分财务支持。政府的政策目的是允许父母为子女选择学校。较好的学校会有超收学生的情况，学校附近的房价升高，因为那些中产阶级父母都希望搬到学区附近居住。从廉租房来的穷孩子只能选择教学水平较差的学校，恶性循环周而复始。

　　幼儿园及托儿所教育在英国参差不齐。英国人并没有享受免费幼儿教育的权利。有些地方比其他地方的教育水平更高、更完善。

That's a Bit Hypocritical, Isn't It?

Marie: You know, I'm really worried about where we're going to send Olivia to school. I mean, the local primary school has got an awful OFSTED inspection report, and half the kids there don't speak English as their first language.

Greg: That's a bit racist, isn't it? What's wrong with that?

Marie: I know it sounds awful, but I want the best for Olivia, and I don't think she's going to get it stuck with a load of kids from the local council estate who have to learn English before they can learn anything else. I know it sounds bad, but there are all kinds of social problems there.

Greg: Hmmm... well, if it wasn't for this obsession with choice that the government keeps going on about, we wouldn't have this problem, would we? Each school would have a catchment area, and that would be that.

Marie: I know. But it looks like we're going to have to start going to mass on a Sunday.

Greg: What do you mean?

Marie: I mean that we'll have to get Olivia baptised as a Catholic, and I'm going to have to take her to church every Sunday and get known by the priest there to show that we're practising Catholics. That way, we can get her into the local Catholic primary school; its OFSTED report is much better.

Greg: That's a bit hypocritical, don't you think?

Marie: Well, I know, but what do you want to do? I mean, lots of people move house just to get into a better state primary school, but we can't move house to a better area, and I am a Catholic, after all...

Greg: No, you aren't!

Marie: I am so! I was baptized and I went to a Catholic school as well.

Greg: Yeah, but you aren't religious. You don't even believe in god, do you? And you never go to church...

Marie: Well, I do believe in something... I mean, I am spiritual, Greg. I do think there's something out there... you know?

Greg: Hmm.

你不觉得这样做有点虚伪吗?

玛丽:你知道吗,我真不知道要送奥莉维亚到哪里上学。我是说,附近小学的教学评估报告成绩很差,而且有一半学生的母语不是英语。

格雷:你这有点种族歧视,不是吗?那里有什么问题吗?

玛丽:我知道,这听起来有点糟,但是我想要给奥莉维亚最好的教育,而且我不想让她和一些从廉租房来的小孩在一起，那些小孩在学任何东西之前还得先学英语。我知道这听起来很差劲，但是那里存在很多的社会问题。

格雷：噢，如果不是政府一直强调可以选择学校，我们就不会有这个问题了，对吗？每个学校会有自己的学区，那就没有什么好选择的了。

玛丽：我知道。但是看来我们得开始每个星期天去教堂了。

格雷：你是什么意思？

玛丽：我是说，我们得让奥莉维亚受洗成为天主教徒，而且我得每个星期天带他上教堂做弥撒，让神父觉得我们是虔诚的天主教徒。这样的话，我们就可以让奥莉维亚进入天主教小学，那里的评估成绩好多了。

格雷：你不觉得这样做有点虚伪吗？

玛丽：噢，我知道，可是你想怎么办？我是说，很多人搬家就是为了能让小孩进入好一点的国立学校，但是我们现在没法搬去好一点的地区，而且毕竟我是天主教徒……

格雷：你才不是呢！

玛丽：我是！我受过洗，而且我也上过天主教学校。

格雷：是吗，但是你并不虔诚。你一点也不信上帝，对不对？

玛丽：噢，我是相信那个……我是说，我是有信仰的，格雷，我相信世上有那个存在……你明白吗？

格雷：哼。

Public Transport

大 众 交 通 工 具

High-quality mass public transport is one of the things that Britain just cannot seem to get right. If it's not late-running or cancelled trains and underground services, it's engineering works or 'the wrong kinds of leaves' blocking the train lines in the Autumn. When we go to Germany and Holland we are put to shame by the efficiency, speed, punctuality and cleanliness of the trains and trams, and we know for a fact that, if Parisians had to put up with the kind of service delivered by London Underground, they would riot and burn the stations down. Why do the British accept this state of affairs? They hate causing a scene, making a fuss or drawing attention to themselves.

Rail and bus transport was privatised by the Tory government in the early 1990s; since then, it has deteriorated in quality and the cost of travel has increased enormously. Even the London Underground has been effectively privatised. There have been sporadic protests in recent years; for instance passengers on First Great Western, one of the private rail franchises, recently got together and refused to pay their fares in protest against bad service, and the government recently had to bring the rail network (but not the train services) back under state control because the private operator was so poor. However, these protests are few-and-far-between, and because all parties believe that private is good and public is bad, there is neither the political will nor the popular pressure to bring public transport comprehensively under state control.

Rail travel in Britain is provided by private rail franchises (a bit like McDonalds's or EF Language Schools), and the service provided is "walk-up", so if you are prepared to pay the astronomical prices, you do not need to book train tickets in advance. It is often cheaper to fly but, for the very best-value prices, and if you book in advance, you can travel by coach. It is very difficult to travel by bus in rural areas because neither the bus companies nor the government want to subsidise ticket prices.

大众交通工具

　　高品质的公共交通在英国似乎是一件永远都无法实现的事。不是火车和地铁误点或取消班次，就是工程检修或秋天"树叶误落"阻塞了火车轨道。当英国人去德国或荷兰看到人家公共交通工具的高效、快速、准时和清洁时会自惭形秽。而且，英国人也深信，如果巴黎人不得不忍受伦敦地铁这种服务品质，他们绝对会发起暴动并烧毁车站。为什么英国人可以忍受这种服务呢？因为他们不喜欢吵架，不愿意小题大作或吸引别人的目光。

　　在上世纪90年代初期保守党执政时，他们将火车和公共汽车系统私有化。自此之后，公共交通的品质逐渐下滑，而票价则大幅上升。即使是伦敦地铁也被私有化了。最近几年有一些零星的抗议事件，例如铁路私营公司之一的大西方公司就曾遭遇乘客集体拒付车票抗议他们低劣的服务。政府最近也因为这些私营公司表现太差而将铁路系统收归国营（火车服务不包括在内）。但是，这些抗议事件非常少见，而且各党派都认为私营比国营好。因此，无论政治意愿还是来自民众的压力都不足以将公共交通系统再度改回国营。

　　在英国，火车服务是由特许连锁的私营公司经营的（有点像麦当劳或英孚语言学校）。车票不需预订，上车前购买。服务是自助式的，所以如果你准备付一大笔钱的话，你就不用事先订票。搭飞机有时候比坐火车还便宜，但是只要你事先订购车票，搭乘大巴是最经济实惠的出行方式。在乡村搭乘公共汽车很困难，因为民营的巴士公司和政府都不愿意补贴票价。

Planning a Trip

Gang: OK, we need to get down London by Friday evening next week. That gives us a week. Let's have a look on the Internet to see if we can get a good deal.

Lei Lei: Ok, here it is. Let's see. Go to the 'Quick Timetable' and type in Newcastle in the 'leaving from' window, and London King's Cross in the 'going to' window. Now, 'outward date' 09/05, then go.

Gang: What about the time and the return date? Shall we put down that we're leaving at 12. 00 and put the return date as 12/05, also travelling 12. 00?

Lei Lei: All right. Click on "get times".

Gang: Gosh! That's typical! The site doesn't recognise the apostrophe in King's Cross! Why is it only foreigners who know how to use apostrophes in English? Just type 'Kings Cross'.

Lei Lei: OK. Here it is... outward journey, Friday 9th May from NCZ to KGX, depart 12. 25, arrive 15. 44, duration three hours and nine minutes. Right, click on 'view' for the details... National Express East Coast. Shall I click on 'send to my mobile'?

Gang: No. They'll just charge you extra for that. Now, click on 'OK' under 'Buy Rail Tickets', then type in 'leaving from' and 'Going To' and the dates and times. 'Journey Type' is return and two adults. Oh, don't forget to type in 'Young Persons Railcard'. Ha! They've forgotten the apostrophe again. Now, click on 'Saver Return' and then on 'Buy'.

Lei Lei: Ok... looks like we have to change trains at York on the way back. It's First Capital Connect to York, then National Express East Coast to Newcastle. Now it's asking if we want to book One Day Travelcards for the Tube . Shall we do that? It'll save queuing at King's Cross. Right, we'll need zones one to three because we're going to Walthamstow Central, but it's off-peak, so we can get zones one to four cheaper. Let's do that. Right... click on 'Continue'.

Gang: Right. There's the itinerary. Oh no, there's a replacement bus service between Stevenage and Peterborough because of engineering work on the line. That's always happening! I don't know why they put up with that kind of thing here.

Lei Lei: I know what you mean but, at least we can book this online and they'll post the tickets out to us. Right. What do we do next?

Gang: Let's see... 'Saver Return. This ticket allows travel on any permitted route. ' What does that mean? Sounds like stating the obvious, to me. Anyway, click that you have understood the terms and conditions; that box there, and then 'Continue'.

Lei Lei: Oh look; it's giving us a choice. We can have them sent out by first class post for a pound, we can pick them up at the self-service ticket machine at the station for 50p. Next day, special delivery is £ 6 and same-day delivery is £ 10. What shall we go for? I think we should ask them to post them out first class.

Gang: No. If they don't arrive, we'll be stuck. Let's pick them up at the station next Friday. Click on that, and choose 'email my reference number to' and type your email address in there. Now... next page... you need to log onto your account. Right... check that the address details are correct, type in your password and date of birth, and continue.

Lei Lei: Right now. Here' the shopping basket page. Now, what's this? Insurance? We don't need that. Let's click on 'Remove' that. Now, continue to payment.

计划旅行

王刚：嗯，我们下星期五晚上要到伦敦去，只有一个星期的准备时间。我们上网看看能不能找到便宜的票。

蕾蕾：嗯，到这个网站看看。去"时刻表"这一栏，在"出发地"输入纽卡斯尔，在"目的地"输入伦敦国王十字火车站。然后在"出发日期"输入5月9号。

王刚：那出发时间和回程日期呢？我们要不要输入出发时间为12：00，然后输入回程日期为5月12日，也是坐12：00的火车。

蕾蕾：好了，按下"取得时刻表"。

王刚：天啊！真是要命！这个网页不认得所有格符号！为什么只有外国人才知道怎么使用所有格符号？你只要输入"Kings Cross"，不要输入所有格符号。

蕾蕾：好了，时刻表出来了，出发行程，5月9日星期五，12：25由纽卡斯尔出发，下午3：44分到达伦敦国王十字火车站，搭乘时间3小时零9分。按一下"查看键"，看一下详细资料……是东海岸快线。我要按一下"发送至我的手机"吗？

王刚：不要，他们会另外收取费用。在买票下方那个"OK"键按一下，然后输入出发地及目的地，还有出发日期及出发时间，"旅程型态"选取"往返"，然后人数选择两个成人。对了别忘了输入"青年卡"的卡号。哈！他们又忘了所有格符号。好了，按一下"优惠价往返票"，然后再按一下"买票"。

蕾蕾：好了，看起来我们回程还得在约克换火车。从伦敦搭"第一首都快线"到约克，然后换"东海岸快线"到纽卡斯尔。这上面问我们要不要买伦敦地铁的一日票。我们需要买吗？我们可以节省在国王十字站排队买票的时间。对了，因为我们要到沃森斯道，所以得买一到三区的地铁票，但是到时候是非高峰时间，所以买一到四区的票比较便宜。好，我们就买一到四区的票，然后按一下"下一步"键。

王刚：嗯，这是行程表。哦，天啊，从斯蒂夫内奇到彼得堡之间因为工程检修所以没有火车，由大巴取代。这种情形常常发生！我真不懂为什么这里的人可以忍受这种服务。

蕾蕾：我明白，但是至少我们能上网买票，他们会把车票寄给我们。好了，我们还要做什么呢？

王刚：我来看看……"优惠价往返票。可以用这种车票在任何许可路线上搭乘火车。"这是什么意思啊？这么明显的事还用说吗？不管了，在"了解权利及条件"那个键按一下，然后选"下一步"。

蕾蕾：哦，看这里，用平邮寄车票给我们收取一镑，我们在火车站的自动贩卖机取票只要50便士。隔日快捷邮件收取6镑，当天快捷邮件收取10镑。我们要选哪一种？我想我们可以请他们用平邮寄来。

王刚：不要，如果寄丢了，我们就没法出发了。我们下个星期五到火车站取票就行。按一下那个键，然后选取"将我的订票号码电邮至"，然后把你的电邮地址输入。然后……下一页……。你需要登入到你的帐户。确认一下住址是否正确，输入你的密码及出生年月日，然后按"下一步"。

蕾蕾：好了，这里是购物车，这是什么？保险？我们不需要保险，按一下"移除"键。好，到下一步"付款"去。

Chapter 19

Safe as Houses?

像房屋那样安稳吗?

There are two old sayings in Britain: 'an Englishman's home is his castle', based on the long-held assumption that no government agent can enter a British home without a warrant, unlike in certain 'foreign tyrannies', and 'safe as houses', which means that a house is the best investment anyone can make because the value will never go down. Well, our homes might be castles in the metaphorical sense, but they are actually the smallest homes in Europe. In fact they are downright pokey, with only an average usable floor space of 76m sq. Britain's houses are no longer as safe as the myth would claim due to market crashes in the early 1990s and 2008.

Owning your own property is extremely popular, and programmes about houses and house prices are very popular on TV. However, despite the widely held perception to the contrary, Britons are not Europe's most prolific homeowners. The Spanish own more of their homes than the British, although the French and Germans own fewer.

During the 1980s the government allowed people in council houses to buy their homes, but Britain still has the highest number of council or housing association dwellings in Western Europe. France has the second highest provision of council houses, while Spain barely has a social sector at all, with only 1%.

■ ■ ■ ■ ■ ■ ■ ■ ■ ■ ■ ■ ■ ■ ■

在英国有两句谚语形容英国人的家，一句是"英国人的家就是他的城堡"，这句话基于长久以来的一个假定：政府官员除非持有搜查证，否则不能擅闯民宅，这可不像"那些专制国家"。另一句是"像房屋那样安稳"，其含义是房子是最好的投资，因为房价只会涨，不会跌。英国人的房屋也许可以被比喻为城堡，但实际上在欧洲可算是最小的住居了。英国的房子真的很小，平均使用面积只有76平方米。经过上世纪90年代及2008年房价暴跌，英国的房屋也不再像谚语所形容的那样保值了。

拥有房产是非常普遍的事，电视上关于房子及房价的节目大受欢迎。但是与预期相反，在英国并没有很多人拥有房屋。虽然英国拥有房地产的人比法国和德国多，但是却比西班牙少。

　　在上世纪80年代，政府允许住在廉租房的人可以将房屋买下作私人住宅。但是现在英国居住在政府廉租房和住房协会共有产权房的人数还是高居西欧之首。法国的廉租房数量算是西欧第二高，西班牙几乎没有什么公有房，仅占房地产的百分之一。

It's So Stressful Buying a House!

Gang: Hey, Greg, how much is your house worth?

Greg: Well, the estate agent valued it at £ 250,000.

Gang: Is that a lot — I mean, in comparison to the market?

Marie: I think it's an outrageous amount, actually. I mean, look at it's only a two-up-two-down! It only cost us £ 63,000 when we bought it back in 1997. House prices have spiraled since then, though. I think we were lucky to get it when we did. I feel really sorry for young couples these days — they just can't get a foot on the housing ladder.

Greg: I know. It's awful. The point is that so much foreign capital has flooded into the country because there are so few restrictions, and anyone with the money can buy property here — there are no rules on residency or nationality — so you get all these foreign speculators buying up property and pushing up the prices.

Marie: Yeah. And young people here are priced out of the market.

Gang: Well I certainly couldn't afford a house here. I'd have to club together with some friends to buy one.

Greg: Well, you could do that. In fact, that's what lots of young professionals do — they'll get together, buy a house and have their own rooms and share the kitchen and bathroom. Then, when they want to leave the others buy them out.

Gang: So, how do you go about buying a house, then?

Marie: Gosh. It is so stressful, buying a house. They say that it's the next most stressful thing to a divorce. You have to spend ages searching websites and estate agents' windows. Estate agents have a really bad reputation here — they're just cowboys.

Greg: Yeah. It's quite hard, actually, and a lot of the stages overlap, but first you need to decide where you want to buy property, taking into account what you can afford, local amenities and so on. You need to save up a deposit, like 5% of the value of the property. You can go direct to a building society or use a mortgage broker. You have to fill in a very detailed mortgage application, stating your occupation and your salary and your savings and debts. The bank carries out a credit check to assess you as a risk and to see whether you are creditworthy or not and, after you've shown bank statements and pay slips to show that you have a secure income, they'll give you a 'decision in principle'.

Gang: Why, 'in principle'?

Marie: Because once you have found a property you want, you make an offer and, if the vendor agrees on the price, you ask him to take it off the market. That's when you go back to the mortgage lender and tell them which property you want to buy. The lender can always pull out if they think it's too risky.

Greg: You also need to locate a property solicitor to carry out the conveyancing — that's the legal aspects of the process and draw up any agreements. You need to instruct the solicitor to act on your behalf, and contact the vendor's estate agent and solicitor and liaise with your mortgage lender. He will start contractual proceedings.

Marie: Yeah, and you also have to find a surveyor and ask for a home-buyer's report or a ̶uctural survey to be carried out to check that the house is in good condition. — The ̶age lender will carry out an independent valuation of the property, and you will be ̶to pay for a mortgage survey. Only when the mortgage lender sees the property ̶d reexamines your application will they release the money through your solicitor.

Greg: Haha. Then you're in debt for the next twenty years, and they can always take the house back if you don't keep up with the mortgage payments.

Gang: Yes, but at least it means that you get the house now and, as long as you keep working, and house prices go up you'll be all right.

Marie: Ah! That's the whole point. Don't get sick or lose your job!

买房太累人了！

王刚：嘿，格雷，你家房子值多少钱？

格雷：噢，房屋中介估算大概值 25 万英镑。

王刚：这算很贵吗？我是说跟市场价格比较而言？

玛丽：事实上，我觉得这是天价。你看，我家只有楼上楼下各两间房。1997 年我们买它的时候只花了 63000 镑。房价从那时起就节节高升，我想我们很幸运当时买了它。我觉得现在的年轻夫妇很可怜，他们是买不起房的。

格雷：我知道，真的很糟糕。关键是英国对外国资金的限制很少，所以很多外国资金流入英国，任何人只要有钱就可以在英国买房地产。很多外国投机商都到英国炒作房地产，把房价炒得很高，因为英国对购房者的居民身份和国籍都没有要求。

玛丽：对啊。所以英国的年轻人因为房价太高而被挤出房屋市场。

王刚：噢，我绝对负担不起。我得跟朋友们集资，才能在这里买得起房屋。

格雷：对啊，你可以这样做。事实上，这里有很多年轻的上班族集资合买房屋。他们有自己的房间，然后跟其他人共用厨房和浴室。如果有人想退出，其他人会把他的股份买下。

王刚：那要如何才能买到房子呢？

玛丽：天啊，买房压力真的很大。大家都说买房的压力仅次于离婚。你得花很多时间在网络上及房地产中介商处搜寻好的目标。在英国房地产中介商可算是声名狼籍，他们就像一群牛仔。

格雷：对啊，买房的确很累，有很多重复步骤。首先你得要决定买在哪里，同时得考虑你付得起多少钱，还有周围的生活设施等等。你还得存一笔钱当保证金，一般是房价的 5%。你可以直接去房屋抵押贷款协会或其它抵押中介去抵押，先要很详细地填写申请书，注明职业、收入、存款及债务。银行会作信用调查，评估你的信贷风险，了解你的信用状况。在确认过你的银行对帐单及薪水单，证明你有固定收入后，他们会核发"原则同意抵押"的决定。

王刚：为什么是"原则同意"呢？

玛丽：一旦你找到理想的房子，你的报价被卖方接受时，你会要求卖方将房屋从销售市场上收回，然后你把你想要买的房屋的资料提供给贷款方。贷款方如果觉得你所选的房地产价值与抵押金额相较太冒险时，他们随时可以否决同意抵押的决定。

格雷：你同时还需要一位房产律师处理不动产转让手续，处理所有的法律程序及草拟合同。你需要指派律师代表你行事，同时与卖方的中介、律师以及你的银行保持联系。律师会准备签约事宜。

玛丽：对了，你还要请一个房产检视员帮你作一份买屋报告或房屋结构报告，确认房屋的状况良好。你的贷款也会作一份独立的估价报告，并会要求你付这份报告的钱。当银行看到估价报告，并再次审核你的申请表后，才会将抵押款汇到你的律师的帐户。

格雷：呵呵，之后的 20 年你就得背负房债，而且如果你付不出按揭，银行可随时把房屋收回。

王刚：噢，可是至少你现在拥有了房屋，只要一直有工作而且房价一直涨，那就没问题了。

玛丽：哈，这才是问题所在。你绝不能生病或丢掉工作！

Chapter 20

Do It Yourself

自 己 动 手 做 (DIY)

Everything connected to homes and home building in Britain — from estate agents to builders — seems to be connected to some form of 'cowboy' economy. Because the economy is so "deregulated", there is less government control over standards than in some other European countries. The political consensus is that this is good, but on a personal level British people never stop complaining about the poor quality of building work and the dodginess of builders in general. One of the results of this is the enormous surge in the popularity of DIY since the 1960s.

You might have seen a new store in China called B&Q. In the UK this is an extremely popular lower-end builders' merchant which caters to home owners and which reflects the fascination and obsession that British people have with DIY and home-improvements. For the British, a house is not just something that you live in or that you have; it is something that you actively work on. Almost the entire population is engaged in some form of DIY, and it has been found that British people spend more than £ 8,500 million per year on DIY, and that only 2% of British men and 12% of women say that they never do any form of home improvements.

As with everything in Britain, class pervades everything from the type of furniture and fittings that a house has to the names people use for the items in the house. It is generally believed that upper-class houses have older shabby, frayed furniture which is of a very high quality and has been handed down through the generations. In fact, a former Conservative politician was snobbishly ridiculed by his colleagues for having bought all his own furniture. Middle class or working-class *nouveaux riches* homes might have new, more showy and expensive furniture along with expensive wide-screen digital TV and music centres which are the focal point of the living room or lounge. Traditional symbols of working-class and middle-class British homes which are becoming less common are the net curtains and the cluttered floral chintz furniture of the stereotypical country cottage. A more modern 'tasteful' look now is the plain white-walled house with bare stripped floorboards and minimalist furniture. 'Shabby-chic' is a popular look among young professionals.

Whatever their social class, all British people moan and say what a nightmare it has been renovating it when they are talking about their home. They will never talk about how much it cost, though. Only the most vulgar of the new rich will advertise their wealth when talking about their homes. It is, however, all right to talk about the current value of your home, because that is something outside your control.

■ ■ ■ ■ ■ ■ ■ ■ ■ ■ ■ ■ ■ ■

在英国，任何与房屋及建筑相关的行业，从房屋中介商到建筑商，似乎都跟"牧童经济"*扯得上关系，因为他们太"没规矩"了。英国政府对标准的设定比其他欧洲国家都更为松散。这从政治角度上看，大家一致认可，但是对个人而言，英国百姓对低品质的建筑工程及建筑工人偷鸡摸狗行为的抱怨从未间断过。因此，从上世纪60年代后，自己动手做（DIY）在英国大受欢迎。

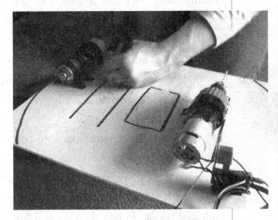

你在中国可能见过"百安居"这家店。在英国，"百安居"是热门的低阶层、建筑工人的采购地，他们同时也接待屋主，反映了英国人对自己动手建房或装修房屋的偏爱。对英国人来说，一栋房屋不只是住的地方，同时也是可以不断折腾的地方。几乎全民都从事不同程度的DIY活动。调查显示，英国人每年花在DIY上的钱约有8500万镑，只有2%的男性及12%的女性从未自己动手做过家庭装潢。

和所有的事一样，在英国，等级主导一切，从哪种式样的家具和装饰，到哪个品牌的小物件。一般而言，上流社会的家庭会使用历代流传下来的高品质破旧磨损的家具。事实上，一位前任保守党政治家曾被他的同事嘲笑，说他的家具都是新买的。中产阶级或是工人阶级的新贵则拥有最新、最华丽及最贵的家具，并把昂贵的数字宽屏电视及音响设备当作是起居室的焦点。在工人阶级和中产阶级家中，传统的装饰是网纹窗帘及典型乡村网格的印花棉布，不过现在已经很少见了。取而代之的是"有品味"的效果：大白墙、不铺地毯的条纹木地板、极少的家具。"新怀旧风"已成为年轻一代所青睐的装潢风格。

无论哪个等级，当讨论到自己的家，所有的英国人都会抱怨重新装潢是他们的梦魇，但他们却从不讨论花了多少钱。只有庸俗的暴发户才会在谈及自己房屋时炫耀他们的花销。不过，说说你房子的市值是可以的，反正它也由不得你。

---

*牧童经济：指那种能耗大、效率低、损害环境的粗放型经营模式。

At Jean and Jim's House

Lei Lei: This is a really nice house, Jean. It must have cost you a lot.

Jean: Oh! Ha ha ha... [cough cough]

Marie: Ha ha.

Jim: Well... not really. You know, house prices are absolutely absurd these days. We picked this place up for quite a reasonable price, but, you know, prices have gone up so outrageously. We had it valued the other day, and you know what the agent said it was worth? £450,000! Can you believe it?

Marie: Gosh! That's amazing.

Jean: Yes, but the problem is that if you want to trade up it's the same story. You'd have to trade down in order really to make any money.

Greg: Yes, it's terrible really. I don't know how youngsters manage to get onto the housing ladder these days.

Jean: Well, their parents have to help them find the deposit, or they have to go in with friends, don't they?

Greg: Or they have to move into privately-rented accommodation where they get ripped off by slum landlords. I mean, there are no council houses any more since the government allowed people to buy their council houses.

Lei Lei: Well I think your house is beautiful, anyway. You must be really pleased with it.

Jean: Well... [sigh] ... the estate agent was a complete idiot... totally sly and incompetent.

Greg: Well, what do you expect... they're like used-car salesmen, aren't they? Thick as two short planks!

Jim: You're telling me!

Jean: Yes, and the process took forever. It was a nightmare.

Gang: I think this room is really nice... there's a lot of natural light in it.

Jean: Well, it's not what we would have chosen, but I suppose we'll just have to live with it for now. We haven't done this room yet, as you can see. Ha ha. But, I know what you mean; it does have potential, doesn't it?

Jim: Yeah... we had to rip out the awful tiled fireplace and pull up the patterned carpet in the lounge, but it's going to take time to do the rest. The floorboards are all original, and there are some other interesting features like an old conservatory on the back wall. I want to go for the minimalist, shabby-chic look. We'll need to rip out the old kitchen soon, of course.

Jean: Well I hope you just don't end up taking forever and leaving the whole place covered in plaster and dust of weeks and weeks.

Jim: Don't worry… I'm going to get some help to do it. We can order the kitchen online, I'll phone up a skip-hire firm and I'll go down to B&Q and pick up a couple of Eastern European guys to do the labouring… they all hang out down there looking for work.

Marie: Well, be careful.

在珍和吉姆家

蕾蕾：珍，你家真的很漂亮，一定花了你不少钱。

珍：哦！呵呵呵……［咳嗽声］

玛丽：呵呵。

吉姆：噢，不尽然。你知道，近来房价真的高得离谱。我们买的时候价格还算合理，但是现在已经涨的很离谱了。我们前一阵子请人来估价，你知道那个房屋中介估多少钱吗？45 万英镑！你能相信吗？

玛丽：天啊，那真是令人吃惊。

珍：对啊，不过，问题是如果你想换大一点的房子就会花更多的钱。你得换小一点的房子才能赚钱。

格雷：对啊，真的很糟。我真不知道现在的年轻人要怎么样才能买到房。

珍：噢，他们的父母得帮他们筹到保证金，或是他们跟朋友合伙买房，对吗？

格雷：或者，他们搬进私人出租的住所，被房东们剥削。我的意思是，自从政府允许人们买下他们住的廉租房，现在已经没有所谓的廉租房了。

蕾蕾：噢，我认为你的房子真的很漂亮。你一定很满意。

珍：嗯……唉，那个房屋中介商真是一个白痴！非常的狡猾而且无用。

格雷：噢，你还能期待什么?! 他们就像卖二手车的，不是吗？笨得跟猪一样！

吉姆：这还用说嘛！

珍：对啊，而且办个手续拖了很久。真像个噩梦。

王刚：我觉得这个房间很好……光线很好。

珍：噢，这不是我们想要的房子，不过我想我们现在得凑合着住一段时间了。你可以看得出来，我们还没装饰这个房间，呵呵。但是我明白你的意思，这个房间很有潜力，不是吗？

吉姆：对啊，我们得把这个丑陋的壁炉拆掉，把客厅的地毯换掉，但是其余部分就得花点时间。这地板是原木的，还有一些不错的特色，像后面的温室。我想要极简主义的做旧效果。当然我们还得把旧的厨房换掉。

珍：噢，我倒希望你别干个没完没了，把整个家埋在泥巴和灰尘里。

吉姆：别担心，我会找人帮忙的。我们可以在网上买厨具，我会打电话给垃圾箱出租公司，然后到百安居去找一些东欧工人来帮忙，他们都在那附近转悠找活儿干。

玛丽：噢，小心点儿。

Chapter 21

Religion

宗 教

Marx said that religion was the opium of the masses because in the 19th Century rich people could afford to smoke opium but the poor couldn't, so they turned to religion to escape from their hard lives in industrial Britain. These days, although Britain is often seen as a Christian country by the Chinese, and the British government plays on its religious heritage to attract tourists, most British people do not actually attend church services, and are ambivalent about their belief in god. In fact, to say that you are religious is to be seen as a bit uncool and weird — as Tony Blair admitted when he left office.

The word *Christ*, in English, means *Jesus*. The main branches of the Christian religion are Catholic, Protestant and Orthodox. The Chinese language distinguishes between *Catholics* and *Christians*, but it is, in reality, distinguishing between *Catholics* and *Protestants*. When the Chinese refer to *Christians*, they are referring to *Protestant Christians*. The fact is that Catholicism, Protestantism and Orthodoxy are all different branches of the Christian religion, and these branches are subdivided into many sects.

Catholicism is the largest branch of Christianity, and is centred on Rome. The Pope is the head, and the Roman Catholic Church was a massive political force during the early modern period. Britain was Catholic before the 16th Century. Protestant Christianity arose as a reaction to corruption and immorality in the Catholic Church in Europe during the late middle ages, and England and Scotland separated from the Roman Catholic Church for political as well as religious reasons in the 16th Century. Henry VIII (the fat king with the six wives!) founded the "Church of England", or the "Anglican" Church, in 1536, because the pope wouldn't let him divorce his first wife, and his daughter, Elizabeth I, consolidated it in 1569, and it is this branch of the Church which is considered to be quintessentially English. In fact, the government-promoted tourist image of Britain focuses on old churches which are actually Anglican churches taken over from the Catholic Church 400 years ago. Although intended to be a Protestant church, it is in fact a typical English "fudge" or compromise, and it contains branches which are more Catholic and branches which are more Protestant. This is why if you visit some of these old churches and cathedrals in England you might think that they are Catholic when, in fact, they belong to the Church of England. In fact, to say you are a member of the Church of England is to say that you are middle-of-the-road, moderate and do not hold extreme opinions.

Generally speaking, most English and Scots gradually became Protestants from the 16th Century onwards, while most people in Ireland remained Catholic, and Catholics became a persecuted minority in Britain for 300 years. From the time of the Industrial Revolution in the 19th Century, however, the Catholic population has increased again in Britain because of migration from Ireland and Southern and Eastern Europe. At the same time, immigration has resulted in large Muslim communities from Pakistan, Somalia and Bangladesh, and you will see mosques and people who are readily identifiable as religious Muslims all over Britain. In addition to this there are large Sikh and Hindu communities in Britain as well. The people who practice these faiths were often born here in the UK of Indian parents. The Jewish community in the UK seems to be getting smaller since its heyday in the early twentieth century when many Eastern European and Russian Jews came to Britain to escape persecution at home.

■ ■ ■ ■ ■ ■ ■ ■ ■ ■ ■ ■ ■ ■ ■

马克思说"宗教是人民的鸦片",因为在 19 世纪时,只有有钱人才可以负担得起鸦片,穷人只能靠宗教去逃避他们在英国工业时代所面临的苦日子。虽然英国被中国人视为基督教国家,而且英国政府也使用宗教遗产来吸引游客,但是大多数的英国人并不去教堂,而且对上帝的信仰也很矛盾。事实上,如果你说你有宗教信仰,会被认为是怪人,正如托尼·布莱尔在卸任时所承认的那样。

基督这个词在英文里是耶稣的意思。基督教里最大的分支为天主教、新教及东正教。中文里的天主教徒及基督徒实际上应该是天主教徒与新教徒。中国人说的基督徒指的是基督新教徒。事实上,天主教、新教及东正教都是基督教的分支,这些分支又被细分为更多的派别。

天主教是基督教下最大的分支,以罗马为中心,教皇是天主教的领袖。在近代的早期,罗马天主教拥有强大的政治力量。16 世纪以前,英国是天主教国家。在中世纪晚期,为了反抗欧洲天主教会的腐败和堕落,新教应运而生。英格兰与苏格兰于 16 世纪因政治及宗教因素脱离了罗马天主教会。亨利八世(娶过 6 个老婆的胖国王!)于 1536 年因为教皇不允许他与第一任老婆离婚而创立了英国国教,或称"圣公会"。他的女儿伊丽莎白一世女王更于 1569 年巩固了英国国教的地位。这个教会被认为是完全属于英国的宗教。事实上,英国政府对游客所推广的英国形象主要体现在在 400 年前英国国教从天主教会手中夺来的老教堂。英国教会虽然表面上是一个新教徒的教会,实际上是一个典型的英国式的幌子,一个妥协让步的结果。你可以发现有些教堂比较倾向天主教,而有些则倾向新教。这就是为什么当你在英格兰参观一些教堂及主教座堂时你会认为它们是天主教教堂,但事实上它们属于英国国教会。实际上,当有人开玩笑说他是英国国教徒时,他其实是说他是中间派,温和、没有极端的意见。

　　一般而言，16 世纪后，大多数英格兰人和苏格兰人逐渐转变为新教徒，大多数的爱尔兰人则保持了天主教信仰。英国的天主教徒在之后的 300 年里变成受迫害的少数。但是，从 19 世纪工业革命开始，从爱尔兰、南欧及东欧来的移民潮使得天主教人口又开始在英国激增。同时，从巴基斯坦、索马里及孟加拉国来的移民使得英国拥有庞大的穆斯林社区。你可以在英国各地看到清真寺及特征明显的穆斯林。除此之外，英国还有庞大的锡克教和印度教社区。那些锡克教和印度教的教徒往往是在英国出生的印度后裔。犹太移民的全盛时期为 20 世纪初，当时，为了躲避国内的迫害，很多犹太人从东欧及俄罗斯移民到英国。现在，犹太社区在英国逐渐势微。

They're Just Religious Nuts!

Gang: Hi Greg, some people came to the door this morning and they gave me these leaflets.

Greg: Let's see. "Jesus loves you!?" "Do you ever wonder what we're here for!?" "Prepare for eternal life!?" Tsk! God botherers!

Gang: Sorry?

Greg: They're religious nuts; some weird sect. You should have ignored them. Erm… you didn't talk to them, did you?

Gang: Well, actually, I invited them in for a cup of tea. We had a very interesting chat; they told me all about their Bible study group and how to spread the word, and that we need to be born again, to pray to our heavenly father and to know Jesus as our saviour!

Greg: Look, Wang, nobody believes in that mumbo jumbo any more except weirdos and religious maniacs… people who can't live without a crutch, something to give meaning to their lives.

Marie: Come on, Greg. Not all religious people are nutters. There are some very genuine people who believe in doing good and want some spirituality in their lives.

Greg: Ooooh… spirituality. If you want that, you can become a Buddhist and go off to India… or maybe China. Wang should know all about that… they're more spiritual in the East.

Gang: Actually, a lot of Chinese think that Christianity is more spiritual than what we have in China.

Marie: Well, I was brought up in the Catholic Church, and that always seemed quite boring… not very spiritual at all, and Grey used to be Church of England but, as you can see, he's very much an Atheist now. You know, here in England, lots of young people experiment with Eastern religions like Buddhism and Hinduism because they think that they offer something deeper than Christianity.

Gang: Well, I'm going to go down to their Church service on Sunday to see what it's all about.

Greg: Don't do it Gang! Don't let them brainwash you! They prey on vulnerable naïve students like you who are away from home. Remember all those lectures on rationality and logic, evolution and science. You can't seriously believe that some supernatural power created the world! Anyway, what about all the wars and famines and poverty and injustice in the world? You can't tell me there's a god when the world is in such a mess!

Gang: Who am I to say that there's a god or not? I'm just curious. Anyway, you guys keep telling me that I need to go out and socialise and integrate culturally.

Marie: I think Gang's right. I mean, if I were studying in China, I'd want to visit Taoist temples and stuff.

Greg: Hallelujah! Praise the Lord! Amen!

他们是宗教狂人！

王刚：嗨，格雷，今天早上有人来敲门，还给我这些传单。

格雷：我来看看。"耶稣爱你!?""你是否怀疑过我们生存的意义!?""为永生做准备!?"呸！恼人的上帝崇拜者！

王刚：什么？

格雷：他们是宗教狂热分子，一些怪人。你不应该理会他们。噢，你没跟他们说话吧？

王刚：噢，事实上，我请他们进来喝了茶。我们聊了一些有趣的事。他们告诉我有关他们读经班的事情以及如何散播福音，还有我们要怎样才能重生、如何祷告及认识我们的救世主耶稣。

格雷：听着，王刚，除了怪胎和宗教狂热分子，没人再相信那些胡言乱语了。那些人不信点什么就没法活。

玛丽：格雷，别这样。不是所有虔诚的信徒都是怪胎。有些真诚的人希望做些好事从而得到精神上的支柱。

格雷：哦……精神上的依靠。如果你想要那些，你应该成为佛教徒去印度或中国。王刚应该对那些很了解，东方人比较崇尚精神生活。

王刚：事实上，有很多中国人认为基教徒比我们中国人更崇尚精神生活。

玛丽：噢，我是在天主教环境中长大的，但是对我来说这些非常无趣，谈不上什么精神生活。格雷曾经是英国圣会教徒，但你可以发现他现在差不多是个无神论者。你知道吗，在英国有很多年轻人尝试东方的宗教，像是佛教和印度教，因为他们觉得这些宗教比基督教更有内涵。

王刚：噢，我星期天想去教堂做礼拜，看看他们都做些什么。

格雷：王刚，别去！不要被他们洗脑！他们专找脆弱天真的学生，像你这样远离家乡的人。想想你上过的所有关于理性、逻辑、进化及科学的课程。你不会真的相信是超自然的力量创造了世界吧！还有，你怎么解释这世上所有的战争、饥荒、贫穷和不公道的事呢？这个世界这么乱，你怎么能说有神的存在呢？

王刚：我哪能说有没有神存在呢？我只是觉得很好奇。还有，你们老是说我需要到外面走走，多与人交往，融入当地文化。

玛丽：我觉得王刚是对的。我是说，如果我在中国求学的话，我也会去道观走走。

格雷：哈利路亚！赞美神！阿门！

Chapter 22

Superstitions

迷 信

From murdered brides and headless horsemen to screaming skulls, from giant worms and dragons to griffins, British folklore is full of spine-tingling ghost stories, myths and legends. Terrified witnesses speak of seeing ghostly Roman armies marching through the fog, hanged pirates searching for hidden treasure and monks chanting in ruined monasteries.

Scientists would say that there is no such thing as supernatural beings — whether they be gods, ghosts, pixies, fairies, elves or goblins. However, human beings everywhere seem to have a need to believe in phenomena which cannot be explained through scientific research. Because of this, despite living in the home of the Enlightenment, modern scientific discoveries and the Industrial Revolution, British people can be surprisingly superstitious. Historically, adults have told ghost and other frightening stories to children; in Europe, the tales of the Brothers Grimm are a collection of stories from European folklore, and the recent Harry Potter series attests to the global popularity of the supernatural among children and adults all over the world.

Christians are not supposed to believe in ghosts and the supernatural. The main Christian Churches officially condemn belief in ghosts, dreams, witches and so on. They say that the dead cannot communicate with the living. However, they do ask their followers to believe in the phenomenon of life after death — that when people die they go either to be with God in Heaven or with the Devil in Hell. Some Churches also ask people to believe in angels and saints, and say that if people pray to saints they will intercede with God on behalf of the people who pray.

Most schoolchildren have some understanding of the main notions of Christianity and, if they go to a faith school they will have a more in-depth knowledge of religious dogma and doctrine. They also learn ghost stories and legends from their local area, and these are often collected and published in booklets in local tourist information offices, local history centres and public libraries. Schoolchildren often do projects on these stories and put posters and stories up on the walls of their classrooms.

There are lots of everyday practical superstitions in Britain such as not walking under a ladder, not walking on the cracks in the pavement, avoiding the number thirteen and so on. The number seven is supposed to be ominous or special; if you are the seventh son of a seventh son you will be a bad sort or the black sheep of the family.

　　被谋杀的新娘、无头骑士、嚎叫的骷髅头、巨型蠕虫、恶龙及鹫头飞狮，英国的民间故事充满了让人毛骨悚然的神怪传说。惊吓过度的目击者诉说看到罗马士兵的鬼魂在雾里行军、被吊死的海盗到处寻找宝藏，还有修道士的鬼魂在修道院的废墟中诵经。

　　科学家会说世上没有超自然的事物，无论是神、鬼、精灵、仙女、小矮人或是妖魔。但是，不管哪儿都有人相信那些无法以科学解释的超自然现象。因此，即便是住在启蒙运动之乡、科学发明和工业革命重镇的英国，人们还是非常迷信。过去，大人们会对小孩讲述鬼怪或其它的恐怖故事。在欧洲，格林兄弟便是由欧洲传说演变而来的一系列神怪故事集。最近的哈利·波特系列也证实了超自然现象受到全球大人及小孩们的喜爱。

　　基督徒不应该相信鬼魂和超自然现象。基督教会公开谴责对鬼魂、幻想、女巫等等事物的迷信。他们认为死者无法与生者沟通。但是，他们要求信徒相信死后的生命——不是到天堂与上帝在一起，就是去地狱见恶魔。有些教会要求信徒相信天使与圣者，并说如果人们向圣者祈祷，圣者会代他们向上帝说情。

　　大部分小学生对基督教教义有些许了解，如果他们在教会学校受教育，会对宗教教义及教条有更深入的认识。他们同时也会学到关于他们区域的一些鬼怪传说，这些传说通常会被收集并出版成小册子放在当地的游客服务中心、历史景点及图书馆。小学生们常常以这些传说为科研项目，制作海报贴在教室的布告栏上。

　　在英国有很多迷信的说法，例如不要在梯子的下方穿过、不要走在人行道的裂缝中、避免数字13等等。7是不吉利的数字，如果你是第7个儿子所生的第7个儿子，你会是个坏种，家族的祸根。

That Sounds Terrifying

Gang: Greg, I saw this horror film on TV last night, and I had nightmares all night. I tossed and turned and had to keep the light on. I was terrified!

Greg: What was the film?

Gang: It was called *Dracula Has Risen from the Grave*. There was this scene where there's a girl walking through a dark forest. She sees this old black horse-drawn hearse through the trees, and gets scared and starts running. The black horses start trotting after her pulling the hearse behind them. She

I was terrified!,,,

starts panicking and running faster and looks back and sees that Dracula — his eyes burning red and his face twisted — is driving the horses forward and cracking a whip...

Greg: Gosh! That sounds terrifying. I used to watch horror films when I was a kid, and I always had to cover my face and go and hide behind the settee. I like the older horror films; they're much darker and psychological than the modern ones. I think the modern ones rely too much on technology and blood and guts — but they aren't really that frightening. I mean, one of my favourite ones is called *The Shining* — it really builds up the pressure and tension to breaking point.

Gang: I'm not so sure about that, Greg. I've seen some recent films that are really horrific and disturbing; films like *Ring* and *The Eye*. Then there's that film *The Others*. The end is so shocking it really takes you by surprise. I like those films like *The Lord of the Rings* — you know, fantasy films based on mythology.

Greg: Do they like horror films in China, Gang? I think I saw a couple of Chinese horror films; one of them was called *Rouge* — it was set in Hong Kong, and was about a young couple involved in a suicide pact because the boy's parents wouldn't agree to him marrying the girl. She died and he didn't, and years later her ghost came back to him. It was kind of nostalgic and tragic and frightening, but it was witty and humorous as well.

Gang: Yes I know that one, and there's a film which is actually called *A Chinese Ghost Story*, and there are lots of films which are based on myths and legends — you know, *Crouching Tiger*, *Hidden Dragon* and stuff like that. Do you have any local myths and legends here?

Greg: Well, there is the story about the son of the local lord went fishing in the local river. He caught a big worm and threw it back into the water. Later on he went abroad to fight in a war, and when he was away the worm grew to an enormous size and started terrorising the local peasants and eating their animals. The lord's son came home, dressed up in spiked armour, and chopped the giant worm to pieces. What about in China?

Gang: Well one of the most classical sources is *Strange Tales from a Chinese Studio*, by *Pu Songling*. It's full of tales about ghosts, fantastic beasts, vixen spirits and Taoist exorcists. It's got some really weird things like flying umbrellas and demons carrying people off in boats. The interesting thing about it is that it is ironic and turns expectations on their heads by making the supernatural characters good and the humans bad, a bit like in that film, *Rouge*, that you saw.

Greg: Yeah. You're right.

听起来真吓人

王刚：格雷，我昨晚在电视上看了一部恐怖片，害得我整晚做恶梦，翻来覆去睡不着，还得整晚开着灯。吓死我了！

格雷：你看了什么电影？

王刚：我看的是《吸血鬼冒出坟场》。其中有一幕是一个女孩走进黑暗的森林，她看到一驾由黑马拉的灵车穿过树林，她很害怕，拔腿就跑。那些黑马拉着灵车朝她奔来，她开始惊慌，狂奔。当她回头时看到吸血鬼红着眼、满脸狰狞地驾着灵车追来，手上挥动着马鞭……

格雷：天啊！听起来真吓人。我小时侯常看恐怖片，而且常常用手遮住眼睛，躲在沙发后面。我喜欢老旧的恐怖片，比现在的恐怖片更黑暗，更能制造心理恐惧。现在的恐怖片太依赖科技手段和血腥场面，其实并不会让你感到恐惧。我最喜欢的恐怖片是《闪灵》，真的把恐怖气氛营造到了极点。

王刚：格雷，我不是很确定。我看过一些最近的电影，真的非常恐怖，像是《午夜凶铃》，还有《见鬼》。另一部是《小岛惊魂》，结局非常惊人，让你觉得十分意外。我比较喜欢魔戒三部曲那样的根据神话创作的魔幻电影。

格雷：王刚，中国人喜欢看恐怖片吗？我想我看过几部中国的鬼怪片，其中一部叫《胭脂扣》。场景设在香港，是关于一对情侣因男方的父母反对迎娶女方，所以相约自杀的故事。那个女的自杀身亡，但是男的没死，几年后女方的鬼魂回来找他。这部电影有点惆怅、悲情还有一点惊悚，不过也拍得非常机智幽默。

王刚：噢，我知道那部片，还有一部叫《倩女幽魂》。我们有很多电影是根据神怪故事及传说拍摄的，像是《卧虎藏龙》之类。你知道有哪些英国神怪故事或传说吗？

格雷：噢，有个故事是说一个地主的儿子到河边钓鱼，他捉到一条大虫，又把大虫丢回水里。不久后他到外国去打仗。他不在期间那条虫变得非常巨大，吓唬当地农民，并吞食农民所养的牲畜。地主的儿子打仗回来，便穿着盔甲将大虫碎尸万段。你们中国有什么神怪故事及传说呢？

王刚：噢，最经典的是蒲松龄的《聊斋志异》，那里面充满了光怪陆离的故事。有些非常诡异的事物，比如会飞的伞，还有会把人捉上船的鬼怪。最有趣的是故事的讽刺性，鬼怪都性情善良，人类则阴险邪恶的，有点像《胭脂扣》里的情景。

格雷：噢，有道理。

Chapter 23

Christenings, Weddings and Funerals

洗 礼、婚 礼 及 葬 礼

Your opinions of British weddings may have been formed by films like *Four Weddings and a Funeral*. Although most British people would not be able to afford the lavish weddings portrayed, this film is broadly accurate in terms of the rituals and ceremonies shown and the attitudes of the participants. In the film the hero, Hugh Grant, plays his usual bumbling, clumsy, socially-inept self, and this is a remarkably apposite take on the attitude that most British people have around ceremonies of this kind. The British 'do' formality very well, but they do not actually like formality; they do not go in for extreme displays of emotion at formal rites of passage like engagement parties, graduation ceremonies, weddings, funerals and christenings. They feel stilted and stiff, and this uneasiness reflects a deep ambivalence in the British character — a need for formality and ritual, but a deep discomfort when taking part in it. If the ceremony is in a Church and is too overtly religious it makes people feel uncomfortable, causing them to squirm and shuffle their feet, even if they profess to belong to one of the Christian denominations. This is perhaps why copious amounts of alcohol are served at many of these ceremonies as a social lubricant and as a way of getting the stiff-upper-lipped British to loosen up a bit. The problem with this is, of course, that things can go too far, the best man might give a drunken speech and a reserved wedding reception can turn into wild party later on.

A christening — or a baptism — is a formal ceremony which welcomes a child into a particular Christian denomination, and is held in a church. Holy water is sprinkled on the child's forehead by a priest or minister, and it is usually only close family and godparents who attend.

At a big white wedding in a Church, people will dress formally, with the groom and the best man and the bride's father wearing a morning suit and the bride in white with the bridesmaids in coloured frocks. The guests will all dress up, and the women will often wear hats, revealing dresses and high heels, as at Ladies' Day at the horse racing. Many people prefer to go for a smaller, less formal wedding at a register office.

Most church weddings consist of the following: the wedding procession — or entrance of the bride with her father — with the groom and the best man waiting at the altar with the priest. That is followed by music, literature, and poetry or wedding readings from the Bible. The couple make their vows and exchange rings, the groom kisses the bride and the priest blesses them. The couple and witnesses then follow the priest into a side room to sign the register and the marriage certificate.

Funerals are perhaps the most difficult ceremonies to deal with. The pain of bereavement and loss compounds the natural difficulty that the British have with social situations, and greetings and condolences can appear even more cold and stilted. An embarrassed, "sorry for your trouble", or "he'll be sadly missed", is what you will most often hear coming from guests at a funeral. Only very close friends and family will hug or kiss each other.

■ ■ ■ ■ ■ ■ ■ ■ ■ ■ ■ ■ ■ ■ ■ ■

你所了解的英式婚礼也许是从电影《四个婚礼和一个葬礼》而来，虽然大多数英国人无法负担像电影中那么豪华的婚礼，但是电影里所表现出的仪式与参加婚礼者的心态却与事实很接近。在片中，男主角休·格兰特扮演他一贯的角色，笨手笨脚又少根筋的人，这非常精确地演绎出英国人在这些仪式上的表现。英国人可以将形式做得很好，可是却很不喜欢形式。他们不喜欢在一些正式的仪式上，像订婚仪式、毕业典礼、婚礼、葬礼及受洗礼等，流露太多的情感。他们会觉得拘束不自然，而这种拘束感反映了英国人非常矛盾的心态，他们一方面需要有固定的仪式，但是对于参加这些仪式感到相当的难受。如果仪式是在教堂举行而且搞得太庄重，那么即使参加的人曾公开承认是教会的一员，也会觉得不自在而手足无措。这也许就是为什么在这些场合会有大量的酒供应，酒作为润滑剂能让拘谨的英国人稍微放松一点。但问题是太多的酒也会让大家轻松过头，伴郎也许会在演讲时胡言乱语，而正式的婚宴也会变成狂欢派对。

受洗礼是在教堂里欢迎一个小孩进入基督国度的一种正式仪式。这个仪式是由一名天主教神甫或新教牧师将圣水洒在小孩的额头上，通常只有近亲和教父母才能参加。

在教堂举办的大型白色婚礼上，人们会穿正式服装，新郎、伴郎及新娘的父亲穿晨间礼服，新娘穿白色婚纱，伴娘们则穿其他颜色的长裙。客人们也会盛装出席。女士们通常会戴帽子、身着礼服及高跟鞋，像是要参加女士日的马赛。许多人喜欢参加小型的，不那么隆重的，在登记处举办的婚礼。

大多数的教堂婚礼首先是步入礼堂仪式，新娘在她父亲陪伴下从教堂门口走入，而新郎及伴郎、教士则在教堂内的法坛处等候。之后会有音乐、诗词朗诵或圣经朗读。新郎及新娘宣读誓言并交换戒指，新郎亲吻新娘，新人接受教士的祝福。之后，新人及证婚人会跟随教士到旁边一间屋子签署结婚证书。

葬礼也许是最难处理的仪式了，居丧的痛苦加上英国人在这种场合拙劣的应对能力，使得相互问候及慰问显得非常的冷漠及不自然。在葬礼上客人说得最多的话莫过于一句尴尬的"为你的麻烦感到难过"或是"我们会悲伤地怀念逝者"。通常只有非常亲近的朋友及家属才会互相拥抱或亲吻。

At the Wedding

Priest: Dearly Beloved, we are gathered here today in the presence of these witnesses, to join Jim and Jean in matrimony, which is commended to be honorable among all men; and therefore — is not by any — to be entered into unadvisedly or lightly — but reverently, discreetly, advisedly and solemnly. Into this holy estate these two persons present now come to be joined. If any person can show just cause why they may not be joined together — let them speak now or forever hold their peace.

Priest: Jim, do you take this woman to be your lawfully wedded wife, to have and to hold from this day forward, for better for worse, for richer for poorer, in sickness and in health, to love and to cherish and forsaking all others to be faithful to her from this day on, till death do you part?

Jim: I do.

Priest: Jean, in the presence of God and these our friends do you take this man to be your husband, promising with Divine assistance to be unto him a loving and faithful wife so long as you both shall live?

Jean: I do.

Priest: You may now exchange rings.

Jim: Jean, with this ring, I thee wed, with my body, I thee worship, and with all my worldly goods I thee endow. In the Name of the Father and of the Son and of the Holy Spirit, Amen.

Jean: Jim, I give you this ring as a symbol of my love and faithfulness. As I place it on your finger, I commit my heart and soul to you. I ask you to wear this ring as a reminder of the vows we have spoken today, our wedding day.

Priest: You may now kiss the bride.

* * *

Marie: Aw. Doesn't she look beautiful?

Mother: Yes. Absolutely radiant. I think I'm going to cry.

Father: He'd better take care of her!

* * *

The After Dinner Speech

Best man: Ladies and gentlemen, I was honoured when Jim asked me to be best man at his wedding. I have known him since we were both four years old. On his first day at school he ran out of the class crying for his mum. Of course, that was not unusual for a four year old kid, but we did find it strange that he was still doing it when he was sixteen... [ha ha] ... I think he's grown out of it, though. I just hope he doesn't go crying to his mum tonight! Now, when he was in the Army, of course, he was the one who... and when he met Jane... [ha ha] ... I remember, once, we were travelling in France on holiday and he met this girl... and she... and so he said... [ha ha ha] ... so, ladies and gentlemen, I hope you will be upstanding, raise your glasses and join me in a toast to the bride and groom!

Everyone: The bride and groom!

Greg: How does this compare to weddings in China, Gang?

Gang: Well, of course there's lots of toasting and drinking there as well. The thing is, though, that the bride has to change dresses lots of times. Usually, they go to the registry office, then straight to a hotel for the wedding reception. The guests file in and hand over a red envelope containing cash for the bride and groom, and the envelopes are opened in public and the amount put down in a big ledger.

Marie: What!? We would never do that here! You mean everyone can see how much you've given to the bride and groom?

Gang: Of course.

Greg: God! Nobody would ever do that here. Flaunting your wealth like that.

Gang: We don't think it's showing off. We think it's all part of being generous and helping the young couple. And, of course, the favour is always returned when the next person gets married. It's all part of *guanxi*.

Anyway, here you have wedding lists. So everybody knows what gift you bought for the bride and groom. In China we just cut to the chase!

在婚礼上

教士：亲爱的朋友们，我们今天聚在这里共同见证吉姆和珍的结合，这是最崇高的结合，所以不可以被轻忽或儿戏，应以虔诚、慎重、深思熟虑及庄重的态度来进行。这两人到这神圣的殿堂里结合，任何人如果有任何原因认为他们不可以结合，请现在表达出来，否则请永远保持沉默。

教士：吉姆，你愿意接受这个女士成为你合法的妻子，从现在开始无论生活好坏、贫穷富裕、生病或健康，屏除一切对她忠诚、永远爱护并珍惜她直到死亡将你们分开吗？

吉姆：我愿意。

教士：珍，在上帝与我们的朋友面前，你愿意接受这个男人为你的丈夫，在神护佑下保证一生一世成为他钟情及忠实的妻子吗？

珍：我愿意。

教士：你们可以交换戒指了。

吉姆：珍，我以这枚戒指娶你，用我的身体崇拜你，给与你我全部的财富。以圣父、圣子、圣灵之名阿门。

珍：吉姆，我给你这枚戒指象征我的爱与忠诚。当我将戒指为你戴上时，我将我的心及灵魂委托于你。我希望你戴着这个戒指，把它当作我们结婚誓言的信物。

教士：你可以亲吻新娘了。

* * *

玛丽：哇，新娘看起来真美！

新娘母亲：对啊，光彩照人！我想我快要哭了。

新娘父亲：他得好好照顾她！

* * *

在喜宴上

伴郎：各位先生及女士们，当吉姆邀请我当他的伴郎时我觉得非常荣幸。我们

从4岁起就认识了。他第一天上学时，哭着跑出教室找妈妈。当然对4岁小孩来说这并不稀奇，但奇怪的是他到16岁时还这样……哈哈……不过我想他已经不那样了。我只希望他今天晚上不要哭着找妈妈。当他在军队时他是那个……当他第一次跟珍见面……哈哈……我记得有一次我们到法国度假时他遇到这个女孩……她……所以他说……哈哈……所以，各位先生及女士们，请你们起立，举杯与我一起敬贺新郎及新娘！

所有人：敬新郎和新娘！

格雷：王刚，这和中国式的婚礼比起来怎么样？

王刚：噢，在我们那里当然也要敬很多的酒。还有，新娘会换好几套礼服。通常我们会先去登记处办证，然后直接到饭店举办婚宴。客人们会到婚宴处签名，然后将装了钱的红包送给新娘及新郎。在现场红包会被打开，金额记录在账本里。

玛丽：什么!？我们这里绝对不会这么做！你是说每个人都可以看清你包了多少钱给新郎新娘？

王刚：当然。

格雷：天啊！在英国绝对没有人会这么做，把钱在大家面前招摇。

王刚：我们不会认为这是在作秀。我们认为这是很慷慨的事，这样可以帮助新婚夫妇。而且，下一对夫妇结婚时这钱还可以收回来。这全都是在维护关系。还有，你们这里也有结婚礼品清单，每个人都会知道你送了什么礼物给新郎新娘。在中国我们只是更直接罢了！

Chapter 24

Multicultural Britain

英 国 的 多 元 文 化

One of the things which most surprises Chinese students when they come to Britain is that a large proportion of the people do not seem to be 'English' or 'British'. Because of the stereotypes of the British that exist in China, many Chinese expect British people to be 'white'. The reason why there are so many different ethnicities in Britain is, of course, that Britain has always attracted immigrants because of its colonial past and its modern economic and political freedoms. In addition to this, though, recent British governments have adopted multicultural policies, and these policies allow immigrant communities to maintain their own cultural norms and practices to a greater degree than in other European countries.

Multiculturalism is a philosophy which recognises ethnic and cultural diversity within society and encourages the celebration of differences and the positive contributions that immigrant communities make rather than trying to make society homogenous. The analogy that is often used by proponents of multiculturalism is that it creates a 'stir fry' society rather than a 'melting pot'.

Because of this, you will often see communities — especially in larger cities — where the people do not speak English and where they appear to have nothing in common with the majority 'white' culture of the UK. In London, for instance, you will find areas like Newham, where most of the population appears to be Asian and African, Haringey, where there is a large Turkish community, and Brixton, where people are mainly Afro-Caribbean. Most areas of Britain now also have large Chinese and Eastern European communities. The fact that so many of the most recent immigrants are white now means that it is acceptable to discuss immigration in a way which would have been previously unacceptable for fear of being accused of racism.

There has been a reaction against multiculturalism in the past few years. Critics say that the policy encourages communities not to integrate and assimilate into British society, and that it favours the celebration of minority differences over what is common to the majority. They say that the policy is a misguided attempt at political correctness and that it actually does minority communities a disservice by keeping them isolated.

An interesting point about the use of the word 'Asian' to describe people in British English is that it refers to people from the Indian sub-continent — Indians, Pakistanis, Bangladeshis and Sri Lankans. Chinese, Japanese and Koreans would be referred to as 'East Asian' or 'Oriental', although some people consider the latter term condescending and old-fashioned.

■ ■ ■ ■ ■ ■ ■ ■ ■ ■ ■ ■ ■ ■

中国学生到英国来后最惊讶的一件事就是，很多人看起来不是"英国人"。英国给人的固定印象让很多中国人认为英国人都是白人。实际上，英国有很多不同种族的人，这是因为英国以前的殖民统治以及英国在经济和政治上的自由吸引了很多的移民。除此之外，近年来英国政府施行了多元文化政策，外来移民可以保有他们自己的文化规范及生活习惯，这比其他欧洲国家宽容得多。

多元文化理念认可社会上种族及文化的多样化，鼓励差异化，认可移民带来的贡献，而非将整个社会同化。多元文化的提倡者经常以"炒菜"而非"熔炉"来比喻多元化的社会。

因此，尤其是在大城市里，你常会看到一些社区里的人根本不会说英语，而且与英国大多数的白人文化似乎一点交集也没有。例如在伦敦，你会发现诸如纽厄姆这样的社区，当地绝大部分的人口为亚洲人和非洲人，而哈林盖则有庞大的土耳其社区，布里克斯顿聚集了许多的非裔加勒比人。目前在英国的大部分地区都有庞大的中国人及东欧人的社区。事实上，因为最近的移民多是白人，大家现在可以讨论一些移民问题，不至于像以前大多数移民为非白人的时候，讨论移民问题会被视为种族歧视。

在过去几年曾有人反对多元文化。批评者指出多元文化的政策不鼓励外来移民融入英国社会，过于强调少数民族的特色而非社会大多数人的共同点。他们认为这种政策是政治正确性的误导，孤立并危害了少数民族。

有趣的是在英国"亚洲人"这个词指的是从印度次大陆来的人，如印度人、巴基斯坦人、孟加拉人及斯里兰卡人。中国人、日本人及韩国人，则被称为"东亚人"或"东方人"，虽然有些人认为"东方人"是种老旧的自贬身份的称呼。

Who Is British?

Gang: Your next-door neighbours are not British, are they, Greg?

Greg: Who? Aslan and Benazir? Actually, they are. They were born here.

Gang: But they are Muslims, aren't they? They are from Pakistan.

Greg: Well, they are Asians, but they are British citizens; I think their parents must be from Pakistan.

Marie: The thing is that here in Britain citizenship isn't based on ethnicity — it's based on residence. So, if you were born here of British parents or you have become naturalised, then you are British. Most of us are from other places originally, anyway. I mean, my grandfather is Italian and one of my grandmothers was Irish.

Greg: Yes, and my brother's wife is from Jamaica originally. When her parents came to Britain, Jamaica was a British colony so they were all British citizens anyway.

Gang: Hmm. It seems to me though that some of the ethnic minority communities in Britain don't subscribe to British values like tolerance and respect for individual liberty. I mean, last night on TV there was a documentary which argued that immigration and multiculturalism had brought no benefits to Britain and that some communities were actively and violently opposed to Britain and its values.

Greg: Well, many communities don't subscribe to 'British' values because they see them as corrupt and immoral. They see a decline in family values, the collapse of religious belief and selfishness masquerading as freedom. Many immigrant communities have different values to the majority "white" community, and these values need to be respected.

Marie: What? Values like forced marriage, honour killing and violence against women? That's just cultural relativism, Greg. Multiculturalism has resulted in the isolation of some communities — they are ghettoised. I think there needs to be more assimilation and that minority communities need to accept our essential values like democracy, the rule of law, equality and respect for this country and its shared heritage. If it hadn't been for misguided multicultural policies, the 7/7 bombers would never have been radicalised in the way they were. You know, it isn't racist to say that multiculturalism is mistaken — all citizens should have the same rights and duties, no matter what their ethnic background.

Gang: Well, in China we have fifty six ethnic or national groups which are all part of China. They are all Chinese.

Marie: Does the government treat them differently? I mean, do they have the same rights and power as the majority Han Chinese community or does the government treat them differently?

Gang: Well, actually, some minority ethnic groups get favourable treatment when they apply to university, and ethnic minorities are not subject to the one-child policy either.

Greg: Ah, but do they all subscribe to common shared Chinese values? Do they all see themselves as part of the same Chinese nation?

Gang: That's difficult to say. Obviously there are communities in most countries that do not want to be part of that country, but the difference in China is that the ethnic minorities have not come from outside China like in Britain. They were already living within the historical borders of China.

谁才算英国人?

王刚:格雷,你隔壁的邻居不是英国人吧?

格雷:谁? 阿斯兰和班纳尔? 事实上,他们是英国人,他们都是在这里出生的。

王刚:但他们是穆斯林,不是吗? 他们是从巴基斯坦来的。

格雷:噢,他们是亚洲人,但他们是英国公民。我想他们的父母是从巴基斯坦来的。

玛丽:在英国,公民的界定取决于居留权,而不取决于民族。如果你在这里出生,父母是英国公民,或者你入了籍,那你也可以成为英国人。大多数人都是从其他地方来的,我是说,比如我的祖父是意大利人,而我的祖母是爱尔兰人。

格雷:对啊,我的弟媳妇是从牙买加来的。当她的父母从牙买加搬到英国时,牙买加还是英国的殖民地,所以无论如何他们都是英国公民。

王刚:噢,在我看来,有些在英国的少数民族并不认可英国的价值观,像是宽容及尊重个人自由等等。我是说,昨天晚上电视上有个纪录片,就在讨论移民及多元文化政策并未对英国带来任何好处,而且一些移民还以暴力活动来反对英国及英国的价值观。

格雷:噢,有很多移民并不接纳英国的价值观,他们认为这些价值观是腐朽而且不道德的。他们看到家庭观念的淡化,宗教信仰的衰落,还有以自由为伪装的自私。许多的移民社区与绝大多数的白人社区有很不同的价值观,这些是该被尊重的。

玛丽:什么? 你说的那些价值观是不是包括强迫结婚、为家族荣誉而杀人以及对妇女的暴力行为? 格雷,多元文化政策导致了一些少数民族被孤立,他们被隔离了。我认为他们需要被同化并接受我们基本的价值观,比如民主、法律、平等以及尊重这个国家并分享这个国家的传统。如果不是多元文化政策的误导,像 7 月 7 号伦敦爆炸案的那些犯人就不会那么激进。你知道吗,指责多元文化并不是种族歧视的言论,所有的公民,不论是什么种族,都应该有相同的权利与义务。

王刚:噢,在中国我们有 56 个民族,都是中国的一部分。大家都是中国人。

玛丽:政府对不同民族的待遇有差别吗? 我是说,他们都和占人口大多数的汉人同样享有同样的权利与义务吗? 还是政府对他们有不同的优待?

王刚:噢,事实上,少数民族申请大学会得到特殊优待。还有,少数民族不受独生子女政策的约束。

格雷:噢,但是他们接受普遍的中国价值观吗? 他们把自己当作中国人吗?

王刚:怎么说呢,很明显在很多国家总有一些人不希望被当作那个国家的一分子,但是中国不同,中国的少数民族不像英国移民一样是外来的,他们原本就住在中国境内,原本就是中国人。

Chapter 25

English Heritage and the National Trust

英格兰文化遗产协会及英国国家基金会

The British in general are obsessed with ancient buildings and monuments. Not for them the Chinese idea that new houses are better than old ones. Their sense of patriotism is this comfortable, homely sense of tradition and continuity, rather than outright nationalism expressed by some other cultures. Two organisations which exist to preserve and protect Britain's physical cultural heritage are English Heritage and The National Trust. The former is a quasi-governmental body which receives money from the government through taxation and is responsible for over 370,000 listed buildings, while the latter is a charitable organisation charged with protecting open spaces and country houses and other threatened buildings. It receives its money from subscriptions, entrance fees and legacies. It is staffed by volunteers.

Members of the public can join both organisations, and membership confers the right to visit hundreds of historical buildings and sites around the country from mediaeval castles to Victorian gardens and World War II coastal defences. Visit any English Heritage or National Trust site at the weekend, and you will see that most members of both of these organisations are white, middle class and middle aged or older. You will see relatively few non-white faces, and most of these will be foreign tourists.

The commentator, Jeremy Paxman, says that English Heritage and the National Trust seem to typify a certain strand in British culture which harks back to comforting myths and notions of the past, and the idea that Britain has a glorious past which has been somehow lost.

■ ■ ■ ■ ■ ■ ■ ■ ■ ■ ■ ■ ■ ■ ■ ■ ■ ■

一般说来，英国人对古老的建筑及纪念物非常着迷，不像中国人认为新的房屋比旧的好。英国人的爱国主义体现在传统和延续性带来的舒适和安全感，不像其他一些文化只强调国家主义。在英国，有两个组织致力于英国物质文化遗产的维修和保护，即英格兰文化遗产协会和英国国家基金会。文化遗产协会是一个半官方的组织，其资金来自政府的税收，管理超过370,000座登记在案的古迹。国家基金则是一个慈善机构，负责保护一些开放空间、乡村宅第及其他濒危建筑物。它的资金来源是认捐、门票及遗赠。员工都是志愿者。

一般民众可以加入这两个组织，会员可以参观全国数百座历史建筑及古迹，从中世纪城堡、维多利亚时代的花园到二战时期的海防工事等。在周末参观任何一座这两个组织管理的遗址，你都会发现两个组织的会员大多数都是中产阶级的中老年白人。也有少数非白人面孔，大多都是外国观光客。

评论家杰里米·帕斯门认为，这两个组织反映出英国文化中一股希望回复美好过去的潮流，还有对曾经拥有的光荣历史的怀念。

I Never Knew About All of This

Marie: Right. We're here: Alnwick Castle. This is where they filmed *Harry Potter*, you know, Gang. It was the interior of Hogwarts School in the film, and it was, in *Robin Hood*, *Prince of Thieves* and *Elizabeth* too.

Gang: Wow. I thought it looked familiar. It's pretty impressive. Does anyone actually live here?

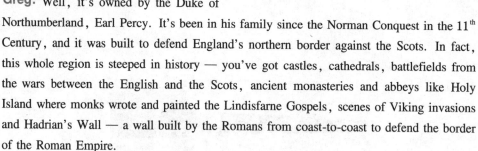

Alnwick Castle.

Greg: Well, it's owned by the Duke of Northumberland, Earl Percy. It's been in his family since the Norman Conquest in the 11th Century, and it was built to defend England's northern border against the Scots. In fact, this whole region is steeped in history — you've got castles, cathedrals, battlefields from the wars between the English and the Scots, ancient monasteries and abbeys like Holy Island where monks wrote and painted the Lindisfarne Gospels, scenes of Viking invasions and Hadrian's Wall — a wall built by the Romans from coast-to-coast to defend the border of the Roman Empire.

Gang: I never knew about all of this.

Marie: I know. Most tourist guides concentrate on London and the South of England, and most tourists don't know anything about the bleak and windswept beauty of the north. I mean, up here we've got absolutely breathtaking natural scenery — the Lake District where the original Romantic poets like Wordsworth lived, Hadrian's Wall, which was the old frontier of the Roman Empire and the Pennines — the mountains and moors where the famous novel *Wuthering Heights* was set.

Greg: Let's have a walk around the gardens. These are world-famous. They were planted by the wife of the Duke. The town here is very beautiful and historical as well; it's on the Great North Road, which is the original route from London to Edinburgh. Do you have any ancient sites like this in China, Gang?

Gang: Of course. There's the Great Wall, the Summer Palace, The Forbidden City and all of those places.

Marie: Yes, but I heard that the Great Wall had been rebuilt in places. Not like Hadrian's Wall, where it's the real thing.

Gang: Well it's true that many sites in China have been reconstructed, so they are not actually the original buildings. That's because in China, we knock things down and rebuild them all the time. We don't have this reverence for ancient buildings just because they are old. It's the actual site that's more important than the building in China.

Marie: Yeah. I heard that it was all to do with the feng shui of the place.

Gang: Kind of. I mean, we believe that buildings should be in harmony with the natural surroundings; that's why we use geomancers to divine where we should build and to search out where the *qi* flows in a place. The thing is, though, that it's the place, not the building, that is important.

我从来都不知道这些

玛丽：噢，我们到了，这里就是安尼克城堡。王刚，你知道吗？这就是电影哈利·波特拍摄的地方。霍格沃茨魔法学校的内景就是在这儿拍的，还有《侠盗罗宾汉》及《伊丽莎白女王》，也是在这里拍摄的。

王刚：哇，我就觉得有点眼熟，的确令人印象深刻。真的有人住在这里吗？

格雷：噢，这座城堡的主人是诺森伯兰郡公爵珀西伯爵，他们家族从 11 世纪诺曼征服时便拥有了这座城堡，当时建筑这座城堡是为了保护英格兰北部边界，防止苏格兰人的侵略。事实上，这个区域在历史上的地位非常重要，这里有城堡、大教堂、英格兰与苏格兰对抗的战场、古老的修道院比如神圣岛，修士们在那里撰写并绘制了《林地斯梵福音书》，还有北欧海盗入侵的遗址和哈德良长城，一座由罗马帝国沿海岸修建的防御城墙。

王刚：我从来都不知道这些。

玛丽：我知道为什么。大多数导游都专注于伦敦及英格兰南部的介绍，所以绝大多数游客都不了解北部苍凉无边，狂风劲吹之美。我的意思是，在这里我们有令人屏息的大自然美景，比如湖区，浪漫诗人华兹华斯就住过那里，哈德良长城是罗马帝国的边界。还有奔宁山，那里的高山及沼地就是著名的小说《呼啸山庄》所描述的地方。

格雷：我们到花园走一圈吧。这些花草可是世界闻名，由公爵夫人亲手栽种的。这个城镇非常美而且历史悠久，位于北方大道上。从伦敦到爱丁堡的大道原本会经过这里。王刚，你们在中国有像这样的古老遗迹吗？

王刚：当然有。我们有万里长城、圆明园、紫禁城还有其他很多地方。

玛丽：对啊，不过我听说长城有些地方重新修建过，不像哈德良长城全部都是古时建造的。

王刚：噢，在中国有很多的古迹都被重建过，所以不能算是原始的建筑。我们常常会将建筑物打掉重建。我们并不觉得建筑物够老就该被尊重。我们觉得遗址比建筑更重要。

玛丽：对啊，我听说这与风水有关。

王刚：有一点儿。我是说，我们认为建筑物要与周遭环境融合，所以我们请风水师卜卦决定应该建于哪里，气会朝哪里流动。重要的是地点，而非建筑物本身。

Chapter 26

Families

家 庭

British family structure is quite different from family structure in China. Apart from the obvious fact that most Chinese couples have only one child, it is very rare in Britain to find an extended family where grandparents live with their children and grandchildren. Some Chinese people are shocked at the fact that older British people often end up living in care homes rather than with their families. The reasons for this phenomenon are, of course, to do with complex economic and social factors and does not mean that British people do not care for the older generation or that Chinese people care more.

The makeup of British families has changed radically during the last two hundred years. The traditional family structure before the Industrial Revolution was the extended family in which it was common for three generations to live under one roof. The early twentieth century saw the growth of the nuclear family in which parents and a small number of children would constitute a single household. The last thirty years, however, have seen a breakdown of the typical nuclear family. Increased divorce rates, later marriage and a move away from marriage altogether has resulted in phenomena like reconstituted families, where divorced parents will form new relationships and take their children with them and couples living together and having children without getting formally married. It has been reported recently that over 50% of children are now born to parents who are not married. Some of these are couples — others are single mothers.

Some minority communities keep to the extended family structure, and it is not uncommon to find families from the Indian sub-continent where there are three generations living under one roof. They say that apart from maintaining traditional family ties, it provides security for older people when they cannot work any more. They point to the phenomenon of other old people living in care homes and believe that this indicates that many old people in the wider community are abandoned in their old age.

The government has recently introduced the concept of civil partnership as an alternative to marriage. This is an attractive option for many modern couples who do not want to marry but want the economic benefits of a formal partnership. Many gay couples choose this option as a way of formalising their relationship and ensuring that when one partner dies the other can inherit property and money. Some gay couples have children by other partners and, although social conservatives find this shocking, British notions of freedom and tolerance seem to accept this.

　　英国家庭结构与中国家庭结构有相当大的差异。除了绝大多数的中国家庭只有一个小孩外，另一个较明显的差异是，在英国很少家庭是三代同堂的。有些中国人对于英国老人住在养老院而非与自己的家人同住感到非常吃惊，造成这种现象的原因多与复杂的经济及社会因素有关，并非英国人不如中国人孝顺他们的长辈。

　　过去两百年来，英国的家庭结构有很大的转变。工业革命以前，传统的家庭结构为三代同堂。20世纪初，由父母与子女构成的小家庭逐渐增加，而过去30年来典型的小家庭也逐渐瓦解。离婚率的激增、晚婚及同居的盛行导致新的家庭结构出现，离婚的男女各自带着子女与新的伴侣另组家庭，也有人同居生子却不结婚。最近的报导指出，超过50%的小孩出生于非婚之家，其中有部分是父母同居但不婚，有些则是生于单身母亲。

　　有些少数民族还保有传统的大家庭结构，印度次大陆来的家庭中三代同堂也很普遍。这种家庭结构除了可维持传统家庭关系外，也给老年人在无法工作后带来一点保障。他们把其他老人住在养老院的现象视为有很多老人被遗弃。

　　最近英国政府提出了将民事伴侣关系当作是结婚关系的另一个选择。这对于一些既不想结婚，又想拥有因正式关系所带来的经济利益的人很有吸引力。许多同性恋伴侣用此种方式将他们的关系正式化，以确保当其中一人过世后，另外一方可以继承财产。有些同性恋伴侣通过其他伴侣获得小孩，虽然保守派的人非常震惊，但是英国人自由、宽容的观念却又容许这种事。

You Seem to Be Happily Married

Gang: Greg. Do you think Lei Lei would make a good wife?

Greg: Who for? For you? Oh, I don't know. Are you planning to ask her?

Gang: Well I like her, and I think that after we graduate we should get married and have a child.

Greg: Have you asked her?

Gang: Not yet. I mean, I wanted to ask your advice. You and Marie seem to be happily married and you have a beautiful daughter. It all seems very nice.

Greg: Well, actually, Marie and I are not married. We just don't think that we need to get married to show our love or that we are good parents. Anyway, we couldn't agree on what kind of wedding to have; it would have been a nightmare trying to reconcile parents and family and everything and, after all, marriage is just a piece of paper in the end, isn't it?

Gang: I suppose so, but there's no way our families in China would accept that. The thing is, it would be a great loss of face for our families if we just lived together, and our parents would disown us. There's also the money aspect, of course. You can get a lot of red envelopes when you get married.

Greg: Well, I don't know, but I think you need to be absolutely certain that you want to get married before you take the leap. It's supposed to be for the rest of your life, after all. You know, over half of all British marriages end in divorce these days.

Gang: I guess so. I mean, nobody gets married with divorce at the back of their minds, but I suppose that divorce is getting more and more common in China as well. I mean, traditional values are breaking down as people get wealthier and travel more. I think that the frenetic pace of change in China is putting pressure on people to concentrate on things outside the family.

Greg: I suppose you're right. They say that the Internet is causing marriage breakdown as well!

Gang: How's that?

Greg: Well, people are meeting other people online more; you know, a friend of mine met his old girlfriend online on a website for former school friends. Both of them were married with kids; they ended up divorcing their partners, getting back together and taking their kids with them. Now they have a new family with two kids from their ex-partners and a new one on the way! How about that?

Gang: Unbeleivable! I don't know if that would go down well in China. The neighbours would talk!

Greg: Well neighbours gossip here too, you know. Everyone likes a bit of tittle-tattle. Anyway, if you look at soap operas on TV, all the families are like that.

Gang: Well, in China we have a one-child policy. You can only have one child per couple, unless you are in a special category like an ethnic minority or married to a foreigner.

你们看上去婚姻美满

王刚：格雷，你觉得蕾蕾会是个好老
婆吗？

格雷：对谁而言？对你吗？噢，我不知
道。你要向她求婚吗？

The Internet is causing marriage breakdown as well!

王刚：嗯，我喜欢她，所以我想等我们
毕业后跟她结婚，生个小孩。

格雷：你问过她了吗？

王刚：还没。我想先听你的意见。你和
玛丽看起来婚姻美满，还有一个漂亮的
女儿，真的很幸福的样子。

格雷：噢，实际上，玛丽和我并没有结婚。我们觉得并非一定要通过结婚才能证明
我们爱对方，或证明我们是好父母。还有，我们没办法决定举行哪一种结婚仪式，
才能让双方父母及亲友都满意，还有一大堆事要协调，那会是个噩梦。毕竟，结婚
只是多一张纸，不是吗？

王刚：我想也是，但在中国，我们的父母是没办法接受未婚同居的。我们如果同居，
那我们家会很没面子，父母会不认我们的。还有钱方面也是一个问题，你结婚时会
收到很多的红包。

格雷：噢，我也说不好了，但是在你做决定前，你一定要十分确定你想结婚。毕竟
结婚是一辈子的事。你知道吗，在英国有超过一半以上的婚姻以离婚收场。

王刚：我想也是。没有人在结婚时会想到以后会离婚，但是我想离婚在中国也越来
越普遍了。当人们变得更有钱，更见多识广时，传统的价值观念也逐渐瓦解了。我
想，中国的急速变化让人们把心思放在家庭以外的事上。

格雷：你说得对。大家都在说互联网也是造成婚姻破裂的原因。

王刚：怎么讲？

格雷：噢，大家在网上可以碰到更多人。我的一个朋友在一个校友网上遇到他以前
的女友。他们都各自结了婚，也有小孩；结果最后他们都离了婚，带着孩子组建了
新的家庭。现在他们有两个上一次婚姻带来的小孩，他们自己的小孩也快要出生了。
有意思吗？

王刚：太不可思议了！我不知道在中国行不行得通。邻居们一定会在背后说闲话的！

格雷：在这里邻居也会说长道短。每个人都喜欢传些小道消息。你如果看电视上的
连续剧，就知道所有的家庭都是那样的。

王刚：噢，在中国我们实行独生子女政策。一对夫妇只能有一个小孩，除非你是例
外，像是少数民族或是跟外国人结婚等。

Chapter 27

Charity Shops

慈善商店

Two interesting features of the British tendency towards eccentricity are the car-boot sale and the charity shop. Both of these are variations on the theme of the garden fete, is aimed at selling goods to raise money for charitable causes.

Charity shops were founded in the early twentieth century by groups like **Oxfam** and **The Salvation Army** which wanted to raise money to carry out charity work. People would donate bags of old clothes and other items like books, records, ornaments and small items of furniture which could be sold on to the public at low prices. Over the last ten years there has been a revolution in the charity shop sector in the UK, with new market-led management, and some charity shops in well-to-do areas are as expensive as up-market retailers. Go into any charity shop on a Saturday morning and you will find people of all ages and classes rummaging around looking for a bargain; it might be a rare CD, a book for a university course, a brand-name shirt or an antique vase.

Car-boot sales are equally popular, but they do not have the overt aim of raising money for charity. This is a way for people to have a good clear out and get rid of old possessions that they don't want any more and to make a bit of money at the same time. Car-boot sales take place at weekends in fields on the edge of all towns in Britain. Here you will see individuals, groups of friends and families with a trestle table set up at the back of their car, selling all kinds of things out of the boot of their car. Although there are asking prices for the items on sale, there is plenty of room for negotiation and bargaining in a car boot sale.

As with everything in Britain, class anxiety features in people's behaviour around charity shops and car-boot sales. Some people will be very proud of having got a good bargain and will readily tell their friends. In fact, charity shops in up-market areas will sell very high quality clothes at quite high prices. Other people who are forced to buy clothes in charity shops, though, might be deeply embarrassed and ashamed.

　　有两件事体现英国人的怪异偏好；逛汽车跳蚤市场和慈善商店。这两者都是由慈善清仓大拍卖演变而来的，慈善清仓大拍卖的目的是以变卖物品来筹措慈善基金。

　　慈善商店创建于20世纪初，由慈善组织，如乐施会及救世军等所筹办，目的在于筹措资金做慈善工作。人们会捐赠旧衣物以及其他物品，如书、录音带、装饰物以及其他小型家具等，再以低价卖给普通群众。在过去的十年间，英国的慈善商店有很大的改变。在新式的市场化管理下，有些富人区的慈善商店卖得和高级零售店一样贵。在星期六的上午到任何一家慈善商店，你会发现男女老少，不分等级在店里东翻西找挑选价廉物美的商品，也许是一张稀有唱盘、一本大学教科书、一件名牌衬衫或是一个古董花瓶。

　　汽车跳蚤市场同样受欢迎，但是他们的目的并不是为了筹措慈善基金。人们可在这儿处理掉一些不要的旧东西，并且从中赚一点钱。汽车跳蚤市场通常在周末举办，地点是位于英国各城镇边缘的空地。在那里你可以看到人们单个、结伙或是全家出动，在车后架起折叠式的桌子，贩卖各式各样的商品。虽然每样商品都有标价，但是绝对有很大的议价空间。

　　和所有在英国的事情一样，等级焦虑就算在慈善商店和汽车跳蚤市场的买卖中也表现无遗。有些人会很骄傲地告诉朋友们他们买到了便宜货。事实上，很多在富人区的慈善商店会以高价出售高品质的衣物。有些人因家境较差而不得不在慈善商店里买衣服，他们会因此觉得难为情。

At a Car-boot Sale

Marie: How much is this vase here?

Woman: It's £ 49. 99, dear.

Marie: £ 49. 99? That's a bit much. Look — it's chipped.

Woman: I know, dear, but it's a genuine antique — Chinese, Ming Dynasty.

Marie: Hey, Gang. This lady's saying that this is a genuine Ming vase. Is she right?

Gang: Well let me see...

Marie: Gang's Chinese — he'll know.

Woman: Well, I was sure it was Ming — I mean, it's been in my family for years and my mother told me it was Ming.

Gang: Well it's got the right blue glaze and it looks old. Look here on the bottom, though. It says Coalport. It isn't Chinese.

Marie: Hmm... I knew it!

Woman: OK. Look, I'll let you have it for £ 20. How about that?

Greg: Let me have a look. Hmm... I don't think it's worth £ 20. Could you go a bit lower? I'll give you a fiver for it.

Woman: Look, love. It's cost me £ 30 just for this pitch today. I'm not even going to cover my costs if I give these things away.

Marie: All right, we'll leave it then. Let's go guys.

Woman: All right, all right. I'll let you have it for a tenner.

Gang: £ 7. Here you are.

Woman: All right, then. You lot are robbing me blind, but I've got to make a living.

Marie: Do you have car-boot sales in China, Gang?

Gang: We don't have car-boot sales, but we do have flea markets. *Panjiayuan* is one of the most famous ones in Beijing. If you go there you can get all kinds of second-hand stuff, bric-a-brac and even genuine antiques. Most of the antiques are fake, though.

Greg: My friend went to China and he came back with loads of things from the Cultural Revolution — you know, Red Guard hats, Little Red Books, revolutionary posters...

Gang: I suppose Western tourists like that kind of thing. We Chinese find them a bit tacky and naff, though. There are factories that churn out these things because they know tourists want them. Some parts of China also have night markets.

Marie: I suppose it's like Chinese tourists buying plastic policeman's helmets and Union Jack T Shirts when they come to London. Greg, we're really going to have to have a good clear out at home and bring all of our stuff to a car-boot sale, and if we can't flog it we'll have to give it to a charity shop.

在汽车跳蚤市场

玛丽：这个花瓶多少钱？

女人：49.99 镑，亲爱的。

玛丽：49.99 镑？太贵了吧，你看这上面还有缺损。

女人：我知道，可这是真正的古董，中国明代的花瓶。

玛丽：王刚，这位女士说这是真正的明代花瓶。她说得对吗？

王刚：噢，我来看看。

玛丽：王刚是中国人，他会懂的。

女人：噢，我确定这是明代的，摆在我们家很久了。我妈妈告诉我这是明代的。

王刚：噢，这蓝釉没错，而且看起来很老旧。看一下花瓶的底部，这里写着科尔波特瓷器，这个不是中国的。

玛丽：哈，我就知道！

女人：好了，我就卖你 20 镑，如何？

格雷：我来看看。噢，我觉得这个花瓶不值 20 镑。可以卖便宜一点吗？我出 5 镑。

女人：喂，我今天花了 30 镑租了这个摊位，如果我把东西便宜卖，都不够本的。

玛丽：好吧，放下，我们走吧。

女人：好了，好了。我就卖你们 10 镑吧。

王刚：7 镑。这给你。

女人：好吧。你们这是在打劫我，没办法，我还得过日子。

玛丽：王刚，在中国你们有汽车跳蚤市场吗？

王刚：我们没有汽车跳蚤市场，但是我们有旧货市场。潘家园就是北京最有名的旧货市场之一。如果你们到那里可以买到各式各样的二手货、纪念品以及古董。但是大多数的古董都是假的。

格雷：我有一个朋友到中国去，带了很多文化大革命时期的东西回来，像红卫兵的帽子、毛泽东的红宝书，还有一些文革时期的海报。

王刚：我想西方游客会喜欢那些东西。我们中国人会觉得那些有点俗气。有些工厂会大量制造那些东西，因为他们知道游客想买。中国有些地方还有夜市。

玛丽：我想，这就像一些中国游客到伦敦会买塑料制的警帽和英国国旗 T 恤一样。格雷，我们应该好好清理一下家里的旧物，拿到汽车跳蚤市场来卖，如果卖不掉就只好送给慈善商店了。

Chapter 28

Down the Pub

去 酒 吧

Pubs are to Britain what teahouses are to China, and traditional pubs, with their distinctive appearance, are major draws for overseas visitors to the UK. There are about 60,000 public houses — or 'pubs' — in the United Kingdom and, apart from selling alcoholic beverages to the public, they also serve an important social and cultural function. Going 'down the pub' is routinely listed as the most common pastime for many British people, and 'the local' has replaced the village church or the post office in many places as the most important venue in the community. In this respect, they are not simply bars or drinking houses. Different pubs and bars cater to different clientele. Many pubs are designed and decorated in the style of cosy living rooms, with comfortable sofas and armchairs and wooden panelling and bookshelves. Others have more plain, functional interiors with long wooden tables and benches and wooden flooring, designed for large groups of younger drinkers. Yet others are fitted out in futuristic metallic décor with large screens on the walls, and cater for music or sports fans. Many pubs also serve bar food or 'pub grub' at lunchtimes. You order and pay for the food and drinks at the bar, then take a table and wait for the waiter to bring it.

Many Chinese students spend four years in the UK without ever setting foot inside a pub, and those who do go enter gingerly and uncomfortably because they haven't acquired the social habits and techniques associated with pub culture and ordering drinks. Because of this, they are missing out on one of the most important experiences of British social life. There's no need to feel uncomfortable in pubs; once you have worked your way around the draught beer pumps on the bar and the optics behind it and worked out the conventions of rounds and the strange references to 'pints' and 'halves' and 'spirits', you'll be fine.

Many of the bar staff in London or in the larger student cities are students themselves, or from overseas. Bar work is traditional area for young Australians, New Zealanders and South Africans, but Eastern European staff are becoming more common because of the expansion of the EU. Always, remember to say "please" and "thank you", when you order drinks. You'll hear British people using the word 'mate' to the barman; that will sound a bit weird coming from you, though.

Over 75% of adults in Britain regularly go to pubs, and over a third are 'regulars' at their 'local'. The pub is a democratic and egalitarian place where people can bond socially. The bar counter is one of the few places in Britain where it is socially acceptable to strike up a conversation with a complete stranger. There is no waiter service in a pub, and many foreigners will sit for ages at a pub table without realising this; drinks have to be bought and paid for at the bar and then carried to the table.

There is no visible queue at the bar, but the barman or barmaid will always know who is next, so if you try to order before it is your turn, he'll say, "sorry, who's next?"

■ ■ ■ ■ ■ ■ ■ ■ ■ ■ ■ ■ ■ ■ ■ ■

酒吧之于英国人就像茶馆之于中国人,而有特殊外观的传统酒吧最能吸引外国观光客。全英国约有60,000家酒吧,除了贩卖含酒精的饮料外,酒吧还兼具了重要的社交和文化功能。对很多英国人来说,"去酒吧"是最主要的休闲活动。而在乡下,当地酒吧取代了村里的教堂和邮局,成为社区中最重要的聚会地点。从这个角度来看,酒吧并不只是酒馆或喝酒的地方那么简单。不同的酒吧迎合不同的顾客。有些酒吧设计装修得像家里的客厅,有舒适的沙发、扶手椅、木板墙及书柜。另一些酒吧的装潢就比较简单和功能化,有长木桌、板凳适合成群的年轻顾客。还有一些酒吧用未来主义风格的金属装潢,墙上有大屏幕,适合喜欢音乐的人或运动迷。许多酒吧在午餐时段还提供食物。你先在柜台边点好食物和饮料,付完款,然后选一张桌子坐下,等侍者将你点的食品送来。

许多中国学生在英国待了4年却从未涉足酒吧,有些人即使进了酒吧也是战战兢兢地浑身不自在,那是因为他们还不习惯英国的社交习俗,也不熟悉酒吧文化和点酒的技巧。他们因此错失了英国社交生活中最重要的经验之一。其实你不必紧张,一旦你搞清吧台上那些生啤酒泵和量杯、帮朋友们买酒的习俗及一些奇怪的术语像是一品脱、半品脱及烈酒,你就会觉得很自在了。

在伦敦及一些大型的学生城,很多的酒吧工作人员都是学生,或是其它外国人。酒吧工作一向都是年轻的澳洲人、新西兰人及南非人的地盘,但是有越来越多的东欧人也因为"欧共体"的扩张而加入进来。在酒吧点酒时永远记得说"请"和"谢谢"。你会听到英国人称呼酒保"哥们儿",但如果是中国人这么叫,他们可能会觉得很奇怪。

75%的英国成年人经常光顾酒吧,约有三分之一的常客经常到当地酒吧喝酒。酒吧是个自由平等的地方,人们可以轻松地交流。在英国,酒吧的柜台边算是少数几个人们认可的可以与陌生人交谈的地方之一。酒吧待者不会到桌边接受点单,有很多外国人坐在桌边等很久还不知道怎么回事。你必须到柜台边点单并付钱,然后等待者把饮料端到你坐的地方。

在酒吧柜台边并没有明显的排队,但是酒保们总是知道谁是下一个客人,所以如果你想要插队,他们会发现并问:"下一位是谁?"

A Pub Lunch

Greg: Right, Gang, what are you having?

Gang: Erm, I don't know. What do they have?

Greg: Well, there's beer on draught — lager, bitter or Guinness. There's cider — draught and bottled. They also have bottled cider and lager behind the bar in the chiller cabinet, and there's alcopops as well.

Gang: What're alcopops?

Greg: They're like lemonade or fizzy orange juice with alcohol in them. They're quite sweet and strong — about 5% usually.

Lei Lei: I'll have an alcopop, please?

Gang: Erm, can I have a beer, please? A pint of lager?

Greg: Sure. Laura and Marie, what do you want?

Laura: Oh, I'll have a gin and tonic, please.

Marie: Can I get a dry white wine, please?

Greg: Right. Could we have a pint of lager, a breezer, a dry white wine and a gin and tonic.

Barman: Single or double?

Laura: Double, please. Ice and lemon, as well.

Greg: Oh, and I'll have a pint of Guinness. Shall we get something to eat as well? Let's have a look at the menu. Right, what do they have?

Laura: Ooh. I like the look of that — steak and kidney pie with chips and peas.

Marie: Mmm. I fancy something a bit lighter, actually. Could I get the chef's salad?

Lei Lei: Erm what's breaded scampi?

Laura: It's like seafood a bit like prawns, coated in breadcrumbs. I'm going to have it.

Lei Lei: That sounds nice. I'll have that.

Gang: I think I'll have the cheese burger and chips.

Greg: Right. I'll have the baked potato with beans. Did you get that?

Barman: Yes. There's your drinks. Here's a number. Just take a seat, and the waitress will bring your food over. That'll be £ 40. 25 altogether, please.

Greg: What?! OK. Do you take debit cards?

Barman: Sure. Just pop your card in the reader... right, just tap in your PIN, please... there you go... here's your receipt. Thank you, sir.

Greg: Thanks, mote.

112

酒吧午餐

格雷：王刚，你想喝什么？

王刚：嗯，我不知道。他们有什么？

格雷：噢，这里有生啤酒——淡啤酒、苦味啤酒和黑啤酒。还有散装的和瓶装的苹果酒。冰柜里也有罐装的苹果酒和淡啤酒，此外还有含酒精的果汁饮料。

王刚：什么是含酒精的果汁饮料？

格雷：像是柠檬汽水或气泡式橙汁再加上酒精，通常很甜很烈，酒精浓度大约有5%。

蕾蕾：麻烦给我含酒精的果汁饮料。

王刚：嗯，请给我啤酒。一品脱的淡啤酒。

格雷：没问题。劳拉，玛丽，你们要什么呢？

劳拉：哦，麻烦给我金汤尼。

玛丽：请给我一杯干白葡萄酒。

格雷：好，请给我们一品脱的淡啤酒，一瓶百加得冰锐，一杯干白葡萄酒，还有一杯金汤尼。

酒保：金酒要一份还是双份？

劳拉：双份，还要加柠檬和冰块。

格雷：哦，我要一品脱的黑啤酒。我们要不要吃点东西？看一下菜单……嗯，他们有什么呢？

劳拉：哦，我喜欢这个，牛排腰子派加上炸薯条和青豆。

玛丽：嗯，我喜欢清淡一点的，可以点厨师沙拉吗？

蕾蕾：嗯，什么是面包海螯虾？

劳拉：那是一种海鲜，像虾子，裹上面包屑。我要点这个。

蕾蕾：听起来不错。我也要一样的。

王刚：我想我要乳酪汉堡和炸薯条。

格雷：好，我要烤马铃薯和炖豆。你都记下来了吗？

酒保：是的。这是你的饮料，这是你的号码牌。请找个地方坐下，服务员会把你的食物端过去。总共是40镑25便士。

格雷：什么?! 嗯，好吧，你们收现金卡吗？

酒保：当然，请你把卡插入刷卡机……好，请输入密码。好了，这是你的收据。先生，谢谢你。

格雷：谢谢你，哥们儿。

Chapter 29

British Cuisine

英 国 菜

"Surely there's no such thing!" I hear you saying as you read the title of this chapter. How can bland, boring British cooking possibly compare with the delightful variety of Chinese food, the spiciness of Indian, the sophistication of French food or the all-conquering popularity of Italian pizza and pasta? Well, you'd be surprised. British food actually acquired a reputation for blandness during the nineteenth and twentieth centuries because all great national cuisines are based on poor peasant dishes, and since Britain had become an industrialised society, working people had lost their connection with the countryside.

A formal British meal consists of three courses; soup or starter, the main course, which traditionally consists of meat, potatoes and two other vegetables all served on the same plate, and then a dessert followed by cheese, fruit and coffee. The staple diet of 'meat and two veg' is so ingrained in the British psyche that we laugh when we see Chinese students piling their plates with totally incongruous combinations of food in university canteens, walking up to the cash register and paying four times as much as they should have because they have put four main courses together instead of one main course with a carbohydrate and vegetables.

Because of Britain's colonial past, the most popular take-away and restaurant food in Britain are Indian and Chinese, but the dishes served would probably not be recognisable to an Indian or a Chinese person. Rice, and especially pasta, are now popular alternatives to potatoes and bread, and supermarkets are now full of all kinds of foreign food from exotic fruit and vegetables to tinned and processed foods.

British cooking is currently enjoying a renaissance. Celebrity chefs like Gordon Ramsay and Jamie Oliver have made British food cool, and the TV schedules are full of cookery programmes like *Saturday Kitchen*, *The Naked Chef* and *Jamie's School Dinners*. Nowadays, lighter Modern British Cuisine sits alongside more the traditional cuisine of gentlemen's clubs with its focus on heavy meat-based dishes, pies and game, puddings and cheeses.

　　当你看到"英国菜"这个标题时，我想你一定会说"英国哪有什么好吃的菜！"平淡无味的英国菜怎么能与美味多变的中国菜、充满香料的印度菜、精致的法国菜及大受欢迎的意大利面和比萨相提并论呢？让人意外的是，英国菜之所以让人觉得平淡无味，是因为所有国家的菜肴都是从贫穷农家的饭菜演变而来的，英国在19及20世纪成为一个工业化社会，人民与乡村断绝联系，英国菜因此而平淡无味。

　　正式的英国餐包含了3道菜：汤或前菜，主菜（传统的主菜将肉、土豆及两样蔬菜全部盛在一个盘子上）、甜点及乳酪、水果、咖啡。这种以一种肉搭配两种蔬菜的饮食方式深植于英国人的心中，所以当他们在大学餐厅看到中国学生在餐盘里堆满了不协调的食物，并付了4倍的钱时，他们感到非常惊讶。那些中国学生买了4份主菜，而不是一份主菜搭配淀粉类和蔬菜。

　　因为英国过去的殖民地文化，最受欢迎的外卖和餐厅是印度菜及广东菜。但是端出来的食物对印度人和中国人来说可能很难辨认。米和意大利面成为取代土豆的最佳选择，超市里更是摆满了各式各样的异国食品，从外国水果、蔬菜到罐头及加工食品。

　　英国的烹调目前正处于复兴时期。知名的大厨像戈登·拉姆齐和杰米·奥利佛，让英国菜变得更流行了。电视上烹调节目扎堆，比如《星期六厨房》、《原味主厨》及《大城小厨学生餐》等。现在有很多清淡的新式英国菜与传统绅士俱乐部所提供的重口味的肉食、派饼、野味、布丁和乳酪等并存于市。

We Would Never Put Those Things Together

Gang: Marie. I'm not sure about what I should eat on the same plate. At the university today, these British students were sniggering and nudging each other and looking at the food on my plate.

Marie: What were you eating?

Gang: Erm, Spaghetti and meatballs, fish and baked beans and some boiled egg salad. Does it sound a bit strange?

Marie: Uuugh! It sounds disgusting. We would never put those things together. I mean, you've got alternative forms of protein and carbohydrate all mixed up on the same plate there. Then you've got eggs on top of that. No wonder people were looking at you funny. The standard is soup at the beginning of the meal, followed by meat and two veg — that means meat or fish or a meat pie, plus some form of potato like chips or mash and two other vegetables like carrots or peas or cabbage. You can put gravy on the meat if you like. Then, to finish off, you can have a sweet — something like apple pie and cream or rhubarb crumble and custard.

Gang: It's very confusing, Marie. Things are much more easy-going in China. Basically, you can eat whatever you like there. We all dip in and share from communal dishes in the middle of the table: etiquette here seems to be more formal than at home.

Marie: Well, I suppose what you need to remember is that you shouldn't drop your head down as close to the plate as you do in China. Also, it's not the done thing to speak with your mouth full or to chew with your mouth open. Just remember to cut with the knife in your right hand and put the food into your mouth with the fork in your left hand. Etiquette isn't as strict these days as it was a few years ago.

Gang: I've heard that people use different names for the main meals here in Britain. Is that a class thing?

Marie: Well, they say that working-class people call the midday meal dinner, while middle-class people call it lunch. The middle-class refer to the evening meal as dinner, and eat it around 7 to 7. 30 in the evening, while the working-class and lower middle-class call this meal tea, and have it earlier — around 5. 30 or 6. Curiously, the old upper class refer to the evening meal as supper, and they eat it later — perhaps around nine or ten at night. They also might have a light tea in the late afternoon. Traditional afternoon tea — that Victorian meal with cucumber sandwiches and cakes and scones — doesn't really exist any more, except in posh hotels and maybe at garden parties.

Gang: Why is there such a difference in the names of the meals?

Marie: Well, it's all to do with working hours. Workers had to have their main meal during the day in order to keep them going, and they went to bed earlier because they worked so hard. Middle-class people had more evening leisure time, so they could make the main meal more of a social event. The names have carried on even though working patterns have changed.

我们绝不会把这些放在一起吃

王刚：玛丽，我不知道我该点什么菜。今天在学校时，那些英国学生看到我盘里的食物都在暗自窃笑。

玛丽：你吃了什么？

王刚：嗯，意粉和肉丸、鱼和炖豆……还有鸡蛋沙拉。听起来有点奇怪吗？

玛丽：啊，有点恶心！我们绝不会把那些食物放在一起吃。我是说，你把本来只选其一的蛋白质及淀粉类全混在一起了，再加上蛋。难怪其他人在背后笑你。标准的吃法是先喝汤，接着吃肉及

两样蔬菜。就是说，你可以在肉、鱼或是肉派中点一样，加上炸薯条或是土豆泥，再配上两种蔬菜，比如胡萝卜、青豆或是甘蓝菜。如果想要的话，你也可以在肉上加卤汁。最后你可以点甜点，比如苹果派加鲜奶油，或是淋上蛋奶沙司的大黄派。

王刚：玛丽，这真的把我搞糊涂了。在中国比较简单。基本上你可以吃任何你喜欢的东西。我们在桌上放一些菜，然后大家分享。这里的餐桌礼仪比中国要正式得多。

玛丽：我想，你得记住吃饭时不要头低得像是埋在餐盘里。还有，边吃东西边讲话是不对的，不要张开嘴巴嚼食。还要记住用你的右手拿刀切食物，用左手拿叉子将食物送进嘴里。餐桌礼仪已经不像以前那么严格了。

王刚：我听说在英国不同的人对主餐有不同的叫法，这跟等级有关吗？

玛丽：他们说工人阶级称中午的餐点为 dinner，中产阶级的人则称之为 lunch。中产阶级把晚间的餐点称为 dinner，大约在晚上 7 点到 7 点半之间进餐。工人阶级或是较低阶的中产阶级则在 5 点半到 6 点间进餐，称为茶点。奇特的是，古老的上流社会把晚间的餐点称为 supper，约在 9 点到 10 点间进餐。他们有时也会在傍晚时用一些茶点。传统的维多利亚式下午茶，包括黄瓜三明治，蛋糕及英式烤饼，已经不存在了，只在高级的旅馆和花园茶会里才有。

王刚：为什么餐点有那么多不同的称呼？

玛丽：这跟作息时间有关。工人们在中午吃正餐才能保证有体力继续工作，而且他们很早就上床休息了，因为他们工作很辛苦。中产阶级的人晚上有较多的休闲时间，所以他们可以把主餐当作是一种社交活动。虽然工作的模式已经改变，这些称呼却一直延续了下来。

Chapter 30

Breakfast

早 餐

The English breakfast is world famous, and is one of the things that many tourists go for when they stay in a hotel or a B&B in the UK. You might be put off by its greasy appearance but, believe me, it is one of the tastiest and most comforting things you can eat. Most cafes also serve full English breakfasts all day — in fact they are called 'all-day breakfasts', and have challenging names like 'The Gut Buster' or 'The Full Monty'. This meal is so big that you will probably not need to eat lunch if you have it.

So what does it consist of? Well, in its simplest form it is just bacon and fried eggs. However, the full version can consist of fruit juice and cereal with milk, followed by bacon, sausages, fried tomato, mushrooms, hash browns, baked beans, black pudding, fried bread and eggs. The eggs can be fried, scrambled or poached. This is accompanied by toast and tea or coffee. If you want to experience it in the right environment, go to a simple 'greasy spoon' café and enjoy it in the company of builders, office workers, students and traffic wardens on their way to work.

Most people don't actually have the time to cook a full breakfast at home, so they either have just cereal and toast and tea or coffee, or they get something on the way to work.

You don't have to eat the full breakfast, of course. Most places offer a wide breakfast menu which includes sandwiches (a bacon sandwich is a good option), toast, omelettes and croissants. You can also have a healthy breakfast of fruit and yoghurt, fruit juice and muesli. Remember that there is always something that you will find appealing. Order your breakfast, sit at a table with your mug of tea (with milk and sugar) or coffee, pick up a newspaper and you're off.

■ ■ ■ ■ ■ ■ ■ ■ ■ ■ ■ ■ ■ ■ ■ ■ ■

英式早餐闻名于世，也是许多到英国的游客在宾馆或 B&B（提供住宿和早餐的简易旅馆）一定要品尝的东西。你也许会被英式早餐油腻腻的外表吓着，但请相信我，这是最美味、最能安抚你的食物。很多小餐馆也全天供应全套英式早餐。事实上，这些餐点被称为全天早餐，并有很具挑战性的名称，比如"大胃王"或"超级全餐"。这些餐点的分量超大，吃完后你也许就不需要午餐了。

那么，英式早餐到底包含了什么呢？最简单的搭配是培根加煎蛋。全套的英式早餐则先有果汁、麦片及牛奶，接着会有培根、香肠、煎西红柿、蘑菇、薯饼、烤豆、黑香肠、炸面包片及蛋。蛋可以煎、炒或是水煮。最后还有烤面包片、茶或咖啡。如果你想体验真正的英式早餐，可以找一家实惠小店，与那些上班路上来刹一脚的建筑工人、上班族、学生、停车管理员一起享用早餐。

大部分人在家没有时间准备全套早餐，所以通常以麦片、烤面包片及茶或咖啡取代，或是在上班的路上买点吃的。

当然，你也不一定要吃全餐。大部分餐厅提供各式各样的早餐，包括三明治（培根三明治是个好选择）、烤面包片、煎蛋饼及羊角面包。你也可以选择健康的早餐，像是水果和酸奶、果汁和燕麦片。你永远都能找到你爱吃的。点好早餐，坐在那儿享受茶（加奶和糖）或咖啡，拿一份报纸，你就好好享受吧。

Making a Fry Up

Greg: God! My head is killing me. I've got a massive hangover from last night.

Marie: You won't be wanting a fry up, then?

Greg: Actually, they say a fry up is the best cure for a hangover.

Gang: Why's that?

Greg: Because all the fat soaks up the alcohol in your system, and it's comforting. I don't know if it's true or not.

Marie: OK, a fry up it is. Sit down, you two, and I'll make it.

Greg: No. Making it is part of the fun. Let's see what we've got. Right bacon, sausages, eggs, black pudding, baked beans, mushrooms and hash browns. Right, Wang, watch this: first you turn the grill on and put the sausages, hash browns, bacon and black pudding under it. Then you empty a can of baked beans into a pan and put it on a low heat. While you're waiting for the stuff to grill you can boil the kettle to make the tea or coffee, put some bread in the toaster to make toast, and heat some oil in a frying pan, ready to fry the eggs. You turn the stuff you're grilling half way through, so that it gets done on both sides, then you crack the eggs into the oil, butter the toast after it pops up and put it on a side plate, and put some teabags into a teapot and pour the boiling water onto them. By the time you've done that, the eggs will have been fried properly — you can have them crispy or soft, like the bacon. You arrange all of the fried and grilled food on a big plate, then you serve it along with the toast and the tea or coffee.

Marie: Gosh, what a rigmarole. I think I'll just have corn flakes and coffee.

Gang: I'll have that too, along with the fry up.

Marie: OK here you are corn flakes in a bowl . aaagh! What are you doing putting orange juice on your corn flakes???

Gang: Isn't that what you do?

Marie: No. You have to put milk on your corn flakes.

Greg: Let him eat them the way he wants. Actually, I think that corn flakes probably taste quite nice with orange juice on them. What's a traditional Chinese breakfast like?

Gang: Well, actually, you can eat anything you like for breakfast in China — pickles, peanuts, boiled eggs, congee — that's like a gruel made of rice and hot water, soya milk. My favourite breakfast is actually dumplings and fritters.

Marie: Sounds lovely.

做一套油炸早餐

格雷：我的天啊！我的头快疼死了。我的宿醉很严重。

玛丽：喔，那你不想吃油炸早餐了吧？

格雷：实际上，大家都说油炸早餐是治疗宿醉的最好良药。

王刚：为什么呢？

格雷：因为所有的油脂都可以吸收你身体里的酒精，你会觉得舒服。我不知道这是不是真的。

玛丽：好吧，油炸早餐。你们两个坐下，我来做。

格雷：不要，动手做是享受的一部分。噢，我来看看有什么材料。我们有培根、腊肠、蛋、黑香肠、烤豆、蘑菇及土豆饼。王刚，看着。首先，你要把烤箱的电源打开，把腊肠、薯饼、培根及黑香肠放进去。然后，打开一罐烤豆放进锅里，开小火。你在等待的时间里可以煮开水来泡茶或咖啡，把面包放进烤面包机里烤，同时热一些油等着煎蛋。这时记得将烤箱里的东西翻面，那样烤出来的才会两边都熟。接下来，将蛋打进炒锅里，把烤好的面包片涂上黄油，放在小盘子上，再将茶包放入茶壶中，冲入开水。当你做完这些，蛋也煎好了，你可以选择像煎培根一样把蛋煎得焦黄或是松软。现在，将煎、烤的食物盛入一个大盘子里，跟烤面包片及茶或是咖啡一起端出。

玛丽：天啊，真是麻烦。我想我只要玉米片和咖啡就好了。

王刚：我也想要玉米片和咖啡，加上油炸早餐。

玛丽：没问题，这碗玉米片给你。啊呀！你怎么把果汁倒进了玉米片里？

王刚：你们不是这样吃吗？

玛丽：不对，你要放牛奶到玉米片里。

格雷：让他用他的方式吃吧。事实上，我想玉米片加橙汁应该蛮好吃的。传统的中式早餐有些什么啊？

王刚：噢，在中国你想吃什么都可以，咸菜、花生米、水煮蛋，粥——用米跟水熬煮的糊状食物，还有豆浆。我最喜欢的早餐是煎饺和馅饼。

玛丽：听起来很不错。

Chapter 31

Take Aways

外 带 食 品

Fast food, mainly from take away restaurants, is the bane of many a nutritionist's life. Newspapers and TV shows are full of stories about the obesity epidemic and the fact that teenagers are grossly overweight compared to their parents. Some of this can be blamed on the fact that children do not walk to school and that they do less sport and sit in front of computers more than a generation ago, but part of the problem is certainly that fast food is a much more popular option for families with busy working lives. It is now far less common than it was a generation ago for families to sit down and eat a meal that has been cooked at home.

Traditional British take away is fish and chips. Fish and chip shops started in Victorian times, when fish and potatoes were cheap. This food became inextricably linked with the British industrial working class up until the 1960s when Chinese food became popular as an alternative. The most popular Chinese take away food in the UK is Cantonese food, which was introduced to Britain by sailors from Hong Kong in London and Liverpool. The Cantonese food in Britain has actually been changed to make it more appealing to British tastes, much like Italian or other Western food has been changed to make it more 'Chinese' in China. Almost every British town has at least one Chinese take away. In fact, British people equate this kind of sweet food with the whole of China, and are surprised to learn that there are other kinds of Chinese food. Indian take aways are also popular, and most 'Indian' restaurants are actually run by Bangladeshis, not Indians. Again, the kind of curry served by these take aways is nothing like an authentic curry — it has been adapted to British tastes.

The ubiquitous McDonald's opened its first restaurant in London in the 1970s. Since then, hamburgers, pizza and kebabs have spread all over the UK. You will find all the usual chains in the UK — McDonald's, KFC, Pizza Hut and Burger King but, for an authentic taste of post-modern multicultural Britain, you can't beat a special fried rice, a doner kebab or a chicken tikka masala!

快餐通常指从餐厅外带的食物,是营养师眼中的有害食品。报纸与电视节目大谈肥胖症的流行,指出现在的青少年比他们父母小时候胖多了。其中一部分原因是现在的小孩都不用走路上学,比起他们的上一代也不太运动,而且常坐在电脑前。另一方面也是因为快餐成为忙碌生活中更受欢迎的选择。比起上一代,现在的家庭已经很少坐在一起吃自己做的饭了。

炸鱼和薯条是传统的英式外卖。炸鱼和薯条店起源于维多利亚时期,当时鱼和马铃薯都相当便宜。炸鱼和薯条一直与英国工人阶级密不可分,直到上世纪60年代中国菜成为另一种受欢迎的选择。在英国卖得最好的中国外卖是广东菜。广东菜由香港水手传到伦敦和利物浦。为了贴近英国人的口味,广东菜稍做了一些改变,这就像意大利菜和其他西方菜肴到了中国也会为了适应中国人的口味而稍做变化。在英国,几乎每个城镇都至少有一家中餐外卖店。事实上,英国人误认为酸甜的广东菜就代表整个中国菜,所以当他们发现中国还有其他不同的地方菜时,感到非常惊讶。外卖的印度菜也颇受欢迎,但是大部分的"印度"餐厅并不是由印度人经营的,而是孟加拉人。跟其它外来菜一样,印度咖喱菜也经过改良以适应英国人的口味,与真正的印度咖喱不太一样。

无所不在的麦当劳于上世纪70年代在伦敦开设了第一家店。从那时起,汉堡、比萨及烤肉便在英国各地蔓延。你可以在英国找到所有的快餐连锁店,像麦当劳、肯德基、必胜客和汉堡王。但是,如果你想了解英国融合了多种文化的后现代口味,那一定不要错过招牌炒饭、旋转烤肉或是马沙拉鸡。

Ordering a Take Away

Marie: God! I'm starving, Greg! Can we get a take away?

Greg: What do you fancy?

Marie: I could murder a Chinese!

Gang: What?!

Marie: Oh, sorry Gang. That just means I really want to eat some Chinese food.

Gang: Oh. What kind of Chinese food are you going to get?

Marie: Have you got the take away menu there, Greg?

Greg: Here it is. Let's see what they've got. I really fancy Sweet and Sour Pork, Egg Fried Rice and Chicken and Sweet Corn Soup. What about you, Gang?

Gang: Let me see... Chicken Chow Mein OK, that's *ji rou chou mian*... this is all Cantonese, but some of it just sounds made up. Chicken Chop Suey? What's that? I've never heard of it? It isn't Chinese.

Marie: What do you mean? That's one of the most popular Chinese dishes here. People love it. They think it's really authentic, just like Chicken and Sweet Corn Soup.

Gang: You're joking, Marie! We think that's really Western!

Greg: Well, I heard that Chop Suey was actually invented in California by Chinese railway workers in the 19th Century. They were all men, and they just threw everything in the frying pan together and stir fried it.

Gang: Well, stir frying is a common way of cooking in China. That's because, historically, there has always been a shortage of fire wood there, so people had to cook quickly. But we also have other ways of cooking — I mean there's boiling, roasting, baking in clay pots all kinds of things. My favourite food is actually North East Chinese food — it's very hearty and filling — things like meat-filled dumplings and roast and baked meat, and potatoes. Cantonese food is very different — we say that in Guangdong they'll eat anything that flies unless it's an aeroplane and anything with legs except for the table and chairs.

Marie: Really? My brother said he ate snake meat in China once. I couldn't eat that. I had Szchuanese food once, though. I really liked that it's really spicy. Have they got any of that on the menu, Greg?

Greg: Well, there's Szchuan Spicy Chicken. What's that like, Gang?

Gang: That sounds like *gong bao ji ding*. It's nice, if you like chillies.

Marie: Right! I'm going to order that, and I'm going to have Singapore Noodles. Oh, and some prawn crackers too. What about you Gang. Order something really authentic so that we can try it.

Gang: Well, apart from the Szchuan Spicy Chicken, I can't see anything really authentic. Why don't we get some Peking Duck, with pancakes and plum sauce? That's a typical Beijing dish.

Greg: OK. Let's have that. I'll call them up and get them to deliver it.

订外卖

玛丽：天啊！我快饿死了，格雷。我们叫份外卖好吗？

格雷：你想吃什么？

玛丽：我想要"杀"一个中国人！

王刚：什么？

玛丽：啊，对不起，王刚。我的意思是说
我想吃中国菜。

王刚：哦，你想吃什么中餐？

玛丽：格雷，你有外卖的菜单吗？

格雷：在这儿，我来看看他们有什么。
我想吃糖醋里脊、蛋炒饭还有玉米鸡茸
汤。王刚，你想吃什么呢？

I could munder a Chinese !!!

王刚：让我想想，Chicken Chow Mein，
喔，这是鸡肉炒面……这些都是广东菜，但是有些听起来像是捏造的……鸡肉杂烩？
那是什么啊？我从来都没听说过，这不是中国菜。

玛丽：你是什么意思？这是本地最受欢迎的中国菜。英国人爱死鸡肉杂烩了。大家
都认为那是地道的中国菜……就像鸡茸玉米汤一样。

王刚：玛丽，你一定是在开玩笑。我们认为那是很西式的做法。

格雷：我听说杂烩实际上是19世纪由一群在美国加州的中国铁路工人发明的。因为
他们全都是男人，所以只会将所有的菜都丢进锅里一起炒。

王刚：嗯，一锅炒在中国是一种非常普遍的烹调法。因为历史上人民一向缺乏生火
的木材，所以需要一个快速的烹调方式。但是我们还有很多的方式，像是煮、烤、
在砂锅里炖等等。我最喜欢的是中国东北菜，非常丰盛，有满足感，像是水饺、烤
肉还有马铃薯啦。广东菜很不一样。我们说在广东，天上飞的除了飞机，地上跑的
除了桌椅都能吃。

玛丽：真的吗？我哥哥说他在中国吃过一次蛇肉。我可不敢吃那个。我吃过一次四
川菜，很好吃，真的很辣。格雷，菜单上有四川菜吗？

格雷：哦，菜单上有四川辣鸡。王刚，那是什么味道？

王刚：这听起来像是宫保鸡丁。很好吃，如果你喜欢吃辣的话。

玛丽：很好！我要点辣鸡，还要新加坡炒面。哦，还要一些虾片。王刚，你呢？你
点一些地道的中国菜让我们尝一尝吧。

王刚：唉，除了辣鸡，我实在是看不到任何地道的中国菜。为什么不点北京烤鸭？
涂上酱，包在饼里吃。那是很典型的北京菜。

格雷：好，点这个。我这就打电话让他们送。

Driving

开 车

One of the first things you will notice about Britain is that they drive on the left, and the steering wheel is on the right. This causes a strange sensation when you sit in the passenger seat of a British car, but you'll soon get used to it. Driving on the left is not as unusual as you might think; about a quarter of the countries in the world drive on the left. Most of them are former British colonies like Australia, South Africa, and Ireland, but Thailand, Japan, Indonesia and Mozambique also do so. This strange quirk perplexes the Chinese and Europeans alike, but there is a perfectly good reason for it: up until the late eighteenth century, everybody travelled on the left-hand side of the road because it was the best way for mostly right-handed people to defend themselves in violent, feudal societies. So when strangers passed on the road, they walked on the left to ensure that their sword arm was between them.

After the French Revolution in 1789, however, the government switched sides as part of a massive social reorganization. Later, Napoleon, extended the change to the rest of Continental Europe. He did this because he was left-handed himself, and he wanted his armies to march on the right so that he could keep his left arm between himself and any opponents. From then on, any part of the world which became part of the British Empire was left hand, and any part colonised by the French was right hand. In North America, the French colonised Louisiana and Quebec, while the Spanish colonized South and Central America, and many parts of what is now the USA. So the British were actually in a minority in shaping the 'traffic', and the US government decided to make traffic drive on the right in order to sever its ties with Britain after it became independent. Because the USA drove on the right, left-side driving was ultimately doomed. Once America became the centre of the car industry, if you wanted a good reliable vehicle, you bought an American-made right-hand-drive vehicle. From then on many countries changed out of necessity.

Today, the EU would like Britain to be the same as the rest of Europe, but this is no longer possible. It would cost billions of pounds to change everything round.

开　车

The last European country to convert to driving on the right was Sweden in 1967, but there were far fewer cars there, and the population was much smaller.

■■■■■■■■■■■■■■■■■■

　　你到英国后一定会首先注意到车是靠左行驶的，而方向盘则是在车的右边。当你坐在驾驶座旁一定会产生一种奇怪的感觉，但你很快就会习惯。左边开车其实没有你想象中那么奇怪，全球大约有四分之一的国家是靠左行驶的。那些国家中除了泰国、日本、印尼和莫桑比克外，其余大多数都是英国的前殖民地，像澳大利亚、南非及爱尔兰。这种奇特的开车方式让中国人和欧洲人觉得非常困扰，但这其实有一个很好的理由。直到 18 世纪末以前，每个人都是靠着路的左边行走，因为这样方便右手活动，这是人们在封建社会的暴力环境中保护自己的最佳方式。当陌生人迎面走来时，大家都走在路的左边，确保他们握剑的手是在他们之间，可以随时拔剑御敌。

　　1789 年法国大革命后，作为大规模社会改革的一部分，法国政府将靠左行走的方式改成靠右。之后，拿破仑又将这个改变推广到欧洲大陆。他这么做是因为他是左撇子，他希望他的军队行进在右侧，这样他就可以让他的左手保持在他与对手之间。从那之后，成为英国殖民地的地区均为靠左行走，而法国的殖民地区则为靠右行走。在北美洲，路易斯安那和魁北克是法国的殖民地，西班牙占领了中南美洲及现今美国的很多地区。因此英国在"交通"问题上反而成为少数。美

国政府在独立后为了脱离与英国的关系，将行驶方向改为右边。由于美国改变行驶方向，左边行驶变得前途黯淡。当美国成为汽车产业的中心时，谁想要买一辆可靠的车，就得买美国制造的适合在右边开的车。从那时起，很多国家为了适应汽车的发展而改成右边行车。

　　如今，欧盟希望英国可以像其他欧洲国家一样靠右边开车，但那是不可能的。要花上几十亿英镑才能将行车方向改变过来。1967 年，瑞典成为欧洲大陆最后一个将行车方向改到右边的国家，但那时汽车很少，而且人口也少得多。

The Car's Really British

Gang: Greg, is your car British?

Greg: Well it's hard to say. I mean it's a Jaguar, but the company which makes Jaguars is owned by Ford. So, when people say that Jaguar is a British brand name, it isn't really. It's like Bentley — that's owned by Volkswagen — and even the world-famous Rolls Royce and the Mini are owned and manufactured by BMW. That's

what the free market has brought to Britain — our whole motor manufacturing industry has collapsed and been bought up by foreign companies whose governments don't play by the same rules. I think we've been sold out.

Gang: So, are there any real British cars? What are the famous names?

Greg: Well, there's high-end sports cars like Aston Martin and Lotus, but even they are partly-owned by foreign firms. In fact, Lotus is owned by Proton, a Malaysian company.

Marie: There is Vauxhall. That's really British.

Greg: Nah. GM owns them. I don't think there are any motor manufacturers that are British-owned. Even MG — Rover was bought by the Chinese a few years ago.

Gang: Actually, you're partly right. Nanjing Automotive Corp does own the MG brand, and they are manufacturing the MG sports car in China, but the rest of Rover is owned by BMW.

Marie: What I can't understand is why our government lets countries that don't follow the same rules, and which don't open up their markets, buy up all our manufacturing industry. I mean, how does that benefit us?

Gang: Maybe you're right. We Chinese are very proud and protective of our own industry. Our government should protect it.

Greg: Hmmm so that's why I think we're going to get nothing out of our prime minister's recent attempts to get China and India to invest in Britain. He's just going to sell off the rest of our companies, and we'll get nothing out of it.

Gang: Well, I've heard that the British motor industry was in decline before foreign companies started buying it up.

Greg: Well, you're right to an extent. Back in the 1970s, the British motor industry was notorious for strikes and bad industrial relations. Japanese manufacturers were producing more reliable cars more cheaply. So, by the time Thatcher came along with her free-market policies in 1979 it was ripe for takeover. The thing is, though, that other governments — like Japan and France and Germany — protected their car industries — ours just abandoned it.

Marie: God! More politics! Will you stop, Greg! Get down off your high horse!

这是真正的英国车

王刚：格雷，你开的是英国车吗？

格雷：噢，这很难说。我的意思是，我的车是一辆捷豹，但是捷豹的制造公司属于福特汽车公司，就像宾利为大众汽车所拥有。即使是世界闻名的劳斯莱斯和迷你车也由宝马公司生产。这就是自由贸易对英国造成的影响。我们整个汽车工业已经完全崩溃了，并且被一些外国公司收购，因为他们的政府根本不遵守相同的规则。我想我们已经被出卖了。

王刚：喔，那么有没有真正的英国车呢？有哪些品牌？

格雷：噢，有一些高级的跑车，比如阿斯顿马丁、莲花等。即使是这两家公司也部分被外国公司所拥有。事实上，莲花的东家就是一家马来西亚公司，普腾。

玛丽：沃克斯豪尔，就是真正的英国车。

格雷：不对，沃克斯豪尔是通用的子公司。我认为英国已经没有任何汽车制造商了。就连名爵汽车也在几年前被一家中国公司收购。

王刚：事实上你只说对了一半，南京汽车制造厂拥有名爵的品牌，也在中国生产名爵跑车，但是罗孚的其余品牌属于宝马。

玛丽：我实在不懂为什么我们的政府让那些不遵守同样规则也不开放市场的国家买下我们整个制造业。我们能从中得到什么好处呢？

王刚：你也许是对的。我们中国人为自己的工业而骄傲，也很维护我们的工业。政府有责任保护自己的工业。

格雷：噢，我们首相最近想吸引中国和印度来英国投资，我想我们从中得不到任何好处。他这样做只会把剩下的英国公司卖光，而我们却一无所获。

王刚：可是，我听说英国的汽车工业在外国公司来收购之前就已经没落了。

格雷：从某种角度来看你说的没错。回溯到上世纪 70 年代，英国的汽车工业就以罢工和恶劣的劳资关系而声名狼藉。日本则能制造更可靠、更便宜的车。所以到了1979 年撒切尔夫人宣布自由市场政策时，汽车工业就到了被收购的成熟期。当其他国家的政府，像日本、法国及德国对他们的汽车工业进行保护时，英国政府却遗弃了自己的汽车工业。

玛丽：天啊！全是政治问题！格雷，你可以闭嘴吗?! 别一副高高在上的样子。

Chapter 33

Cabbies

出 租 车 司 机

The London black taxi is an icon for tourists. It is solid and imposing and dependable, and exudes an air of security. The basic design has changed little since it was first developed in the early twentieth century, although the most recent model is slightly smaller and dinkier, and is preferred by drivers because of it's small turning circle; it can do a complete U-turn on any London street without having to reverse.

Being a taxi driver in London is a job that requires a lot of training. London black cab drivers, or cabbies, have to train for two years and take a test called The Knowledge which then qualifies them to register with the police as a taxi driver. In The Knowledge they must show that they know all the streets in zone one in London, and be able to explain to the examiner how to get from one place to another, describing all the streets, landmarks and buildings on the way. In fact, scientists have proved that a particular part of the London cabbie's brain is larger than a normal person's because of all the memorising he has to do.

All black taxi drivers are registered with the Metropolitan Police or with local councils, and the driver is required to take you anywhere you want to go once he stops for you. Hop in a black cab in London and the driver will treat you to a discourse on everything from the state of the nation to immigration, unemployment, foreigners and famous celebrities. London cabbies have a reputation for being politically reactionary and hard line, and it is common for satirical magazines to mock them, but this reputation is not fully deserved. Being a cabbie is a very well-paid profession, and many cabbies have degrees and even PhDs.

The kind of taxi that is an ordinary saloon car is known as a mini cab. There are mini cab firms everywhere, and you call them up to book a cab, rather than hailing them in the street. Many mini cab drivers are immigrants or people who are moonlighting in order to make some extra money.

Tell a taxi driver that you are Chinese, and he will give you the benefit of his wisdom on everything to do with China from human rights to pandas, and what is amazing is that he will often be able to hold opposing opinions at the same time.

对游客来说，伦敦的黑色出租车是一种象征。它坚固、气派，并且可靠，外型流露出安全的气息。从20世纪初刚普及的时候到现在，它的基本设计几乎没有大的改动，目前最新的款式更为娇小玲珑，尽管目前最新的款型稍小一些，精致一些。司机们更偏爱新款的车，因为新车型的转弯幅度较小，可以在伦敦任意一条路上直接调头，不需倒车。

在伦敦，要想成为出租车司机需要经过很多的训练。伦敦的黑色出租车司机需要经过两年的训练，之后接受知识测验，通过后方有资格到警察机关登记，成为出租车司机。在知识测验中，他们要表现出他们对伦敦一区的大街小巷了若指掌，要向监考员说明从出发处到目的地怎么走，描述经过的街道、路标及建筑物。事实上，科学家们已经证实：伦敦黑色出租车司机脑部的记忆区要比常人的大，因为他们需要记忆大量的资料。

所有的黑色出租车司机必须到本市警察局或当地行政机关处登记。出租车司机一旦为你停下车，他就必须载你到任何你想去的地方。跳上一辆黑色出租车，司机就会滔滔不绝地对你高谈阔论，从国家大事、移民政策、失业状况，到外国人和知名人士。伦敦的出租车司机一向被认为在政治上是强硬的保守派，讽刺性杂志上常常有嘲笑他们的文章。实际上他们名不副实。这是一个待遇相当高的行业，许多出租车司机拥有学位，有些甚至还有博士学位。

另一种出租车是普通轿车，称为迷你出租车。迷你出租车公司到处都有，你可以打电话叫车，比在街上拦车还要方便。许多迷你出租车司机是外来移民，或是晚上兼差赚外快的人。

如果对一位出租车司机说你是中国人，他马上会跟你分享他所知的有关中国的知识，从人权到大熊猫等等。而且你会很惊讶地发现，他们常常自相矛盾。

Hop In, Mate

Gang: Euston Station, please.

Cabbie: OK. Hop in, mate.

Gang: Thanks terrible weather.

Cabbie: Yeah. I blame that global warming. You know, I read in the newspaper yesterday that there's nothing we can do about it because the Chinese are bringing a new coal-fired power station on-stream every week. I mean, look around here look at all the cars and the oil that goes to make them and the pollution they cause. Are you Chinese, then?

Gang: Yes, I am actually.

Cabbie: Isn't it terrible — that news about the earthquake there. All those poor people who've lost their lives? I saw it on the news last night. Shocking! I'm so sorry.

Gang: Yes, it's bad news.

Cabbie: Are you from anywhere near there? I mean, the place the earthquake struck?

Gang: No. I'm from the North East but I called home and they said that the shock was felt all over the country.

Cabbie: Mind you, I must say, it's very impressive the way your government has mobilised the PLA to deal with it. Very decisive and you're letting the world see it as well; the Chinese authorities are behaving in a way we've never seen before — not like in Burma when that cyclone struck. They don't want anyone to know about it there, and they won't accept aid from any outside countries.

Gang: Well China is not like Burma we have the resources to deal with natural disasters ourselves. *Wen Jia Bao* has said it's "a major geological disaster — time is life," and he should know — he's a geologist by training.

Cabbie: Yeah I suppose so, but we've always thought that China was a very secretive country. I mean, years ago they would never have broadcast news about something like this.

Gang: Well, the thing is that China is really changing; it's been opening up to the world ever since *Deng XiaoPing's* open door policy, and as time goes on it opens up more and more. It's a process, isn't it?

Cabbie: Yes. China's an amazing country; I think it's fascinating the way it's developing faster than Britain during the Industrial Revolution, they say. It's going to be the next superpower. The Yanks must be pretty scared. Still, I suppose that earthquake must have come as a phenomenal shock. Especially since the Olympics are only a couple of months away.

Gang: You know, China's goal is peaceful development. It's no threat to America. You Westerners are always going on about that!

上车，伙计

王刚：麻烦您我要去尤斯顿车站。

出租车司机：好，上车吧，老兄。

王刚：谢谢。天气真是坏极了。

出租车司机：是啊。我认为这得归咎于全球变暖。你知道吗，昨天报纸上说中国每周都有一座新的燃煤发电厂建成，所以我们对此一点办法都没有。看看吧，要有多少汽油才能发动这些车，因此又会带来多少污染啊。你是中国人吗？

王刚：是啊，我是中国人。

出租车司机：关于大地震的消息真是可怕啊，所有那些可怜的遇难者。我昨天在电视新闻上看到那些悲惨的情景，真是触目惊心。我很遗憾。

王刚：是啊，真是个不幸的消息。

出租车司机：你是从那儿来的吗？我是说，接近地震的区域？

王刚：不是，我是从东北来的。我打电话回家时，家里人告诉我整个国家都有震感。

出租车司机：我得说，你们政府调派人民解放军去救灾的做法令人印象深刻，非常果断，而且愿意让全世界的人看到了你们救灾的情况。中国政府的表现真是前所未见，一点都不像旋风侵袭时的缅甸。缅甸政府不想让任何人知道灾情，也不接受任何国家的援助。

王刚：中国跟缅甸不同，我们有资源去处理天灾。温家宝总理说这是一个"地质上的大灾难，时间就是生命"。而且他是学地质的，是这方面的专家。

出租车司机：对啊，我想也是。但是我们总认为中国是个非常隐密的国家。我是说，要是几年前他们是不会播报这种新闻的。

王刚：噢，中国真的在变。自从邓小平的对外开放政策实施后，中国真的越来越开放了。这是一种进步，不是吗？

出租车司机：是啊，中国是个令人惊讶的国家。有人说中国比英国在工业革命时发展的速度还要快，实在是十分神奇。中国将成为下一个超级大国；美国佬一定非常害怕。我想大地震一定带来很大的震撼，尤其是在距离奥运会只剩下几个月的时候。

王刚：中国的目标是和平发展，对美国不会有任何威胁。你们西方人老是危言耸听。

Chapter 34

White Van Man

白 色 货 车 人

The British man who drives a white, light commercial vehicle like a Ford Transit van with no company lettering on the side for a living and is notorious for his aggressive driving, poor manners on the road, cutting up other motorists and generally not driving safely is referred to as a white van man. He has taken over from the London cabbie as the 'voice of the people' or the 'voice of the man in the street' who is not afraid to speak out and voice opinions that other people might be too worried to.

The stereotypical white van man is a uniquely British (or Irish) social phenomenon, and is usually a self-employed small businessman from a working-class background engaged in manual work like a builder, a carpenter, a plumber or a removals man. He does not think politically but he believes in low tax, low public spending on things like welfare, disapproves of unemployed people, middle-class liberals, people on welfare and immigrants (although he will have no qualms about employing Eastern European immigrants, and will praise their work ethic). White van man is fervently patriotic (often flying the English Cross of St George flag from his van). He is not averse to expressing racist and sexist opinions, thinks prisons are not tough enough and that the government is too soft on crime. On the other hand, he believes strongly in the NHS and in a fair day's work for a fair day's pay. He works hard and plays hard, does not tolerate losers and reads *The Sun* while he has his big fried breakfast in a greasy spoon 'caff'. In fact, between 2001 and 2003, *The Sun* used a column called *White Van Man* as a way of delivering its editorial opinion.

Although he is probably not very highly educated, white van man is certainly not stupid; he is often ambitious and upwardly-mobile; he will probably live in a house that he owns and he might have a private pension. He will have no job security and will probably work long hours, but he will be able to take holidays in places like Florida, Cyprus and Spain. He might wear an England football top, have his head shaven and have a tattoo on his arm. His wife, who often has a good figure, a bare midriff and blonde hair and a tattoo on her lower back, might wear bling. He sees himself as honest and straight-talking. He says what he thinks, and does not mince his words.

■■■■■■■■■■■■■■■■

在英国，开着车上没有任何公司名称的白色货车，比如福特全顺，送货维生的人通常被称为"白色货车人"。他们因开车横冲直撞，态度恶劣，喜欢超车，不守规则而声名狼藉。这些人取代了伦敦出租车司机成为"人民的声音"或"街头人民的声音"，他们毫无顾忌地说出心声，毫无保留。

白色货车人是英国（或爱尔兰）独特的社会现象。他们通常是不受雇于任何人的小商贩，大多出生于工人阶级，从事体力劳动工作，像是建筑工人、木匠、水电工或搬运工。这些人没什么政治头脑，但是却拥护低税率和降低福利开支。他们不认同中产阶级自由主义者、靠社会福利过活的人及移民尽管他们也毫无愧疚地聘用东欧来的移民，并且称赞东欧移民的工作态度）。白色货车人拥有强烈的爱国主义（通常会将英国国旗插在车上），对于种族及性别歧视的言论毫不避讳，认为监狱不够严格而且政府打击犯罪的手段不够强硬。他们非常认同全民医疗服务，并相信干一天体面的工作就该拿一份体面的工资。他们努力工作，也尽情玩乐；他们不容忍输家，喜欢在实惠小饭馆里一边吃着油炸早餐一边看《太阳报》。事实上，从 2001 年到 2003 年，《太阳报》以"白色货车人"做为他们社论专栏的名称。

这些人也许没有受过高等教育，但是他们并不笨。他们通常很有野心并积极向上，有些还拥有自己的房屋和退休金。这些人没有工作保障，也许需要长时间工作，但他们有足够的经济实力到海外度假，比如佛罗里达、塞浦路斯及西班牙等地。他们会穿件足球衫，剃光头，胳膊上有刺青。他们的老婆通常身材姣好，拥有平坦的腹部及一头金发，后腰有文身，身上带着金光闪闪的首饰。白色货车人认为自己很诚实，心直口快。他们想什么就说什么，绝不会装腔作势。

A Delivery

WVM: Delivery for Mr Harrop? We've got your new kitchen in the back of the van here.

Greg: Oh. Thanks, mate. Do you need a hand?

WVM: Naah. It's OK, I've got the lad with me. Oi Jack! Come and help me shift this gear.

Jack: OK dad.

Marie: Do you want a cup of tea?

WVM: Oh, yes please, love. Strong. Milk and four sugars. Same for the lad.

* * *

Gang: Hello.

WVM: Hello, there! You Chinese, then?

Gang: Yes, I am, as it happens.

WVM: Cor! You speak good English where did you learn it? At school?

Gang: Well I learned a bit at school. Actually, though, I'm a student here. I've learned most of my English here.

WVM: Oh what do you study? English?

Gang: No, I'm studying Business Management and Finance.

WVM: Good choice, mate. You have to put food on the table before anything else. I've got no time for all these kids wasting their parents' money on courses like Sociology and Media Studies. Yeah. People need to work hard and make money. There's too many people want to take a free ride; know what I mean?

Gang: Erm yes.

WVM: Yeah I mean, look at all these immigrants coming in; they all come here and claim asylum cause they know they can get straight down the DSS and get the dole and housing benefit. They get their kids into school and get free medical care. Then they bring their wives and parents and cousins and everyone over here. Yeah they're taking us for a ride. We're going to be a minority in our own country soon. I mean, I'm not being funny, but if you look around here everyone's an immigrant. No offence, mate. I don't mean you, of course.

Gang: Of course not.

WVM: Mind you, you've got to hand it to them — these immigrants. They're bloody hard workers, and they're clever. I mean, they work their way up and they're ambitious. Their kids all do really well and go to university. Not like my boy here — he's thick. And their families stick together, innit? They all look after each other. That's something that we've lost in our culture.

Gang: Hmm.

WVM: I mean, look at families here. It's all falling apart. Single mothers getting council flats, same-sex couples, old people living in care homes with no family to look after them. I don't know what this country's coming to.

Gang: Yes, but all the people who work in the care homes are immigrants, aren't they? I mean, British people don't want to do those jobs, do they?

WVM: Well they would if it wasn't for the European Union. That's the root of all our problems. I think we should get out of it and start sorting ourselves out. Look at all the money we're spending on the war in Iraq and Afghanistan when we've got our own problems to sort out here. Mind you, I think we were right to go in there; I mean, that Bin Laden — he's a nutter, innit? And they're in among us, too...

送 货

白色货车司机：送货给哈洛先生。我们车里有你订的厨具。

格雷：喔，谢谢，哥们儿。需要帮忙吗？

司机：没关系，不用。我带了这小伙子来帮忙。喂，杰克！过来帮我搬东西。

杰克：好的，老爸。

玛丽：你要不要喝杯茶？

司机：哦，好的。浓一点，加牛奶再加4块糖。我儿子的和我的一样。

* * *

王刚：你好。

司机：你好！你是中国人？

王刚：是啊。一看就知道。

司机：噢，你的英文很好，你在哪里学的？学校吗？

王刚：噢，我在学校学了一点，事实上我在这里上学，我大部分的英语都是在这里学的。

司机：喔，那你学什么？英文？

王刚：不是，我在学商业管理和财务。

司机：噢，选得好，哥们儿。挣钱过日子比什么都重要。我可看不上那些浪费父母钱的小孩，念什么社会学和传媒。大家都应该努力工作赚钱。有太多的人想不劳而获，你懂我的意思吗？

王刚：噢，差不多吧。

司机：噢，我是说，看看那些移民，全都到这里申请庇护，因为他们知道他们可以直接到社会福利中心领取失业救济和住宿福利金。他们把子女送到学校，还可以获得免费医疗。然后他们再把老婆、父母还有亲戚朋友一起带来。他们简直是在耍我们。不久我们就会在自己的国家变为少数民族。我不是在开玩笑，我是说真的，看看周围吧，每个人都是移民。别介意，哥们儿。我当然不是指你。

王刚：不会，不会。

司机：说实在的，你不得不佩服这些移民。他们玩命工作，而且又聪明。我是说，他们一路往上爬又非常有野心。他们的孩子书念得不错，都能上大学，不像我这儿子，很笨。而且他们家庭团结，不是吗？他们互相照应，在我们的文化里，那种精神已经消失了。

王刚：噢。

司机：我是说，看看英国家庭，简直是四分五裂。单身妈妈住廉租屋、同性伴侣、老年人住在养老中心没有家人照顾。真不知道这个国家会沦落到什么地步。

王刚：对啊，可是几乎所有的养老中心员工都是外来的移民，不是吗？我是说，因为英国人不想做那些工作，对吗？

司机：噢，要不是欧盟，他们会去养老中心工作的。欧盟是所有问题的根源。我认为我们应该脱离欧盟，集中精力解决我们的问题。看看我们花了多少钱在伊拉克和阿富汗战争上，我们自己还有一大堆问题要解决。不过话又说回来，我觉得加入那些战争是对的，我是说本·拉登，他是个疯子，不是吗？而且我们当中也有他们的人……

Chapter 35

Fashion and Style

时 尚 与 风 格

In 1979, there was an article in the *Daily Mail* about China. It said, 'imagine a country where they've never heard of The Beatles.' China has changed dramatically since then, and now many young urban Chinese look to London — like Tokyo and New York — as a centre of fashion — not the *haute couture* of Paris or Milan, but cool, hip cutting-edge street fashion based on youth movements that developed in the sixties and seventies. Back in the 'swinging sixties' Carnaby St in London was the centre of a young, vibrant fashion scene based around pop and rock music typified by the Beatles and the Rolling Stones, film heroes like James Bond and designers like Mary Quant, and satirized by the *Austin Powers* films in the 1990s. When this image became old and bloated in the late 1970s, a new fashion movement based on punk developed with designers like Vivienne Westwood. In the late 1990s, after the cultural trough of the Thatcher years, the 'New Labour' government promoted a youthful, resurgent Britain under the name of 'Cool Britannia'. So, London has always been a fashion centre which reflects and picks up on what young people themselves are wearing, and this is reflected in the work of designers like Paul Smith, Stella McCartney (the daughter of the Beatle Paul McCartney).

Fashion is important to many people, but there does not seem to be any particular 'in' style any more. Walk around any street in Britain these days, and you will see a whole array of different styles — gone are the days when there was a standard period fashion. Some people dress up, while others dress down, and different styles fit different occasions. Fashion magazines like *Vogue*, *Cosmopolitan* and *Elle* for women, and *GQ* magazine and *FHM* for men seem to be both arbiters and reflectors of fashion, but the fact is that fashion and style begin on the street. Fashion in general is multifarious and changes much more quickly than culture; while it is fundamentally an expression of identity, it is also often criticized as representing the worst aspects of the wasteful, throw-away consumer society. It can also be seen as a way of imposing either individuality or conformity. It could be said that British fashion reflects the multicultural, multi-faceted reality of modern Britain.

　　1979 年，《每日邮报》上有一篇关于中国的报导，上面写着"想象一个从来都没有听过披头士的国家。"中国从那时起已经有了巨大的变化，现在城市里的年轻人把伦敦、东京及纽约当作是流行的中心。他们不再崇尚巴黎或米兰的高级时装，而是以从六、七十年代的青年运动发展而来的又酷又新潮的街头风格为主流。在"摇摆的 60 年代"，伦敦的卡纳比街是年轻充满活力的流行中心，以摇滚乐为主流，典型人物有：披头士和滚石等流行音乐和摇滚乐队、詹姆士·邦德等电影主角、玛莉·昆特等设计师。这些在 90 年代系列电影《王牌大贱谍》里被一一嘲讽。70 年代后期这些形象显得过时浮夸，以朋克为主的新流行风格起而代之，设计师薇薇安·韦斯特伍德的作品具有代表性。在 90 年代末期，历经了撒切尔夫人年代的文化低谷期后，新的工党政府以"酷的不列颠"为名推销年轻、复兴的英国。所以，伦敦一直以来都是一个时尚流行中心，能及时捕捉并反映出年轻人喜好的风格。这种风格反映在保罗·史密斯以及斯特拉·麦卡特尼等设计师的作品上（斯特拉·麦卡特尼是披头士之一保罗·麦卡特尼的女儿）。

　　时尚对很多人来说非常重要，但是似乎已经没有任何风格称得上是"最新潮"。走在英国的任何一条街上，你可以看到各式各样的装扮，那种每一个时期流行一种风格的时代已经过去。有些人盛装出行，有些人休闲随意，并且不同的场合有不同的打扮。女性时尚杂志有《风格》、《大都会》及《Elle》等，而《GQ》和《FHM》则专给男人看。这些杂志似乎是时尚的仲裁者或风向标，但事实上流行起源于街头。一般来说，流行是五花八门的，其变化比文化快很多。时尚基本上是一种个性表达方式，但同时也被批评为消费社会里最浪费的行为。时尚既可表达个性，又可强调共性。可以说，英国的流行时尚反映出现代英国的多元文化特色和社会的多面性。

Super-thin Is In

Gang: Hey, Greg, have you seen this in the paper? It says that they're going to ban models under the age of 16 from London Fashion Week and that all models may have to show a health certificate before they are allowed to walk down the catwalk. What's a catwalk?

Greg: Hmm? Oh, it's the platform that models walk down at a fashion show.

Marie: I think that's a good idea. There are too many skinny models around; half of them have got anorexia and bulimia.

Gang: What does that mean?

Marie: It means that they're ill. They have eating disorders that mean they don't eat or they make themselves sick so that they can stay thin. It's really bad, because the fashion industry encourages them and they are role models for young girls. Fashion magazines are full of them.

Greg: Don't listen to her, Gang. She's just jealous because she's not young and slim any more.

Marie: Shut up, you! Dirty old man! Women become like this and dress in uncomfortable high heels and things because men think it's sexy — that's all. What else does it say, Gang?

Gang: It says that the British Fashion Council is concerned at how thin and waif-like models have become. Super-thin is in, and medical experts are worried that teenagers and women in their twenties are copying the look and risking their health to get to size zero.

Greg: Well, more fool them! Don't they know that men find that look off-putting? I think most British men actually like women to have a bit of meat on them.

Gang: Actually, in China, the ideal is to be tall, slim and willowy with very soft, smooth skin. It's not good to be fat.

Greg: Yes, but I think Chinese 'fat' is different to British 'fat', isn't it? I mean when you say your girlfriend is 'fat', I'd say she's a bit chubby.

Marie: But, Gang! That's an impossible ideal. The vast majority of women can never be like that. Just like most men don't look like Hollywood matinee idols.

Greg: I do!

Marie: Big head!

Gang: Greg，it says here in another article，"Should men wax their swimming trunk line？" What's that？

Marie: Well go on, Greg. Tell him.

现在流行超瘦

王刚：嗨，格雷，你看到报上写的吗？上面说伦敦时装周将禁止使用 16 岁以下的模特儿，而且所有的模特儿要呈交健康证明才可以参加 Catwalk。什么是 Catwalk？

格雷：噢？就是模特儿走秀的舞台。

玛丽：我觉得这是个好主意。皮包骨的模特儿太多了，她们多半都有厌食症和易饥症。

王刚：什么意思啊？

玛丽：就是说她们都有病。她们都有饮食失调症，要么不吃，要么就是吃了之后想办法吐出来，这样才能保持苗条。这真的很不好，因为服装业鼓励她们这么做，而她们又是年轻女性的榜样。时尚杂志上全是她们。

格雷：王刚，别听她说。她只是很忌妒，因为她不再年轻，而且也不再苗条了。

玛丽：你给我闭嘴！糟老头！正是因为男人认为这样很性感女人才这么做，穿上不舒服的高跟鞋和衣服。王刚，报上还写些什么？

王刚：报上还说，英国时装理事会担心模特儿越来越瘦。现在流行超瘦，医学专家们很担心十几岁的少女及二十几岁的年轻女性会模仿她们，牺牲健康去追求 0 尺码。

格雷：噢，真是白痴！她们不知道男生觉得瘦成那样很倒胃口吗？我觉得大多数英国男人喜欢有点肉的女人。

王刚：事实上，在中国要瘦瘦高高有很好的皮肤才算好看。胖是不好看的。

格雷：对，可是我觉得中国人说的胖和英国人认为的胖是不一样的，不是吗？我是说，你认为你的女朋友很胖，可我觉得她只是有点圆。

玛丽：王刚，可那是很理想化的观念。大多数女人没法长成那样，就像大多数男人无法长得像好莱坞偶像一样啊。

格雷：我就是！

玛丽：吹牛！

王刚：格雷，报上还有一篇文章说"男性应该除去泳裤边的毛吗？"那是什么意思？

玛丽：噢，格雷，告诉他啊。

Chapter 36

Youth 'Tribes' and Sub-cultures

年 轻 族 群 与 次 文 化

When you look at Western youth culture and music, you might be forgiven for thinking that young people in the West are either living freely and dressing and expressing themselves exactly as they want or completely disaffected and rebellious. Postcards of London often show Punks with brightly coloured Mohican haircuts or Goths dressed as frightening and sinister vampires with whitened skin and black lipstick and eyeliner. The plethora of youth 'tribes' or sub-cultures which have developed in Britain since the 1950s are all closely identified with different types of music which were originally based on black American music like Jazz, Soul and the Blues, and modified by young whites into different types of pop and Rock 'n' Roll until we have ended up with a dizzying array of styles like Hip-Hop, R&B, Techno, Garage, House, Trance, Metal, Death Metal, Grunge the list is endless. Each group has its own way of talking, its own 'in words' and its own magazines and fanzines.

Hard-core fans of each style will dress in different ways to somehow rebel against mainstream society while still conforming to a particular group. Many students and other young people will dress in what appears to be a rebellious way but will eventually grow out of it, get married, settle down and have families. Others simply become more mainstream as they get older, being embarrassed by the way they looked in their youth.

You will find clothes manufacturers like Gap and Next and Zara adapting their styles to certain sub-cultural ways of dressing, while mixing and matching at the same time. Hence, the popularity of hoodies and Hip-Hop fashion. Although 'pure' members of some tribes might describe these fashions as bland and boring, there does seem to be a lot less rigidity in the 'uniforms' that young people choose to wear than twenty years ago. What is clear, though, is that despite complaints from some conservative politicians, youth sub-cultures are actually a feature of mainstream society in the UK, and the members of these tribes are far more conservative and conformist in their attitudes than they like to pretend. There is, after all, a strong tradition of eccentricity in British dress and fashion.

当你欣赏西方的青年文化和音乐时,你也许很自然地就会认为西方的年轻人过着不受拘束的日子,穿着打扮及表达方式都随心所欲,要不然就是愤世嫉俗非常叛逆。伦敦的明信片常常印着一头彩色莫希干发型的朋克型,或是一身邪恶可怖的吸血鬼装扮、抹白的皮肤、涂黑的嘴唇和眼线的"哥特人"。从上世纪 50 年代开始,青年族群和亚文化群体蓬勃发展,以不同形态的音乐为各自的象征。这些音乐起源于美国黑人音乐,如爵士乐、灵歌及蓝调,通过年轻白人的改造成为不同类型的流行乐及摇滚乐,直到我们眼前这些令人眼花缭乱的曲风,如嘻哈、节奏蓝调、强劲摇头、车库、清风音乐、狂飙电音、金属音乐、重金属音乐等等。每一个族群都有自己的说话方式及"流行词汇",还有专属的杂志及歌迷。

族群的死忠粉丝们有自己的特色打扮,展示出对主流社会的反抗和对特定群体的依附。很多学生及年轻人会以叛逆的方式打扮自己,直到长大脱离族群,结婚,安定下来,建立家庭。有些人随着年纪的增长渐渐融入主流生活,对自己当年的装扮感到羞愧。

你会发现一些服装制造商,像是 Gap、Next 及 Zara 等,大多将其产品与某些亚文化群体的穿衣方式结合起来。连帽衫及嘻哈服饰应运而生。虽然"正牌的"族群成员认为这些服饰平淡无味,但是比起 20 年前年轻人"制服"一样的服装已经很出位了。虽然有很多保守的政治家对青年亚文化群体颇有怨言,但是在英国社会,青年亚文化实际上已经成为主流文化的特色之一。成员们也比他们所伪装的外表更为保守和守旧。总之,标新立异是英国的服装和流行文化的坚实传统。

Hoodies

Gang: What's this in the newspaper, Greg? It says, 'hug a hoodie'.

Greg: Oh, that's the Conservative leader, David Cameron. He's trying to show how cool he is by saying that we should try to be more understanding of hoodies. Ha! Politicians are always doing that — trying to get the youth vote. He's been saying that he likes all these cool bands too, but that's just his advisers telling him to say that.

←A hoodie

Gang: So, what's a hoodie?

Greg: You know those lads with hooded sweatshirts you see hanging around at the end of the street? Well the things they wear are called hoodies, and so are they themselves. The newspapers are always going on about how feral and wild they are and how they're linked to knife and gun crime. Some people are saying that they are completely out of control and some shopping malls have banned them.

Gang: Yeah, I've noticed that there are all kinds of youth groups and some of them seem to dress really outrageously.

Marie: Yeah! They all think they're 'expressing themselves!'

Greg: Yeah, well I suppose we both dressed a bit weird when we were younger. I mean, you went through a Goth phase, didn't you?

Marie: Oh God! Please don't remind me! I'd rather forget that if you don't mind. Anyway, what about you and your Grunge period? When I met you, you looked like someone out of a third-rate Seattle rock band all long shaggy hair and loose clothes. You needed a good wash!

Greg: I know, but come on! People change as they get older. I mean, my dad was a skinhead. Did you know that? He used to wear Ben Sherman shirts, braces, tight jeans and Dr Marten's boots. He was a real hooligan and used to go to football matches just to fight.

Marie: Gosh, I never knew that. He's really mellowed with age. And he's bald for real now. My mum was a bit of a hippy, actually. She liked all of those old rock groups from the sixties and the seventies. There really was a big class division between youth groups in those days, wasn't there? I mean, your parents and mine would probably never have mixed.

Greg: I suppose there still is a big difference. I mean, look at the kids who wear all the Hip-Hop gear and the bling. I mean, you're more likely to find them on a council estate than on a university campus.

Gang: That's really strange. In China it's more like kids with quite well-off parents who would dress in that Hip-Hop gear.

连帽衫人

王刚：格雷，这报纸上写的是什么啊？上面写着："拥抱一个连帽衫人"。

格雷：喔，那是保守党的领袖大卫·卡梅伦。他为了显酷才说我们应该多了解那些穿连帽衫的年轻人。哈！政客们老这么干，不过是想拉到年轻人的选票。他也曾说他喜欢所有的年轻乐团，不过那些都是他的顾问们让他说的。

王刚：那究竟什么是"连帽衫人"呢？

格雷：你知道那些穿着连帽衫，常常在街头闲晃的年轻人吧？他们常常穿连帽衫，所以他们这一类人也被称为"连帽衫人"。报上常报导他们有多凶悍野蛮，他们常常被牵扯上刀枪等犯罪事件。有些人说这些连帽衫人已经无法约束，有些购物中心甚至禁止他们进入。

王刚：是的，我也注意到有很多的年轻族群，有些人的打扮非常夸张。

玛丽：没错，他们认为那样是在做自我表达！

格雷：对啊，我觉得我们年轻时的打扮也有一点标新立异。我说，你不是有一阵子扮哥特人吗？

玛丽：哦，天啊！请你不要再提醒我了！如果你不介意，我宁可忘了那些事。对了，那你和你的垃圾乐时期呢？我认识你的时候你看起来像是从三流西雅图乐团跑出来的角色……乱糟糟的长发还有松垮的衣服。脏得没法看了！

格雷：我知道，但是别这样！随着年龄的增长人会变的。我是说，我父亲以前还剃过光头，你知道吗？他那时都穿宾舍曼衬衫、背带、紧身牛仔裤和马丁大夫鞋。他以前真的是个足球流氓，去看比赛就是为了打架。

玛丽：天啊，我从来都不知道。他真的随着年龄增长变得成熟了，而且他现在可是真秃。我妈妈以前有点嬉皮，事实上她喜欢所有六、七十年代的摇滚乐团。那时候的年轻族群真的有很大的等级鸿沟，不是吗？我是说，我们两边的父母就绝对不会混在一块儿。

格雷：我觉得现在还是有很大的差异。我是说，那些穿着嘻哈服饰还戴着闪亮饰品的年轻人，你不觉得你只能在廉租宅看到他们而不是学校宿舍吗？

王刚：这真的很奇怪。在中国，有钱人家的小孩才更有可能做嘻哈装扮。

Chapter 37

Accents

口 音

Chinese people often talk about British English and American English. In fact, it is common for Chinese language schools to specify that they want a teacher who speaks 'American English' when they are advertising for teachers. The irony is that most language school directors are unable to distinguish between the two.

The Queen's English, Oxford English and BBC English are common names for the accent of British English that is considered prestigious. Linguists call this accent Received Pronunciation (RP) or Standard British English and it is, in fact, a fairly recent development. It was created in the elite public (private) schools in England in the 19th Century as a way of making all the boys, who spoke in regional accents, use a standard form. RP quickly developed as the accent of government, the monarchy and upper classes and the universities. For this reason, it spread throughout the British Empire and became the accent of the colonial administration. When the BBC came into being in the 1920s, RP became the voice of the airwaves and became seen as the accent of authority; people who spoke in this accent became seen as more intelligent and charming — and even better looking! This accent is not linked with any particular region of Britain; it is an artificial form.

Reverence for RP has absolutely nothing to do with any innate linguistic qualities of the accent (there are other accents which are considered more pleasing to the ear), but everything to do with social factors. This is the accent of the elite 0.5% of the population, and when foreigners think of British English, it is this accent that they are probably thinking of.

The fact is, however, that the British people speak in a whole variety of accents and dialects. Indeed, there is a common saying that accents change every seven miles in the UK. Most outsiders would probably not notice the smaller differences, but they would certainly hear the differences between, say, the accent of London and that of Glasgow. Every region in Britain has a distinctive accent and, generally, the more working-class the speaker is, the stronger the accent will be. Some people might even speak in a distinctive local dialect where they use completely different words and grammar. Generally, but not always, the more educated a person is the less of a regional accent he will have and the more his accent will tend towards RP. Linguists also say that it is more usual for women to speak closer to the standard form of English. Next time you are listening to a British person speaking, ask her where she is from and try to identify the features of her accent.

■ ■ ■ ■ ■ ■ ■ ■ ■ ■ ■ ■ ■ ■ ■ ■

中国人常常讨论有关英式英语和美式英语的问题。事实上，中国的语言学校常常在登广告找老师时指明要说美式英语的教师。可笑的是，有很多语言学校的主管常常无法分辨这两者的差异。

女王英语、牛津英语及BBC英语被统称为英式口音，也被视为上流社会的口音。语言学家称之为"被接受的口音"或"标准的英式英语"。事实上，这是近期的发展，19世纪时由私立学校创立，是为了让所有满口乡音的学生们以同一种标准口音来交谈。这种标准口音很快被政府、王室、上流社会和大学所接受并使用，进而迅速扩散至大英帝国所有的地区，成为殖民地的官方语言。上世纪20年代BBC成立后，标准口音成为广播语音，被视为权威语音。使用这种口音的人被认为更具智慧和魅力，甚至长得更好看！其实这种口音与英国任何地方口音都无关联，完全是人造的。

对标准口音的尊崇并无任何语言学上的相关性（有些其他口音会被认为更悦耳），但是却与社会因素相关。这是人口中0.5%的精英使用的口音，当外国人想到英式口音时，他们自然会想到这个。

然而，英国人实际上使用各式各样的口音及方言。有一个通俗的说法是在英国每走7英里口音就会变。大部分的外来者可能无法察觉一些细微的变化，但他们绝对可以分辨出伦敦腔和格拉斯哥腔。英国的每一个区域都有其独特的腔调，一般而言，越是蓝领阶级口音越重。有些人的独特方言甚至使用完全不同的文字和语法。通常来说，当然不是绝对的，教育程度越高的人地方口音就越弱，而且更接近标准口音。语言学家还认为，通常女性的口音会更接近标准口音。你下次听英国人说话时，问一下她是从哪里来的，试着去找出她的口音特色。

Which Is the Best English?

Gang: Greg, I can't understand the postman and the guy in the local grocer's. Their accents are so strong. Where are they from?

Greg: Well the postie's a local guy; he's from round here, and I think the bloke in the grocer's shop is a Scouser; he's from Liverpool. His accent is quite strong, mind. He kind of speaks in a nasal tone with a rasping sound in his throat. It's a bit

sing-song as well, isn't it? A lot of people think that Scouse accents are annoying and whining; don't say that to the postman, though! Is that why you can't understand him?

Gang: Kind of what accent do you have?

Greg: Well, I'm from Durham, in the North East of England, so I have a kind of soft Geordie accent. Geordie is the accent of Newcastle, which is the biggest city round there, and people from Newcastle are called Geordies. The accent is most distinctive in Newcastle and gets softer as you move away from it. Soft Geordie accents are very popular on the BBC and among advertisers — they're seen as friendly, honest and warm.

Gang: Scottish accents are really distinctive, aren't they? They sound like they're speaking Italian or Spanish with that strong 'rrr' sound. I can't do it; it sounds like 'l'.

Greg: Well different parts of Scotland have different accents. I mean, the Glasgow accent is almost a caricature of an impenetrable regional accent, while Edinburgh Morningside is considered 'posh' and educated, but distinctively Scottish. When you get up to the Scottish islands, though, the accent becomes absolutely beautiful — really clear and measured.

Gang: Is London English the best English?

Greg: Well, you can't say 'best', and there are different kinds of accent around London. Many people in the North think that there are just two kinds of accent around London — posh Standard English and Cockney — the working-class accent of East London, and this is a caricature which is perpetuated in films and on TV. The fact is, though, that you won't hear real Cockney in East London now — most of the people who speak it have moved further East to Essex and Kent. Most youngsters in inner London now speak an accent which is influenced by black accents like Jamaican and cool Hip Hop street talk. You know that TV character, *Ali G*? That's what he talks. There's also an accent called Estuary English, which is seen as a more democratic, acceptable and inclusive accent; even Tony Blair used to lapse into it when he wants to sound like a 'man of the people'!

Gang: What's that?

Greg: Estuary English? It's an accent that's developed along the Thames estuary from a mixture of Standard English and modified Cockney. It's what posh people speak when they want to sound cooler and more in touch with ordinary people, and what ordinary people speak when they want to sound posher!

什么是最好的英语？

王刚：格雷，我听不懂邮差和杂货商讲的话，他们的口音很重。他们是从哪里来的？

格雷：噢，邮差是本地人。我想杂货商是从利物浦来的，他的口音很重。他讲话时拖着鼻音，而且带有刺耳的喉音，有点儿像是在唱歌，对吧？很多人都觉得利物浦腔很烦人。你可别跟那个邮差说啊！你是不是因为这个而听不懂他说的话？

王刚：那你是什么口音？

格雷：噢，我是从达累姆来的，那是在英格兰的东北部，所以我有一点轻微的纽卡斯尔口音。纽卡斯尔是那里的一个大城市，从那里来的人被称为小乔治。纽卡斯尔的口音非常独特，离它越远口音就越轻。轻微的纽卡斯尔口音在BBC节目或广告里非常受欢迎，因为它让人觉得友善、诚实，有温暖的感觉。

王刚：苏格兰口音非常独特，不是吗？他们说话时好像在说意大利语或是西班牙语，有很强的卷舌音。我发不出那个r音，听起来很像L。

格雷：噢，在苏格兰，不同的区域有不同的腔调。我是说，格拉斯哥口音简直就是难懂口音的滑稽典型，而爱丁堡口音被认为时髦有教养。当你到苏格兰的北方群岛时，那里的口音就很好听，非常清晰标准。

王刚：伦敦英语是最好的英语吗？

格雷：噢，不能说"最好"的，因为伦敦有很多种口音。很多北方人认为伦敦只有两种口音，一种是时髦的标准口音，另一种是伦敦当地人的口音，也就是伦敦东区工人阶级的口音，电视或电影里常常有关于伦敦佬口音滑稽的场面。事实上，你在伦敦东区已经听不到真正的伦敦佬口音了，大部分有这种腔调的人已经搬到更东边的艾赛克斯和肯特郡去了。现在大部分在伦敦市内的年轻人流行一种黑人口音，混合了牙买加和嘻哈那种街头说话方式。你知道电视角色阿里·G，就是那种口音。还有一种口音称为港湾英语，一般人认为这种口音更能体现民主，更易懂，并具有包容性。当托尼·布莱尔想显示他能融入一般民众时也会使用这种口音。

王刚：那是什么啊？

格雷：港湾英语？那是一种从泰晤士河港湾一带演变出来的口音，夹杂着标准英语及修饰过的伦敦佬口音。上等人这么说是想让自己显得更酷更亲民，而一般人这么说是想让自己显得更时髦。

Chapter 38

Rock Festivals

摇 滚 音 乐 节

When you think of pop or rock festivals, do you think of thousands of young people standing in a big field in the middle of the countryside going wild on "sex 'n' drugs 'n' rock 'n' roll"? Do you think of uncontrolled hedonism, loud music and excitement? Perhaps you think this kind of thing is all *passé* — something that boring old hippies did back in the 1960s when the Rolling Stones were young.

The rock festivals which are a feature of the summer all over Europe and North America began as folk festivals back in the 1960s. They developed into the famous rock festivals of the late sixties like Woodstock, Monterey and Altamont in the United States, Montreaux in Switzerland and The Isle of Wight and Hyde Park in Britain.

The reality is that music festivals have been undergoing a steady revival and increase in popularity over the last ten to fifteen years, after a long period during which they were considered uncool and unfashionable. Indeed, they are so popular now that they have become part of the mainstream, middle-class season, with many older couples taking their children along for a weekend of music and camping.

The kind of music that features at festivals is not generally the type that is popular with younger teenagers. Boybands like Blue, Westlife and The Backstreet Boys or divas like Celine Dion would not generally consider playing, and would probably not be popular with a festival crowd. Some R&B acts might play, and rave acts would also be popular at some festivals.

The Summer is festival season in Britain, and two of the most popular festivals in the UK are Glastonbury and Reading. Glastonbury is the largest music festival in the world, and is famous not only for hosting the latest acts but also for putting on comedy, dance and theatre shows. In 2007 nearly 180,000 people attended the festival, and there were over 700 acts on 80 stages.

　　提到流行音乐或摇滚音乐节，你是否会想到几千个年轻人站在乡村田野上疯狂沉溺于性、毒品及摇滚乐？是否会想到无法控制的享乐主义、喧噪的音乐及刺激的事物？也许你会认为这些全是过时的事，是那些无聊的老嬉皮在上世纪60年代滚石乐队还年轻时的所作所为。

　　摇滚音乐节是全欧及北美洲夏季的一大特色，源自上世纪60年代的乡村音乐节，在上世纪60年代末发展成有名的摇滚音乐节，如美国的伍德斯托克音乐节、蒙特里爵士音乐节、阿尔塔芒特音乐节，瑞士的蒙特勒音乐节，英国的怀特岛音乐节及海德公园音乐节。

　　虽然摇滚音乐节在很长一段时间里被认为是过时的活动，但它在过去10至15年间又慢慢流行起来。事实上，音乐节受到了热烈的追棒，目前已进入主流中产阶级。许多年纪较大的夫妇会带着他们的孩子一起参加周末音乐会及露营活动。

　　在音乐节里演出的音乐并不总是青少年们喜欢的类型。男子乐团像是Blue、西城男孩、后街男孩，还有天后席琳·迪翁通常是不会参加音乐节演出的，在音乐节观众中也许不太受欢迎。有些R&B及锐舞表演在某些音乐节上会受到观众的喜爱。

　　在英国，夏天是音乐的季节。最受欢迎的两个音乐节一个是在格拉斯顿伯里，另一个是在雷丁。格拉斯顿伯里音乐节是世界上最大的音乐活动，其之所以闻名不仅在于它有最新的音乐，还因为它有喜剧、舞蹈及舞台剧等表演。2007年，约有180,000人参加了这项活动。80个舞台上有700个节目的表演。

The Music Was Pretty Good

Gang: Greg, we're thinking of going to Glastonbury this year. You went last year — what was it like?

Greg: Well, last year we got completely rained out... it was a mud bath!

Gang: What do you mean?

Greg: Well the music was pretty good. The Arctic Monkeys, Byork, The Killers, Iggy and the Stooges and The Who were the headlining acts. The weather was so bad though that the field that we were camping in got flooded, and when we went to watch the acts we were stood in a quagmire. We got absolutely soaked, covered in mud and freezing cold.

Marie: Yes, Greg, but that's the whole point. Festivals always get rained on. That's the fault of the British summer.

Greg: Yeah, but it isn't always like that. I mean, me and my mates went to Reading the year before and it was great. The August Bank Holiday weekend was scorching. We camped next to the Thames under the trees and the music was blinding!

Gang: What kind of people go to these festivals?

Greg: Well, all sorts, really. I mean, Reading is quite different to Glastonbury — it's mostly indie, rock, punk, metal and alternative stuff.

Gang: Who did you see?

Greg: Um, let's see — we saw Pearl Jam, Metallica, Kaiser Chiefs and Franz Ferdinand. It can be pretty hairy at Reading though — the crowd is very demanding and if they don't like a particular act they'll bottle them off.

Gang: What does that mean?

Marie: It means that if the music isn't what the crowd wants, they'll pelt the band with bottles and cans filled with all kinds of things until they leave the stage. Like, a few years ago that American rapper, 50 Cent, got bottled off. Not surprising, really — rap music is just not festival music. Ha! It isn't even music.

Gang: Really? Did you do that, Greg?

Greg: No, I dindn't — I'm an old hippy, me. All peace and love, man. I was at the back of the crowd just chilling.

这音乐棒极了

王刚：格雷，我们想去看看今年的格拉斯顿伯里音乐节。你参加过去年的，怎么样？

格雷：噢，去年下了场倾盆大雨，简直就像是在洗泥巴浴！

王刚：什么意思？

格雷：噢，音乐太棒了。去年的重磅演出来自北极猴、比约克、杀手乐团、依基、傀儡和谁人乐队。但是天气非常糟，我们露营的地方淹了水，等我们去看演出时几乎是站在泥沼里。我们全都像落汤鸡一样，满身泥泞，而且冻得要死。

玛丽：对啊，格雷，但那就是重点。每次音乐节都会下雨。要怪就怪英国的夏天吧。

格雷：不过，并不是每次都这样。我是说，我和朋友前年去雷丁音乐节时天气就不错。八月的银行假周末，天气十分炎热。我们在靠近泰晤士河的树下露营，音乐震耳欲聋。

王刚：什么人会去参加这些音乐节呢？

格雷：各式各样的人。我是说，雷丁音乐节与格拉斯顿伯里音乐节有很大差异，大多是独立音乐、摇滚、朋克、重金属及其它东西。

王刚：你看到谁了呢？

格雷：噢，我们看到珍珠果酱、黑色金属、恺撒·切弗斯乐队和弗朗兹·费迪南德。在雷丁音乐节可能会很可怕，观众要求非常高，如果他们不喜欢台上的表演，他们可能会把台上的人轰下来。

王刚：那是什么意思？

玛丽：他是说，如果音乐不是观众喜欢的，他们就会向乐队丢酒瓶、罐头，直到乐团离开舞台。几年前，美国说唱歌手50分就被轰下台。我一点也不意外，说唱根本就不该拿到音乐节来，哈！甚至算不上音乐。

王刚：真的吗？你真的把歌手轰下台吗？

格雷：没有，我是个老嬉皮，待人平和心眼好，伙计。我当时只是站在人群后面乘凉。

Chapter 39

Courtship and Flirting

If you read British tabloid newspapers, watch popular TV programmes or witness the drunken antics of young people on a Saturday night, you might think that the British are very up-front and uninhibited about sex. However, the fact is that if you take away the alcohol, the British are quite awkward and incompetent when it comes to flirting and courtship. The bumbling characters played by actors like Hugh Grant and Hugh Laurie are seen as stereotypically British by many foreigners — clumsy, tongue-tied and self-conscious around women.

Of course, flirting is a basic human instinct common to all ethnic groups, and the British are just as programmed to flirt as anyone else. The problem is that the British tendency to irony and self-deprecation mean that they are not as direct as some other cultures in the way that they do it. For instance, British men might avoid paying women direct complements about their beauty, intelligence and so on for fear of appearing too keen and therefore setting themselves up for rejection. Instead, they often prefer to indulge in mock teasing, insults and banter, or to go through an elaborate series of subtle hints and manoeuvres that are so understated that they might not be noticed at all. British women are used to this vague, ambivalent form of flirting, where neither attraction nor rejection is made explicit, but foreign women find it confusing and often think that British men are just hopelessly shy or arrogant and aloof. Both men and women are uncomfortable with terms like 'dating', or calling each other boyfriend and girlfriend too soon, even though their relationship might already have developed into a close one. This is, of course, also a way of saving face for both sides.

So where do the British do their chatting up? Where do they get off with each other? As with most cultures, shared interests — or pretend shared interests — are the springboard to most romantic relationships, and research shows that workplaces, pubs and nightclubs, educational courses, dance, theatre and cinema clubs, spectator sports events and supermarkets are the best flirting zones. Over 40% of British people say that they met their current partner in the workplace, while almost 30% say they met in a pub. Of course, working with someone gives people time to lose their shyness and alcohol breaks down barriers much more quickly, so this is not surprising. The shared interest factor implicit in educational courses, dance, theatre and cinema clubs and spectator sports breaks down barriers as well but, of course, there is a degree of good-old British hypocrisy in all of this. Everyone knows why they are really there but they have to keep up the pretence. You might wonder how single people would strike up a conversation in a supermarket ("Which is better? Full-fat or semi-skimmed milk?") but, actually, many single Britons do their shopping after work in the evenings, and so it is a natural meeting place. The conversation prompts are similar to those for art galleries and bookshops as well.

- - - - - - - - - - - - - - - -

如果你读英国的八卦小报、看热门的电视节目或目睹星期六晚上年轻人酒后闹事的情况，可能会认为英国人非常直接并且在性方面放荡不羁。但是，如果没有酒精帮忙，英国人在谈情说爱方面是非常笨拙不熟练的。那些由休·格兰特及休·劳瑞扮演的笨手笨脚的角色是外国人印象中的英国男人——碰见女人就手足无措、结结巴巴，心神不宁。

当然，调情对所有种族来说都是共同的本能，英国人也跟其他种族一样具备了这方面的天性。但问题是，英国人爱讽刺及自我调侃的特性使他们在调情方面不像其他文化的人那么直接。例如，英国男人不会直接赞美女性的外表、智力等等，怕表现太明显而被拒绝。取而代之的是取笑、戏弄、侮辱及开玩笑的方式。有些精心设计的暗示及花招因为过于低调而不易察觉。英国女性对于这种暧昧不明的求爱方式非常受用，但是外国女性却对此感到非常困惑，甚至认为英国男人无可救药地害羞、自傲或是冷淡。即使是关系相当密切的男女，对于"约会"这个词也会感到非常不自在，也不喜欢太早称呼对方为"男朋友"或"女朋友"。这当然也是为了顾全双方的面子。

那么英国人通常会在哪里认识对方呢？他们都到哪里约会呢？与其他文化一样，共同兴趣，或是假装拥有共同兴趣，是大部分恋情发展的跳板。研究显示，办公室、酒吧、夜总会、教育课堂、舞蹈班、戏院、剧院、体育场所及超市是最好的调情场所。超过40%的英国人承认他们在办公室认识他们现在的伴侣，有30%的人则是在酒吧认识他们的另一半。当然，一起工作让人们有时间脱离羞涩感，而酒精能让人更快打破藩篱，所以这个结果一点也不会让人讶异。当然，共同兴趣这个调情因素在教育课程、舞蹈、戏院、剧院、体育活动之中能消除沟通障碍，英国人那种虚伪的个性也隐含其中。每个人都知道大家来此的目的，但是却假装毫不知情。你也许会纳闷一个单身汉如何在超市里挑起话题，难道是"哪一种牛奶比较好，全脂还是脱脂？"这样的吗？但事实上，很多单身的英国人会在下班后到超市买菜，所以那里很自然地成为与其他人碰面的好去处。话题的挑起跟在美术馆或书店里没什么两样。

She Fancies Him, Really

Gang: Greg, I was on the bus this afternoon, and these teenagers were really having a go at each other. At least that's what I thought, but then it sounded like they fancied each other. I just don't understand the way British kids flirt.

Greg: What were they saying?

Gang: Well, this boy was sitting with his friend and there were these two girls a couple of seats in front. The boy goes, "God! Let me get my sunglasses! Your dress is so bright it's blinding me!" Then the girl spins round and goes, "Huh! Look who's talking! Did you get that haircut for a bet! Do you really think anyone would fancy you looking like that? You should have spent your pocket money on acne cream instead!" in this really superior tone of voice. Then he goes, "what makes you think I'd fancy you anyway, you slag?" I was really shocked when he said that, but she just tutted and said, "huh! You sad geek!"

Greg: Well, that sounds like typical chat up lines to me. He didn't want to risk being blown out and losing face by showing that he fancied her, and she knew that and played along. It's all just an elaborate mating ritual like in the animal kingdom.

Gang: You're so right! That's what happened in the end, because the boy said, "oh, look, this is my stop" — and he stood up to get off, winked at the girl and said, "see you around." She then immediately turned to her friend and said, "I'm getting off here," and ran after the boy. When I looked out of the window, they were walking down the road holding hands.

Greg: Well that's it, then. It was all a convoluted set-up, wasn't it? Stuff like that always happens. What about the other two? The other boy and girl?

Gang: Oh, they were left looking embarrassed and not talking to each other. The other boy was fiddling with his i-Pod and the girl was pretending to text someone for the rest of the journey.

Greg: Sounds about right. The first two kids used the second two as cover so that they could get off with each other, and the second two were left high and dry — just normal tongue-tied, clumsy teenagers.

她看上他了，真的

王刚：格雷，我今天下午在公车上看到一群年轻人似乎在吵架，至少我是这样认为的。可是听起来他们却又好像很喜欢对方。我真搞不懂英国的年轻人是怎么调情的。

格雷：他们说些什么？

王刚：噢，有个男孩和他的朋友坐在一起，还有两个女生坐在他们前面几排。那个男孩就说："天啊，我得戴上我的墨镜了！你的裙子实在太花俏了，我的眼睛都快被晃瞎了！"然后那个女孩回头用高高在上的语气说："哼！看看是谁在说话！你是打赌输了才剪成那种发型！你真的觉得有人会喜欢你把头发剪成那样吗？你应该把你的零用钱花在买去痘膏上才对！"之后男孩说："你凭什么认为我会喜欢你，你这个笨蛋？"当他这么说时我非常惊讶，不过那女孩只是不耐烦地说："呵，你这个可怜的怪胎！"

格雷：噢，这听起来像是很典型的调情对话。他不想冒险，很怕因为表现出喜欢那女孩而没面子，而那女孩也有所了解，所以用同样的方式回话。这些都是精心编排的求爱仪式，像动物世界一样。

王刚：你说的真对！最后真的像你说的那样，因为那男孩说："喔，我到站了。"他站起来准备下车，然后对那女孩挤挤眼说："下次再见"。那女孩飞快地转头对她的朋友说："我要在这里下车"，然后便跟着那男孩跑下去。当我看向窗外，看到他们手牵手一起走在街上。

格雷：噢，这就对了。这些都是复杂的设计，不是吗？这种事永远都会发生。车上另外那个男孩和女孩呢？

王刚：哦，他们看起来很尴尬，也不说话。那个男孩在玩他的 iPod，那个女孩则在假装发短信。

格雷：就是这样。第一对男女利用其他两个人作掩护，这样他们就可以一起出去玩。剩下的一对则孤立无援，这种笨嘴笨舌的青少年很常见。

Chapter 40

Shopping

购　物

Are you a shopaholic? Do you simply have to buy shoes and handbags, or do you love browsing around bookshops or window shopping? Napoleon Bonaparte once dismissed the British as 'a nation of shopkeepers' who were not capable of challenging French ambitions in Europe. He got a response he was not expecting at the Battle of Waterloo in 1815.

There is still some truth in what Napoleon said two centuries ago. There are still many small independent retailers, but the small butchers, tailors, hardware stores, greengrocers, and other specialist shops that he was referring to are fast disappearing, having been overtaken by large conglomerates which run supermarket chains and out-of-town shopping centres. Many of the small corner shops that still exist are run by immigrants from Pakistan, India, Sri Lanka and Turkey. They charge higher prices because they cannot afford to buy in bulk but, on the other hand, they are convenient and open late.

Supermarkets must, by definition, have a floor space of at least one hundred and eighty six square metres (186m^2), and have three check outs. They are mostly situated next to motorways or large trunk roads, and have parking space. They concentrate on food and drink, and are separated into aisles where food is displayed, and also have counters which sell fresh produce. Many also sell clothes, white goods and household items. The biggest supermarkets in the UK are Tesco, Sainsbury and Morrisons, and many people claim that they are responsible, not only for destroying local communities and independent traders, but of fixing the market to exploit small farmers and other suppliers. There is also a problem with lorries causing traffic jams while delivering supplies. In fact, it is common for local communities to protest every time a large supermarket wants to open a store in their town or village. All supermarkets offer loyalty cards which give points to customers to encourage them to continue shopping there, and some even offer banking and insurance facilities.

Out-of-town shopping centres are extremely convenient for people with cars. They house all of the famous high street names, and these are places where you can buy any designer item or brand label you want. However, they are blamed for causing the decline of the high street in the inner city.

Department stores, like Debenhams, C&A and Marks and Spencer, are divided into different areas which sell a wide range of clothing, electrical goods, furniture and household items. Some of them also have food halls, where they sell up-market ready-made or easy-to-prepare meals for busy people who live in big cities.

If you really hate shopping, you can always log onto your computer and shop online. Many supermarkets and department stores provide online shopping facilities and will deliver to your door. In fact, it is possible to buy anything you want and never leave your house if you have a computer

■ ■ ■ ■ ■ ■ ■ ■ ■ ■ ■ ■ ■ ■ ■

　　你是一个购物狂吗？你是非买鞋子和手包不可吗？还是就喜欢浏览书店或逛逛大街？拿破仑曾说英国是个"小店主之国"，没有能力阻止法国占领欧洲的野心。但是1815年的滑铁卢之役给了他一个意外的回应——被英军击败。

　　在两个世纪前，拿破仑的说法似乎还有一点贴切。现在，英国还是有一些小零售商，但是拿破仑所说的肉贩、裁缝店、五金行，蔬果商及其他专营店正在快速地消失，取而代之的是由大型集团所经营的连锁超市及郊区的大型购物中心。剩下的街头小商店大多由巴基斯坦人、印度人、斯里兰卡人及土耳其人经营。因为无法负担低价大量采购，他们必须收取较高的价格，不过，他们那儿购物方便，而且营业时间长。

　　法律上规定，超级市场需要有186平方米以上的营业面积及3个收银台。这些超市大多设于高速公路或主要干道旁，有停车场。超市内以食物及饮料为主，所有的食物依种类被区分成不同的通道，也有一些柜台出售新鲜食品。有些超市也卖衣服、家电用品及家居用品。英国最大的超市是乐购、桑斯博里及莫里森。许多人认为这些超市不但破坏了社区生态，还整垮了个体商户，同时也剥削了小型的农场及供货商。他们运送货物的卡车也造成了严重的交通阻塞。事实上，每当有大型超市要设立新的分店时，常常会遭到当地居民的抗议。所有的超市都提供积分卡，鼓励消费者持续到店里采购，有些超市甚至提供金融及保险商品。

　　郊区的购物中心对于有车的人来说非常方便。购物中心里有众多的名牌商店，你可以在里面购买你想要的任何品牌的产品。但是，他们被指责为造成市中心商业街业绩下滑的原因。

　　百货商店比如德本海姆、西雅衣家及玛莎百货，分成不同的部门销售服装、电器、家具及日用品。有些百货店还有食品部，出售高档熟食或半成品，卖给住在大城市里工作繁忙的人。

　　如果你讨厌逛街，可以随时上网购物。许多超市和百货商店均提供网购服务，而且送货上门。如果你有电脑，即使足不出户也可以买到任何你想要的物品。

At the Shopping Mall

Marie: Right. Here we are. The Metro Centre! We can get absolutely everything we need here. Make sure you park in a disabled bay, Greg. I don't want to have to go for miles in this wheelchair.

Greg: OK... here goes... do you need any help?

Gang: Do you need any help, Marie?

Marie: No. I'm OK. Just get the wheelchair out of the boot, and let me slide across this board. Right. There we are. Let's go. Where shall we go first?

Greg: Well, I wanted to get some new trainers. Shall we go to *JD Sports*?

Marie: OK

Gang: I'd like to get a new wireless adaptor for my computer. Where can I get that?

Marie: Currys or Dixons, probably.

Greg: Well they're next door to each other on the same floor. Let's get the lift.

....

Gang: I need a WiFi adaptor for my computer.

Assistant: What do you need, like — a stick, or a card?

Gang: What's the difference?

Assistant: Same difference, really. This is a card you just slot it in like this and this is a stick — you plug it into a USB socket at the back.

Gang: Which one is cheaper?

Assistant: Well, this stick is the cheapest option, but there are other more expensive ones. It depends which system you're using. Some sticks aren't really compatible with some systems. It depends which system you're using.

Gang: Windows operating system.

Assistant: Well I've heard that this adaptor works better with Windows.

Gang: OK then, I'll take that one. How much is it?

Assistant: £ 39. 99. Do you need anything else?

Gang: No, thanks. Here you are.

Assistant: That's fifty pounds. Ten pounds and a penny change. Here's your receipt. Do you need a bag?

Gang: No, that's all right thanks.

在购物中心

玛丽：购物中心到了。我们可以买到任何想要的东西。格雷，请停在残障区，我不想推上好几公里的轮椅。

格雷：好，就停这儿，你需要帮忙吗？

王刚：玛丽，你需要帮忙吗？

玛丽：不用，我可以自己来。请帮我把轮椅从后车厢拿出来，再让我滑过这个板子。好了，我们可以走了。我们要先去哪儿呢？

格雷：噢，我想买一双球鞋。我们可以去 JD 体育用品店吗？

玛丽：好。

王刚：我想为我的计算机买一个无线网卡，我到哪儿可以买到呢？

玛丽：到英佳或维客吧。

格雷：他们两家都在同一层的隔壁间，我们坐电梯吧。

....

王刚：我想给我的计算机配一个无线网卡。

售货员：你想要棒状还是卡状？

王刚：有什么差别呢？

售货员：没什么差别。这是卡状，你可以把卡像这样插入计算机，或是把这棒状的插到计算机后面的 USB 槽。

王刚：哪一种便宜些？

售货员：噢，这个棒状的比较便宜，但是还有其他比较贵的。这要看是什么样的系统，有些是不兼容的，所以要看你用的是哪一种系统。

王刚：我用的是 Windows 操作系统。

售货员：噢，我听说这个和 Windows 搭配得很好。

王刚：好，我就买这个。多少钱？

售货员：39.99 英镑。你还需要其他东西吗？

王刚：没有了，谢谢。钱给你。

售货员：收你 50 镑。找你 10 镑 1 便士。这是你的收据。你需要用袋子装吗？

王刚：不用了，谢谢。

Chapter 41

Health and Addictions

健 康 及 上 瘾 问 题

Watch any British news programme or read any newspaper and you'll come across stories about drunken binge drinking, drug crime, obesity and obsessions over. Turn to the soap operas and you could be forgiven for thinking that Britain is in a state of crisis, with young people staggering drunkenly around the streets and fighting, while others are shooting up heroin and smoking crack in the streets. The chattering classes and hip young clubbers are said to be hopelessly addicted to cocaine and ecstasy, council estates are plagued by drugs and super-strength lager and schoolchildren are growing up either stuffing themselves with fast food and sitting in front of computer games or starving themselves to death because of anorexia.

Of course, for every one of these stories, you'll find alternatives about athletic young people actively engaged in sports and hobbies and other weekend activities. Many young people are actively involved in charity work, volunteering and study, but it cannot be denied that both drug and alcohol abuse and weight obsession are issues that British people are concerned about.

Some people blame the dysfunctional British relationship with alcohol on a mixture of pub-licencing laws which restrict drinking times, an unhealthy attitude to the role of alcohol in social relations and just a general genetic addiction to alcohol among some northern Europeans. Other people say that this kind of behaviour is a rite-of-passage for young people and that they grow out of it. Certainly, it can be very disconcerting for some foreigners when they see young British people reeling aggressively around town centres after the pubs close, and the ubiquity of illegal drugs in all areas of society is not helped by the way that the tabloid press focuses on the misfortunes of pop stars like Amy Winehouse and Pete Doherty.

There is concern today that, despite the popularity of organic food and healthy living, people are less fit now. They live a more sedentary lifestyle, eat more junk food and do less exercise than their parents' generation.

　　如果观看英国的新闻节目或翻阅任何报纸，你就会看到关于酗酒、毒品犯罪及肥胖等话题层出不穷。观看肥皂剧你可能认为英国处于危机中，年轻人烂醉如泥地在街头到处打架，吸食毒品，滥服海洛因；爱抱怨的城市中产自由主义者和年轻新潮的夜店客无可药救地沉迷于古柯碱和摇头丸；廉租屋充斥着毒品及烈酒；小学生们不是沉迷电子游戏、狂吃快餐，就是因厌食症而把自己饿得半死。

　　当然，在阅读这些新闻的同时，你也可以发现活跃的年轻人积极参与运动和一些周末活动。许多年轻人积极参与慈善公益活动、做志愿者并努力工作。但是不可否认，滥用药物、酗酒和过胖仍然是英国人关心的议题。

　　许多人把责任归咎于英国人与酒精之间不正常的关系，这包含了酒吧管理法令对饮酒时间的限制、酒在社交生活上扮演的不健康的角色，以及北欧人喝酒成瘾的基因。其他人则认为这种行为是年轻人必经的一个过程，会随着成长而消失。当然，在市中心看到英国年轻人在酒吧打烊后摇摇晃晃、打架闹事的表现，会让一些外国人忧心忡忡。八卦报纸总是关注那些麻烦不断的明星，像流行歌手艾米·怀恩豪斯及皮特·多哈提，这无助于解决无所不在的毒品问题。

　　现在有人担心，尽管有机食品和健康生活的观念越来越普及，但人们还是不如以前健康。大家过着懒洋洋的生活，吃更多的垃圾食物，比起父母亲的年代运动得更少。

A Check Up

Marie: I'm really going to have to get out and do some exercise. I feel that I've just got so fat since I had the baby. I want to get my shape back. I think I'll join a gym.

Doctor: Well, maybe you should just start doing some jogging or cycling. They say that most people who join gyms pack it in after a few weeks, so they end up wasting their money.

Marie: I know, but I just can't seem to get started. Maybe if I got a child seat on the back of the bike, I could take Olivia cycling

I feel that I've just got so fat since I had the baby.

along the sea front. It's really getting me down. I think I'm drinking too much as well.

Doctor: Well, how many units a week are you drinking?

Marie: I don't know. How much is in a unit?

Doctor: Well, one unit of alcohol is like half a pint of normal-strength beer, a small glass of wine, or a single measure of spirits.

Marie: I don't know. I don't drink every night, but maybe three times a week, my husband and I have a bottle of wine between us with dinner. We hardly ever go out, though, because of the baby. And I never get really drunk.

Doctor: Well, that doesn't sound too bad. The government guidelines are getting stricter, mind. Do you smoke at all?

Marie: Gosh, no. I gave up when I got pregnant. Although I have had one or two a week since I had the baby.

Doctor: Hmm. There is no safe level for smoking. It causes cancer and heart disease — absolutely no question about it, so don't listen to those people who tell you, "oh, my father smoked a packet a day all his life " Now, do you take any recreational drugs?

Marie: Well, I did try cannabis and ecstasy and coke when I was younger — you know, when I was a student; everyone does, don't they? I haven't done anything for years, though.

Doctor: What about Class A drugs?

Marie: What? Heroin? Crack? Gosh no; I'd never do any of them. They're for losers, aren't they?

Doctor: You'd be surprised the kind of people who end up addicted to hard drugs, you know. Now, you say you're worried about your weight. Let's check you on the scales

164

right, your BMI is rather high; in fact, you are clinically obese, according to this. I'm going to put you on a low-carbohydrate, low-fat, low-sodium diet, OK? I'm also going to give you an exercise plan. You can do these exercises every day — you don't need any special equipment or anything, and I'd like you to come and see me again in six weeks' time, all right?

体 检

玛丽：我真的要外出做运动了。自从生了小孩以后我越来越胖。我想恢复身材。我得去健身房。

医生：噢，也许你应该慢跑或骑自行车。他们说很多人参加健身房几周后就不去了，白白浪费钱。

玛丽：我知道，但我就是没办法开始运动。也许我该把孩子放在自行车后座上，可以载着奥莉维亚到海边逛逛。这真的让我感到沮丧。而且，我想我也喝得太多了。

医生：噢，你一个星期喝多少单位的酒？

玛丽：不知道。一单位是多少酒啊？

医生：噢，一单位的酒大约是半品脱的普通啤酒，一小杯葡萄酒或是一小份烈酒。

玛丽：我不清楚。我不是每天都喝酒，也许一周喝3次，我和我先生在晚餐时分享一瓶葡萄酒。因为有小孩，我们不常外出。而且我也很少喝醉。

医生：噢，这听起来不是很糟。政府对喝多少酒的建议变得更严格了。你抽烟吗？

玛丽：天啊，没有。我怀孕时戒了，虽然自从生了小孩后我一星期抽一两根。

医生：噢，抽烟是没有安全量的。抽烟会导致癌症及心血管疾病，这是毫无疑问的，所以别轻信有人说"喔，我父亲每天抽一包烟抽了一辈子……"你服用任何毒品吗？

玛丽：噢，我年轻时服用过大麻、摇头丸及古柯碱，你知道的，当时我还是学生，大家都尝试过，不是吗？不过我很久都没用过了。

医生：那甲级毒品呢？

玛丽：什么？海洛因？安非他命？天啊，没有，我从来不碰这些的。只有那些不成器的人才会，不是吗？

医生：如果你知道都是些什么样的人会沉迷于这些毒品，你会很吃惊的。噢，你说你担心你的体重。我们来称称看。噢，从临床来说你超重了。我要帮你设计一个低淀粉质、低脂、低盐的减肥计划，可以吗？我还要给你一个运动计划。你可以每天做这些运动，不需要任何特殊设备，我希望你6周后再来找我，可以吗？

Chapter 42

The Arts

The arts are what many people mean when they talk about culture. Literature, music, poetry, sculpture, theatre, cinema, painting and so on are what express the culture of a nation or an area or a people.

Do you think of Britain as an artistic country? Could you name any British artists if you were asked to? Have you heard of things like the *Turner Prize*? Have you heard of artists like Banksy ad Tracy Emin? Have you heard of architects like Norman Foster and can you recognise any of the buildings he has designed? The fact is that modern writing in English is multicultural and multifaceted, reflecting the vibrant and eclectic nature of modern British society. Which poets and novelists do you think of when you hear the words 'English Literature'? Do you think of Shakespeare, Dickens and Emily Bronte? Do you think of the American writers in your high school English course book? Writers like Mark Twain or Emily Dickinson? Or do you prefer *Harry Potter*?

Despite the rise of the Internet and the plethora of on-line writing and literature, the British book publishing industry has never been more profitable, with more and more books being published each year. A look at the short-lists of the Man Booker Prize, the Orange Prize and the Costa Book Awards — three of the most prestigious literary awards in the UK — will reveal a range of writing from throughout the UK by writers from all kinds of backgrounds, ethnic groups and social classes. It is this vitality and vibrancy in British writing that shows how the English language is not the property of the English people themselves, but has been adopted by all of the minority communities to express the realities of their lives. This is not a new phenomenon.

All of the quality newspapers have supplements which examine and review new writing — both fiction and non-fiction. If you look at the Sunday broadsheets, you will see reviews of recent publications. There are even weekly newspapers — The *Times Literary Supplement* and The *London Review of Books*. Weekly TV programmes like *The South Bank Show* and *Newsnight Review* have round-table discussions where well-known critics examine recent publications.

当人们谈到文化时，他们通常指的是艺术。文学、音乐、诗歌、雕塑、戏剧、电影、绘画等等，这些都能表达一个国家、一个地区或一个民族的文化。

你认为英国是一个有艺术的国家吗？你可以举出一些英国艺术家的名字吗？你听说过特纳奖或是艺术家班克斯和翠西·艾敏吗？你听说过建筑师罗曼·弗斯特，而且能指出他所设计的建筑吗？英国的现代文学是融和了多种文化的多元化作品，充分反应了生气勃勃的、具有折中精神的现代英国社会。当你听到"英国文学"这个词你会想到哪些诗人及小说家呢？你会想到莎士比亚、狄更斯还是艾米莉·勃朗特？还是那些你在高中课本里看到的美国作家，像是马克·吐温和艾米莉·狄金森？或者，你比较喜欢哈利·波特？

尽管互联网的兴起及大量网上作品甚嚣尘上，英国的出版业可是前所未有地财源滚滚，出版的书一年比一年多。看一下英国最有威信的三大文学奖项布克小说奖、橙橘奖及考斯塔图书奖的入围名单，就可以看到各种背景、种族及等级的作者所写的作品。英国文学的活力与生命力展现出英语并不是英国人的特有财产。英文已被所有少数民族所接受并用来表达他们的现实生活。

所有高品质的报纸都有专门增刊，评论新出版的小说及非小说。在星期天的报纸上，你可以看到新书书评。有一些专门周报像《泰晤士报文学评论副刊》及《伦敦书评》。每周也有一些电视节目，譬如"南岸秀"及"新闻之夜评论"，会请一些知名的书评家针对新出版的书籍做圆桌讨论。

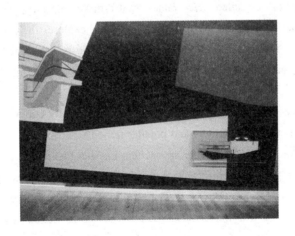

Talking About Books

Gang: Marie, how can I know which are the best books to read in English? I mean, which literature is the best?

Marie: Well, it's hard to say. I mean, I just read the blurb on the back of the book when I'm browsing in the bookshop. Sometimes I get recommendations from friends and sometimes I read the book review sections in the broadsheets.

How can I know which are the best books to read in English?

Greg: They say you should never judge a book by its cover. People like to distinguish between 'high art' and 'popular art', but I guess it depends what kind of book you're looking for. Some people like more 'literary' writing, others like chick lit and some people like thrillers. Sometimes the boundaries are blurred, and it's difficult to classify some writing.

Marie: Yeah. If you like literary or 'quality' fiction, it's probably a good idea to look at the short lists for the Booker Prize, the Costa Book Awards or the Orange Prize. There's some amazing writing out there which really reflects a whole range of cultural identities. I mean, people like Zadie Smith — she's mixed Jamaican and English, and her novel, *White Teeth*, was fantastic, then there's Monica Ali — she's half Bangladeshi and half English; she had a great novel out called *Brick Lane*. And erm Andrea Levy — she was born in London to Jamaican parents and her novel, *Small Island* explores the experiences of Black Britons. There's also older writers like Hanif Kureshi who is Pakistani British and Kazuo Ishiguro who's Japanese, but writing in English. There's actually a British Chinese author, Timothy Mo. His most famous book is *Sour Sweet*.

Greg: Yeah. I guess that's all right if you want to be politically-correct and inclusive, but what about crime fiction and thrillers and popular fiction?

Gang: What? Like Agatha Christie or spy writers like Ian Fleming?

Greg: No. I mean good modern detective novels like the *Rebus* series by Ian Rankin, or *The Blind Assassin* by Margaret Atwood. There's also writers like Frances Fyfield and Colin Bateman who write very witty novels. Do you have any crime fiction in China, Gang?

Gang: Well, I guess *Wang Shuo* is the most famous Chinese crime writer. You can see that he's influenced by Raymond Chandler, though. We have some good literary writers who are well-known internationally too. There's *Ha Jin*, and there's *Gao Xingjian* — he is the first Chinese author to win the Nobel Prize and one of his books, *Soul Mountain*, really illuminates the human condition and journeys deep into the heart of modern-day China.

Oh, and there's a bestselling Chinese novel called *Wolf Totem*, by *Jiang Rong*, which has been translated into English recently.

谈论书籍

王刚：玛丽，我怎么知道哪些是好的英文书？我是说，什么文学是最好的？

玛丽：噢，这很难说。我在书店买书时通常看一下封底的介绍。有时候我的朋友会推荐一些书，其他时候我会看报上的书评。

格雷：大家都说买书不能只凭封面。人们喜欢区分"高雅艺术"及"通俗"，但是我想这应该取决于你喜欢读什么书。有些人喜欢文学，有些人喜欢通俗小说，还有人喜欢惊悚小说。有时候区分不是那么明显，所以很难界定有些作品的种类。

玛丽：对啊，如果你喜欢文学或高品质的小说，最好的方法是参考那些图书奖的入围名单，比如布克奖、橙橘奖或是考斯塔图书奖。市面上有些不错的书，他们真的能反映文化特征。像查蒂·史密斯，她有牙买加和英国血统，她的《白牙》写得很棒。还有莫妮卡·阿里，一个孟加拉及英国混血儿，她的大作《金石街》也很出色。还有安德烈娅·利维，她是出生在伦敦的牙买加后裔，她的书《小岛》深入地描述了英国黑人的生活经验。还有一些老作家，像是英籍巴基斯坦人哈尼夫·库瑞斯和英籍日裔石黑一雄等。事实上，也有一位英籍华裔小说家毛翔清，他著名的小说是《酸甜》。

格雷：对，如果你想表现出政治正确性和宽容度，我想那些书是不错的，但是像犯罪、惊悚及其他畅销小说呢？

王刚：哪些？阿加莎·克里斯蒂或是间谍作家伊安·弗莱明？

格雷：不，我是指一些好的现代侦探小说，伊安·蓝金的"警探瑞拔"系列，或是玛格丽特·阿特伍德的《盲刺客》。其他作家如弗朗西斯·法菲尔德及科林·贝特曼也出版了非常机智的小说。王刚，在中国你们有犯罪小说吗？

王刚：噢，我想王朔算是最出名的中国犯罪小说家。你可以看得出他的小说受到雷蒙德·钱德勒的影响。我们也有一些国际知名的文学作家，像是哈金，还有高行健，他是第一位获得诺贝尔奖的华人作家，他的著作之一《灵山》描述了人类的生存状况，对现代中国进行了深入的描写。喔，还有最畅销的中文小说《狼图腾》，是姜戎写的，最近也被翻译成了英文。

Chapter 43

The Proms

英 国 逍 遥 音 乐 节

The Proms, or Promenade concerts are a season of over seventy orchestral classical concerts and eight chamber concerts held in The Royal Albert Hall in London between July and September each year and are unashamedly patriotic in style and focus. They feature a range of classical composers and world-famous conductors, and are broadcast on the BBC.

The Proms started in 1895 and were deliberately designed as a way of bringing classical music to the masses. The low ticket prices, focus on popular undemanding classical composers like Debussy and Vaughan-Williams, and informal rules on eating, drinking, smoking and walking about attracted people who would not normally attend classical music concerts.

The climax of the season is the Last Night of the Proms, held in the second week of September. At the Last Night, some concert goers (promenaders) dress up in tacky Union Flag hats and suits and wave British flags and sing patriotic songs. The Proms have often been criticised for harking back to myths of Britain's imperial past. In fact, one government minister recently attacked the Proms for being overtly and crudely nationalistic, exclusive and elitist, only to be attacked in turn herself for being out-of-touch with popular sentiment. Defenders of the Proms, however, say that the concerts are not nationalistic, and that the kind of patriotism displayed in the Last Night of the Proms is self-deprecating and humorous in tone — perfectly in line with the knowing irony that is one of the hallmarks of British humour.

Whatever side of the argument you come down on, it cannot be denied that the Proms are a must for anyone who wants to get a taste of British and international classical music in an authentic setting. The tickets sell like hot cakes and big screens are set up in Hyde Park to deal with the overflow. The BBC broadcasts performances live.

英国逍遥音乐节每年从七月到九月在伦敦的皇家阿尔伯特演出厅举行，约举办70场古典管弦乐及8场室内音乐会，从形式到内容都充满了爱国主义。节目内容包括一系列的古典作品，邀请了世界著名指挥，并在BBC播放。

英国逍遥音乐节起源于1895年，主要目的在于将古典音乐介绍给平民大众。音乐会票价低廉，选择对听众水平要求不高的热门曲目，比如德彪西及沃恩·威廉斯的作品。场内不拘礼节，不限制吃、喝、抽烟和来回走动，吸引了原本不会参加古典音乐会的观众。

逍遥音乐节的高潮是在九月第二个星期的最后一场音乐会。在这最后一夜，有些观众（也称逍遥客），会穿戴有英国国旗图案的俗气衣帽，挥舞着国旗并高唱爱国歌曲。英国逍遥音乐节经常被批评为想引导大家重温大英帝国的旧梦。事实上，最近一位政府大臣批评英国逍遥音乐节过度强调民族主义、有排外思想和优越感。她反而被抨击与大众情感脱节。逍遥音乐节的支持者辩称音乐会并未强调民族主义，其呈现出的爱国主义只是一种自嘲、幽默的表现，与英国人的标志之一——英式讽刺性的幽默不谋而合。

不管你赞成哪一种说法，不可否认的是，如果想在真正的音乐厅内欣赏到英国及国际古典音乐，英国逍遥音乐节绝对是最好的选择。音乐会一票难求，海德公园内设立起大型屏幕以满足更多的观众。BBC也会做实况转播。

Patriotic Music

Gang: Look at this leaflet for the Proms, Greg. I'd like to go, but I'm not sure which concerts would be the best ones to see. What do you think?

Greg: Well, let's see what they've got. Ralph Vaughan-Williams, fiftieth anniversary of his death. Oh, I love his music. It is so evocative of the English countryside it brings tears to my eyes, Elgar's *Cello Concerto*, Beethoven's 5th Symphony, Rimsky-Korsakov, Grieg, Sibelius, Albinoni this is all excellent stuff, Gang, but I would suggest The Last Night of the Proms. That's the climax.

Gang: What's that, then?

Greg: It's where they have a whole evening of popular British classics. It always kicks off with Elgar's *Pomp and Circumstance March Number 1* — that's *Land of Hope and Glory*. That's followed by Sir Henry Wood's *Fantasia on British Sea Songs*. That's a sequence that culminates with *Rule Britannia*! The whole concert concludes with Hubert Parry's *Jerusalem*, followed by the British national anthem, *God Save the Queen*. It really is a sight to behold and it can move even a cynic like me to tears.

Gang: *Jerusalem*? I've heard the crowd singing that at rugby internationals. What does that have to do with England or Britain?

Greg: Well, it's become a kind of unofficial English national anthem because some people think it's more stirring and moving than our real national anthem. It started as a poem, by William Blake, in which the writer says that we do not have Jerusalem — or God's City — in England, but that we need to create it in our hearts. It is actually a very revolutionary song but, like many revolutionary aspects of Britain's past, it's been co-opted by The Establishment and made more conservative.

Marie: Listen to you! Who do you think you are? Che Guevara? It's just nice music, that's all. Do you have classical concerts in China, Gang?

Gang: Well, it depends what you mean by classical music. We have what's called *guoyue*, or National Music, which is based on folk songs but heavily influenced by Western classical styles. You probably know *The East is Red*, but the *Yellow River Piano Concerto* is also world-famous. Then we have traditional Chinese music, which is played on woodwind and percussion, bowed stringed instruments and plucked and struck strings. You've probably heard of instruments like the *sheng*, the *erhu* and the *pipa*. These are where that typical Chinese sound comes from.

Marie: Actually, there was a Chinese guy playing some kind of stringed instrument in the shopping mall yesterday. He was flogging his CD, and the music sounded a bit 'poppy.'

Gang: Yeah, I know. That stuff's kind of tarted-up classical and folk music. It's not really Chinese — it's a bit like the food in Chinese restaurants here — changed into something different to suit Western tastes.

Greg: You mean like fish and chips in China?

爱国音乐

王刚：格雷，你看一下逍遥音乐节的节目单。我很想去，可是不知道哪几场音乐会比较好。你觉得呢？

格雷：噢，我来看一下他们有什么节目。纪念拉尔夫·沃恩·威廉斯逝世 50 周年的节目，我很喜欢他的音乐，它让我想起英国的乡村田园，令人热泪盈眶。艾尔加的《大提琴协奏曲》，贝多芬的《第五交响曲》，里姆斯基-科萨科夫、格里格、西贝柳斯、阿尔比诺尼的作品……这些都是很好的音乐，但是我会推荐最后一场音乐会，那是整个音乐节的高潮。

王刚：那是什么？

格雷：噢，整场音乐会全是热门的英国经典音乐。通常第一首曲子是艾尔加的《威仪堂堂进行曲第一号——希望与荣耀之土》。之后有利·伍德爵士的《不列颠海洋之歌幻想曲》，这个系列的高潮是《统治吧！英国》。整个音乐会以赫伯·派瑞的《耶路撒冷》及英国国歌《天佑女王》作压轴，整个场面非常壮观，连我这种愤世嫉俗的人也会掉泪。

王刚：《耶路撒冷》？我曾经在世界橄榄球赛上听到观众们唱这首歌。那和英格兰或英国有什么关系呢？

格雷：噢，这首歌已经成为英国非官方的国歌，因为它比英国国歌更能感动人。这首歌原本是威廉·布莱克的诗，内容阐述的是，英国虽然没有上帝之城耶路撒冷，但是我们可以在心中创造耶路撒冷。这其实是一首非常革命的歌曲，但是就像英国历史上其他的革命事物一样，已经被体制同化，变得保守了。

玛丽：看你说的！你以为你是谁？切·格瓦拉吗？那只是一首好听的曲子而已。王刚，中国有经典音乐会吗？

王刚：噢，那要看你指的是哪一种经典音乐。我们有所谓的国乐，国家音乐，这些音乐大多以民谣为基础，受西洋音乐的影响很深。你大概听说过《东方红》吧，还有《黄河钢琴协奏曲》，这可算是世界闻名的曲子。我们还有传统的中国乐曲，用木管乐器、打击乐器、弦乐器等演奏。你也许听说过笙、二胡和琵琶，这些都是传统中国音乐所使用的乐器。

玛丽：昨天有个中国人在购物中心弹奏一种弦乐器，他在兜售他的光盘，那音乐听起来有一点伤感。

王刚：噢，我懂。那种音乐只是把古典音乐和民谣拼凑在一起，不是纯正的中国音乐，有点像这里的中国餐馆会把菜色做些调整，以符合西方人的口味。

格雷：你是说像在中国的炸鱼和薯条吗？

Chapter 44

The Edinburgh Fringe

爱 丁 堡 边 缘 艺 术 节

Edinburgh is the cultural and political capital of Scotland, and is a beautiful and imposing city with a strong tradition in the arts, literature, science and philosophy. It is the home of The Enlightenment thinkers like David Hume and Adam Smith. JK Rowling, the author of the Harry Potter books, also lived there when she was writing the first book in the series. The city's big rival is Glasgow — a much larger and more industrial city. However, Edinburgh is the capital, and it is the seat of the Scottish Parliament at Holyrood House.

If you travel to Edinburgh by train, you will arrive at Waverly Station, named after a famous romantic novel by Sir Walter Scott. Coming out of Waverly Station, you will see the main thoroughfare, Princes Street, on the right. If you look up to the left, though, you will see the massive imposing structure of Edinburgh Castle looming over the city. Walk up the cobbled stones of the Royal Mile towards it, past the cathedral, and you will experience the true heart of the city.

The Edinburgh Festival Fringe takes place over three weeks in August, and is the largest arts festival in the world with 31,000 performances of 2,050 different shows in 250 venues. It was set up in 1947 as an alternative to the more official Edinburgh International Festival, but has now outgrown the official festival in size and importance. It is a showcase for the performing arts — particularly theatre, dance, music and comedy — and, as well as traditional staples like Shakespeare and Beckett, it showcases *avant garde* and alternative productions by small independent companies and troupes from all over the world. The organisers, the Festival Fringe Society, publish a programme and sell tickets for performances at the Fringe offices on the Royal Mile, but there is no selection committee, so the festival acts as a magnet for small experimental production companies.

In the past, there has been animosity between the Fringe and the official International Festival but, these days, the two events run in tandem, with the International Festival highlighting official performers and troupes from abroad and the Fringe highlighting alternative acts. A favourite pastime for cultural commentators and critics on some national newspapers is to bewail the weirdness of some of the new productions at the Edinburgh Fringe, but the Edinburgh newspaper *The Scotsman* gives an objective review of what is on. The Fringe has always been seen as a testing ground for new comedy and theatre acts which have since become mainstream in their popularity.

■ ■ ■ ■ ■ ■ ■ ■ ■ ■ ■ ■ ■ ■ ■ ■ ■

　　爱丁堡是个风景优美的城市，在富有深厚的艺术、文学、科学及哲学传统，同时也是苏格兰的文化和政治首府。爱丁堡还是启蒙思想家大卫·休谟及亚当·斯密的故乡，也是哈利·波特的作者罗琳撰写这个系列的首部曲时的居住地。爱丁堡的最大竞争对手是格拉斯哥，一个更大更工业化的城市。不过，爱丁堡是苏格兰的首府，而且苏格兰议会所在地也在爱丁堡的豪利罗德宫。

　　如果你搭乘火车到爱丁堡，就会抵达威弗里火车站，这个站名来自瓦尔特·司各特爵士的著名浪漫小说。一出威弗里火车站，在右手边可以看到主要大街，王子街。左手边则可看到雄伟的爱丁堡城堡俯视整个城市。沿着皇家麦尔大道的鹅卵石路而上，经过大教堂，就你可以体验到这个城市的精髓。

　　爱丁堡边缘艺术节为期三周，于八月份举办，是全球最大的艺术节，拥有31000个节目，分散在250个场地举办2050场演出。艺术节始于1947年，是爱丁堡国际艺术节的另一个选择，但是现在边缘艺术节的规模及重要性已经超越了国际艺术节。爱丁堡边缘艺术节主要包括表演类艺术，特别是戏剧、舞蹈、音乐剧及喜剧，同时也展示传统的表演，像莎士比亚及贝克特的戏剧，还有其他来自世界各地小型的独立公司和团体表演的前卫艺术。主办单位边缘艺术节协会出版节目表，并在皇家麦尔大道的办公室出售各项演出的门票。但是该协会并没有评选委员会，所以艺术节像磁石一样吸引了那些小型的实验剧场来表演。

　　在过去，爱丁堡边缘艺术节及爱丁堡国际艺术节之间有些嫌隙，但现在两者之间各有分工。国际艺术节以国外官方表演者及剧团为主，而边缘艺术节则注重形式多变的表演。一些文化评论家最喜欢的消遣就是在一些全国性的报纸上批评在爱丁堡边缘艺术节上表演的一些古怪的新作品，爱丁堡的报纸《苏格兰人》的评论则比较客观。边缘艺术节一向被视为一些新的喜剧及表演的实验场，有些后来也成为受欢迎的主流节目。

At The Fringe Ticket Office

Gang: Right, here we are. Have you got a programme, please?

Assistant: Here you are. Are you interested in anything in particular?

Gang: What about this — *Ricky Gervais at Edinburgh Castle*.

Lei Lei: No, Gang. That's comedy. We'll never understand British humour. I'd like to see something serious like a play or something like that.

Gang: OK. What about this — *Twelve Angry Men* directed by Guy Masterson and starring Bill Bailey and Stephen Frost. It's a courtroom drama starring twelve well-known comedians in uncharacteristically serious roles. That sounds good.

Lei Lei: What's it about?

Gang: It's about a jury of twelve men who have to decide whether a man is guilty or not guilty. I think it was a Hollywood film as well.

Assistant: The reviews of that play have been very good.

Lei Lei: Hmmm. It's three hours long. I don't fancy that.

Assistant: Look. Why don't you try this: *Fringe Sunday*. This is where many of the companies perform part of their shows at The Meadows to give people a little taster. That way you can see what is on offer before you commit to buying a ticket for the full show. Alternatively, if you just walk around the streets near the cathedral and the castle you can see theatre companies doing impromptu street theatre, handing out flyers and telling people about their shows.

Gang: Actually, I'd like to see the Military Tattoo in the castle. They say it's a really impressive show with massed pipes and drums and military bands from all over the world.

Lei Lei: Oh no! I don't fancy that. All that military stuff is just like grown men playing at soldiers like little boys.

Assistant: Actually sir, the Tattoo is very popular with the tourists but, if you want to get tickets, you'll need to go up the Royal Mile to the ticket office. You know, there's more to Scotland than men in kilts playing bagpipes. All that tartan was an English invention anyway!

在爱丁堡边缘艺术节售票处

王刚：我们到了。请问你这里有节目表吗？

售票员：这个给你。你对什么表演有特别的兴趣？

王刚：这个怎么样，《里奇·格威斯在爱丁堡城堡》。

蕾蕾：不要，王刚，那是喜剧。我们理解不了英式幽默的。我想看正经点的舞台剧。

王刚：好，这个怎么样，盖伊·马斯特森执导的，比尔·贝利及斯蒂芬·弗罗斯特主演的《十二怒汉》。这是法庭剧，由 12 位知名的喜剧演员演出没有个性特征的严肃的角色，这听起来很有意思。

蕾蕾：内容是什么啊?

王刚：是关于 12 名陪审员要决定一个被告到底有罪还是无罪。我想这以前是一部好莱坞电影。

售票员：这部戏的影评不错喔。

蕾蕾：嗯，可是得演 3 个小时，我不想看了。

售票员：你们可以看看"边缘艺术节星期天"。很多剧团会在"草地"表演一个片断，让大家开开眼。这样你们可以在买票前先了解这些节目的内容。或是，你们也可以到大教堂及城堡附近走一走，看一些团体在街头做即兴表演、发传单并告诉观众有关他们节目的信息。

王刚：事实上，我想看爱丁堡军乐表演。大家都说那简直棒极了，有大量来自世界各地的管乐器、打击乐器及军乐队。

蕾蕾：嗯，不要! 我不想看军乐表演。那些军乐队，一群大男人就像小孩一样扮军人。

售票员：事实上，军乐表演非常受观光客喜爱，但是如果你想要买票，得到皇家麦尔大道的售票处去。你知道吗? 苏格兰的文化不只是男人穿着苏格兰裙吹风笛，我们还有很多东西。其实，那些花格呢都是英格兰人发明的!

Chapter 45

Soap Operas

肥 皂 剧

The British love soap operas; peak viewing times on the BBC and ITV are when the soap operas are on, and the most watched programme of 2007 was the Christmas episode of *Eastenders*, which is based on the East End of London. Other popular soap operas are *Coronation Street* (this is actually the longest-running programme on British TV, having started in 1952), based in the working-class Salford area of Manchester, *Emmerdale*, which is based in a farming community in the Yorkshire countryside, *Brookside*, which is set in Liverpool and *Hollyoaks*, which is set in the new-rich Northern county of Cheshire.

The term 'soap opera' comes from American TV of the 1950s, when soap powder companies used the commercial breaks during these shows to advertise their products because they knew that housewives would be watching them. So the washing powder companies effectively funded the production of the soap operas. These days, people are more likely to equate the meaning of the word to the 'slushiness' of the storylines.

British soap operas differ from American ones in that they deliberately focus on the day-to-day problems of ordinary working-class and lower-middle-class people. Whereas American soaps are glitzy and glamorous, the British variety focuses on the loves, struggles and disappointments that we all face in our everyday lives. In this way, they claim to hold a mirror up to the reality of peoples' lives.

Some of the main criticisms of soaps are that they are sentimental and emotional — that they focus on the downside of life and that they cram all the worst aspects of human nature into a short period of time. "How can all of these things happen to one person?!" is a common criticism of the lack of reality and the mawkishness of some of the plots. Another is that the characters are shallow and stereotypical, lacking in any real depth.

However, they can be seen as an art form in their own right, and some of them are very cleverly written. Like real operas, they are emotional and over-the-top, but they are also addictive and are seen by some as life-affirming. The plots are on-going; they have no beginning or end — only an endless middle — so it takes some time to pick up on the storylines, but once you have started, you can't stop. Soap operas are also an excellent way of practising your listening comprehension and getting exposure to real English.

■ ■ ■ ■ ■ ■ ■ ■ ■ ■ ■ ■ ■ ■ ■ ■

　　英国人很喜欢看肥皂剧，BBC 和 ITV（英国独立电视台）的收视高峰都是肥皂剧的播放时间。2007 年收视率最高的节目是《伦敦东区》的圣诞节特集，这部肥皂剧以伦敦东区的人物为主角。其他受欢迎的肥皂剧有《加冕街》，1952 开播的英国播放时间最长的剧集，讲的是曼彻斯特索尔福德区的劳工生活；《艾玛谷地》以约克郡的农村生活为主；《小河边》场景是利物浦；《欲望之城》的故事发生在北部新富柴郡。

　　肥皂剧这个名词是上世纪 50 年代由美国传来的。当时肥皂粉公司认为家庭主妇们会观看这类节目，所以包下了广告时间。这样一来肥皂粉公司几乎可以算是出资制作了肥皂剧。现在人们将这个词的含义与贫乏无味的剧情划上了等号。

　　英国与美国的肥皂剧不太一样。英国的肥皂剧着眼于普通工人阶级和中下阶层民众的日常生活。与美国肥皂剧的浮夸花哨不同，英国肥皂剧反映我们每天都要面对的爱、挣扎和失望。它们因此称得上是人们现实生活的镜子。

　　有些人批评肥皂剧太多愁善感，因为它大多表现人生的低潮，把人性中所有坏的方面集中体现在短短的节目中。"怎么可能所有的祸事都发生在同一个人身上?!"是一句经常听到的评语，指责不够实际的、贫乏无味的剧情。也有人批评剧中人物的塑造得太过肤浅刻板，缺乏深度。

　　不管怎样，肥皂剧本身还是一种艺术，有些剧本还算不错。和其他剧情片一样，虽然内容过于感性夸张，肥皂剧容易被看上瘾，还有人认为它有激励人生的功用。肥皂剧的剧情是无限延伸的，没有开始也没有结局，只有没完没了的中间过程，所以需要点时间去理清故事主线，但一旦开始就会让人入迷无法停止。另外，肥皂剧也是很好的练习听力的工具，而且可以接触地道的英语。

I Bet That Got High Ratings

Marie: Wow! That Christmas edition of *EastEnders* was unbelievable! You know, it was so gripping!

Greg: Well I think it's banal. It's superficial and appeals to people's basest emotions. And nobody ever seems to be happy or satisfied in it... life is always a constant struggle against the odds. The characters are jealous, envious, petty, mean-spirited, vengeful, spiteful, angry and greedy.

Marie: It deals with real social issues like alcoholism, drugs, crime, divorce, domestic violence, affairs everything that normal people go through in their daily lives, but there's also love, loyalty, support and real community spirit?

Greg: I didn't see much of that during the latest episode. Do you know what happened on it, Wang?

Gang: No. What?

Greg: This guy, who is a violent alcoholic, beats up his wife and goes and has an affair with his son's fiancée! Nobody knows that he's having this affair. It's their dirty little secret until the girl gets fed up of the guy promising that he'll leave his wife for her that she secretly records them meeting in a hotel room and swaps the DVD with one that the guy got as a Christmas present. Then, on Christmas day, the guy invites the whole family to watch the DVD after Christmas dinner, thinking that it's the latest Hollywood blockbuster! They all see the scene in the hotel room — the guy, his wife, his son and all their relatives. Pretty cool, huh?

Gang: Wow. I bet that got high viewer ratings!

Marie: Well, actually, it was the most watched show over the Christmas break. People went wild.

Gang: I don't think that'd be allowed on Chinese TV. I mean, they do deal with the same issues, but not in such a direct way. There usually has to be some moral message.

Marie: Really? I'm sure Chinese people would love to see something like *EastEnders*.

Gang: Well actually, it's South Korean soaps that are really popular in China — especially among women.

我敢说那个收视率一定很高

玛丽：啊！《伦敦东区》的圣诞节特别节目真是好得不可思议！简直太好看了！

格雷：噢，我觉得无聊透顶。内容肤浅，迎合人们最恶俗的趣味。里面没有一个人是快乐的或是满足的，生活充满了矛盾挣扎。人物无不妒忌、猜忌、心胸狭隘、坏心眼儿、报复心重、恶毒、愤怒及贪婪。

玛丽：这部剧反映了真实的社会问题，比如酗酒、吸毒、犯罪、离婚，家暴、外遇等等，这些都是一般人在日常生活中遇到的问题，而且里面也表现了爱、忠诚、支持及邻居互助，不是吗？

格雷：最新的一集里那些东西都没有啊。王刚，你知道剧情吗？

王刚：不知道。怎么了？

格雷：男主角是个酒鬼，爱打老婆，还与他儿子的未婚妻搞外遇！没有人知道他外遇的事，这是他们之间的秘密，直到他儿子的未婚妻再也受不了他，因为他一直保证会离开他老婆却又迟迟不肯行动。于是她秘密地把他们在旅馆内私会的情景录制成光盘，与他要送给他老婆的圣诞节礼物对调。最后，在圣诞节当天，男主角邀请全家在饭后一起观赏他买的好莱坞大片。他，他老婆，他儿子，还有所有亲戚们，都看到了他在旅馆内的丑事。很带劲是吧？

王刚：啊。我打赌这一集一定有很高的收视率！

玛丽：噢，事实上，这一集是圣诞假期里收视率最高的节目，大家都乐疯了。

王刚：我觉得这样的节目是没法在中国播放的。我是说，中国的节目也有类似的情节，但是不会演得这么直接。我们的节目通常都带有道德意识。

玛丽：真的吗？我想中国人应该也会喜欢《伦敦东区》这样的剧目。

王刚：噢，事实上最受欢迎的是韩剧，女性尤其喜欢。

Sports

The British are said to be passionate about sports — both as participants and spectators — and the TV schedules are crammed with sports coverage. Not only do the BBC and ITV have whole weekends of sport, but there are digital, satellite and pay-to-view channels dedicated purely to sport

Football, the world's most popular game, was invented in Britain among working men in the towns of the Industrial Revolution and Rugby, which Britain has exported to its former Empire as well as countries as far apart as France, Argentina and Japan. Cricket, a peculiar symbol of English village life, has been taken up in Australia, South Africa, the Indian sub-continent and the West Indies. Any sport you care to mention will be played or watched in Britain, and every weekend you will see thousands of fans attending football and rugby matches on Saturday afternoons, playing amateur sports themselves on Saturday and Sunday mornings and going out to the seaside and countryside to take part in water sports and countryside activities.

Events which highlight the British love of sports and their obsession with charitable works are marathons and fun runs. The idea is that people will run in order to raise money for charity and also to fulfil a personal challenge. This area has turned into a massive business sector in recent years, and millions of pounds are raised for a whole host of charities through individual and corporate sponsorship.

The London Marathon is one of the biggest in the world and has been held every April since 1981. It covers a distance of 26 miles and 385 yards (42.195 km). The extra 385 yards were added because at the 1908 Olympics, the Royal Family wanted the run to finish in front of the Royal Box in the stadium. The London Marathon is the biggest fund-raising event in the world and it is estimated that in 2006 it raised £41.5 million for charity. It is second in the number of participants only to the Great North Run — a half marathon which is run every year in Newcastle, in the North of England.

Marathons and fun runs are showcases for English eccentricity. Stand on the roadside as a spectator to cheer the participants on and you will see runners dressed as pantomime horses, giant bananas, butlers and waiters, snowmen and deep-sea divers in lead suits. Remember, the British are a reserved and private people, but events like this allow them to be eccentric and outgoing without breaking social conventions. Very weird!

■ ■ ■ ■ ■ ■ ■ ■ ■ ■ ■ ■ ■ ■ ■

英国人可以说对运动非常疯狂，无论是作为参与者还是观赏者。电视上充斥着体育报导。不仅 BBC 和 ITV 整个周末的体育节目，数字电视台、卫星电视台及各个付费电视台都有专门的体育频道。

足球，世界上最受欢迎的运动，是在工业革命时期及橄榄球的发源地由工人们发明的，之后流传到前大英帝国所属地及其他国家，远至法国、阿根廷及日本。板球，英国乡村生活的象征，在澳大利亚、南非、印度次大陆及西印度群岛等地受到欢迎。在英国，任何你能想到的运动不是有人在参与就是有人在观赏。每个周末，成千上万的球迷在星期六下午观看足球及橄榄球赛，或在星期六及星期天上午参加业余的运动，或去海边从事水上运动，去乡村进行休闲活动。

马拉松及趣味赛跑体现出英国人对运动和慈善活动的热爱。人们参加跑步的出发点是既能为慈善事业筹募基金，又能达到挑战自我的目的。近几年来这些活动已经形成一个庞大的经济体，通过个人及企业团体的支持，可募集到好几百万英镑。

伦敦马拉松是世界上最大型的马拉松赛事之一，自 1981 年起，每年都在四月举行。伦敦马拉松全长 26 英里 385 码（42.195 公里）。这多出来的 385 码是于 1908 的奥运会增加的，原因是英国王室希望马拉松能在体育场内的王家包厢前结束。伦敦马拉松是世界上最大的慈善基金筹募活动，估计 2006 年为慈善机构募集到 4150 万英镑。伦敦马拉松参加人数仅次于"大北方马拉松"。那个长跑只有半个马拉松的长度，每年都在英格兰北部城市纽卡斯尔举行。

马拉松及趣味赛跑是英国人作怪的舞台。站在路边为参赛者们加油，可以看到很多参赛者把自己打扮成童话剧的马、大香蕉、管家及侍者，雪人及深海潜水者等等。要知道英国人是很保守并强调隐私的民族，但是这些活动却让人们将爱作怪的一面表现出来，又不会违反社会习俗。真是一帮怪人！

Going For a Run

Gang: Are you going out for your training for the Great North Run again, Greg? It's so late! it's nearly midnight.

Greg: I know, but the streets are empty at this time and it lets me think and switch my brain off. Anyway, I'm a bit behind in my training and I need to catch up.

Marie: Yes. Well, don't make a noise when you come back in. I don't want you waking the baby up.

Greg: All right I won't. I promise.

Gang: Why are you doing this, Greg? I mean, what drives you to do it?

Greg: Well, a couple of things, really. First and foremost, it's personal achievement. I want to prove to myself that I can do it. They say that the buzz you get when you cross the finish line is out-of-this-world. And, in fact, even though it's knackering I feel really great every time I do a training run.

Marie: Sounds like masochism to me.

Greg: Well, I think humans are programmed to feel like that. You know what they say, "no pain, no gain."

Gang: I know what you mean, Greg. I play basketball, and I feel really good afterwards.

Marie: You men are weird.

Gang: What else do you get from this, then, Greg?

Greg: Well, there's the camaraderie on the run itself. You make so many new friends on the run, and you urge each other on because there's a feeling that you're all in it together. This year I'm running in a team made up of people that I met on the course last year.

Gang: I know what you mean. I saw a poster in the Students' Union today about the London to Brighton Cycle Ride. I'm going to get a team together from the Chinese Society. We're going to do it to raise money for Cancer Research. Will you sponsor me?

Greg: Of course. As long as you sponsor me; I'm running for the Spinal Injuries Association. Put me down for a fiver.

Gang: Erm doesn't that mean we cancel each other out? I mean, we might as well just make separate donations directly.

Greg: I know what you mean. I actually think charity is a cop-out in many ways; it exists in some Capitalist economies because governments are scared of taxing people in order to provide the services they need. So what happens is that essential areas of health and education get left to the charitable sector. The point is, I guess, that doing this gives a sense of personal fulfilment and achievement.

Gang: I know what you mean, but it is going round the houses a bit, isn't it? Why can't the government pay for these things directly?

Greg: People don't like paying tax. Anyway, it's the FA Cup Final on the telly tomorrow. Let's sit down with a six-pack and watch it, eh?

Gang: Yeah. It might destroy your six pack, though. Ha ha.

出去跑一圈

王刚：格雷，你又要为了参加大北方马拉松赛去练习了吗？已经很晚了！快要半夜了。

格雷：我知道，可是现在街上几乎没人，我可以趁夜深人静好好想想事情。我的练习有一点落后，我得赶上进度。

玛丽：好吧。回来时小声点，别把孩子吵醒。

格雷：好，我保证不会制造噪音。

王刚：格雷，你为什么要参加长跑？你的动力是什么？

格雷：噢，有好几个原因。首先，第一，这是个人的成就。我想要证明我可以做到。有人说，当你越过终点线时那种感觉真叫腾云驾雾。虽然每次练习后非常累，但是我觉得很开心。

玛丽：听起来像是一种自我虐待。

格雷：噢，我想人类有这种天性。你没听说过"一分耕耘，一分收获"吗？

王刚：格雷，我了解你所说的感觉。我每次打完篮球后都觉得非常快乐。

玛丽：你们男人真是很奇怪。

王刚：格雷，那你还能从长跑中得到什么呢？

格雷：噢，还能获得一些友谊。你可以交到很多新的朋友，大家互相鼓励，总觉得大家是在面对同一件事。这次，我和去年长跑时认识的一些朋友组成一个小队，一起参加比赛。

王刚：我懂你的意思。我今天在学生俱乐部里看到一张海报，宣传从伦敦到布赖顿的自行车活动。我想去中国同学会组一个队参加比赛，筹一些钱给"癌症研究基金会"。你会资助我吗？

格雷：当然，只要你也资助我。我这次长跑是帮脊髓伤病协会募款。我会赞助你5镑。

王刚：噢，我们这样不是相互抵消了吗？我的意思是说，我们不如就直接捐给我们所赞助的机构好了。

格雷：我了解。我觉得慈善事业只是一种逃避的行为，它存在于资本主义的体制里，因为政府害怕向人民收税去提供人民所需的服务。这样一来导致一些基本服务，如医疗及教育，只能由慈善事业来承担。我想，关键是，参加慈善活动能获得个人成就感。

王刚：我懂，但这有点像是在兜圈子，不是吗？为什么政府不能直接支付这些费用？

格雷：因为人民不喜欢纳税。明天电视上有足球决赛。我们可以坐下来摆一盒6瓶啤酒，一起看球赛。

王刚：好啊。可是那会毁了你的6块腹肌，呵呵。

Chapter 47

Holidays

度　假

Where do Chinese people go for their holidays? Do they go down to Hainan to get away from the bitter cold of Northern China during the Chinese New Year holiday, or to Qingdao or some other resort during the summer? Do they go further afield? Australia, perhaps? Maybe they are adventurous and go to Europe or the United States. What about British people, though? Are they culture vultures who want to do a modern version of the Grand Tour[1], taking in the ancient sites of Greece and Italy and the art galleries and famous palaces of Continental Europe? Do they like to get off to exotic, far-flung destinations — beachcombing on the palm-fringed beaches in the Caribbean, scuba diving off the Great Barrier Reef or taking in a safari on the Serengeti Plains of East Africa? Or maybe they just want to grab a cheap package tour to Spain, Cyprus or Florida, where they can chill out on a beach for a couple of weeks of sun, sea and sand. Some British people prefer to call themselves travellers rather than tourists, because they do not want to be lumped in with those who just go to another country and don't really get to know the local people. Many young people take a gap year, during which they go backpacking around the world, living cheaply and sometimes working to pay for their trip. You may have seen young Western backpackers in China. Some of them teach English there — but that is another story!

Since the 1970s, travel has become cheaper for ordinary British people, and this has culminated in the current plethora of budget airlines flying all over the world. The most popular destination by far for British tourists is Europe. More than 80% of holidays are taken there, and the five most popular destinations are Spain, France, the USA, Ireland and Italy, with seaside holidays being the most popular. There were nearly 14 million visits to Spain by British people in 2005, and about 11 million

---

1. Grand Tour. A long trip around Europe taken by rich young men in order to complete their Classical education during the 18th and 19th centuries.

2. Source: International Passenger Survey, Office for National Statistics.

to France, and between 2001 and 2005, visits by British people to the USA increased by 6% to 4.2 million. In fact the number of visits abroad by British citizens has tripled to over 66 million since 1985, and risen tenfold since 1970. Seventy five percent of these trips were holidays, and nearly half were package tours. Almost 43 million trips were made by air, nearly ten million by sea and just over six million using the Channel Tunnel[2].

Most British people take their holidays in the summer, in July and August, but second holidays are becoming more popular, with skiing breaks in the Swiss Alps in the winter and short city breaks at other times of the year.

■ ■ ■ ■ ■ ■ ■ ■ ■ ■ ■ ■ ■ ■ ■ ■

　　中国人都到哪里度假呢？北方人是不是会到海南岛避寒度过农历春节？会不会去青岛或其他度假胜地避暑？会去更遥远的地方像是澳大利亚吗？还是冒险选择欧洲或美国？那英国人怎样？他们会不会是文化饥渴者，到希腊、意大利等遍布古迹的国家，或是欧洲大陆的美术馆及宏伟宫殿作一番大旅行[1]？还是比较喜欢去充满异国情调的偏远地区——长满棕榈树的加勒比海滩、可潜水的澳大利亚大堡礁、可徒步探险的东非塞伦盖蒂平原？也许他们只想订一趟便宜的去西班牙、塞浦路斯或佛罗里达的包价游，享受几周的阳光、海洋和沙滩。有些英国人喜欢称自己为旅行者而非观光客，因为他们不想跟那些到了外国只是走马观花而不与当地民众交流的人归为一类。许多年轻人花一年的时间背着背包环游世界，住便宜旅馆，有时靠打工支付旅费。你也许曾看到年轻的西方人背着背包在中国旅行。他们之中有人会在中国教英文，不过那又说来话长了。

　　从上世纪70年代以来，旅行对普通英国人来说不再昂贵。近几年各种廉价航班更是能让你满世界跑。到目前为止，最受英国人喜爱的观光地区是欧洲。超过80%的假期是在欧洲度过的，而其中最受欢迎的前5个国家是西班牙、法国、美国、爱尔兰及意大利，而这之中海边假期又是最受人们喜爱的。2005年到西班牙旅行的英国人约有1400万人次，到法国度假的英国人约有1100万人次。从2001年到2005年，到美国旅行的英国人约有420万，增长了6%。事实上，从1985年至今，英国人到海外的人次已增长了3倍，约有6600万，而这个数字约为1970年的10倍。这里面大约有75%的人出国度假，其中约有半数为包价游。几乎有4300万人次是搭飞机出国，近1000人次搭船，仅有600万人次使用英法海底隧道[2]。

　　大多数英国人会在七八月夏天时安排他们的假期，但是越来越多的人会在冬季安排去瑞士山脉滑雪，或是在年底安排一些短的假期去其它城市旅行。

---

1. 大旅行。在18至19世纪，有很多富裕家庭的年轻人会在欧洲做长时间的旅行，借此完成他们的古典教育。

2. 资料来源：《国际旅客调查》，国家统计局。

Talking About Trips

Gang: Hi Greg. I've been looking at this brochure for skiing holidays in Austria. Do you think Austria is nice?

Greg: Well, I've never been skiing. I've been to Vienna, but I think it's overrated, but Salzburg is nice — that's Mozart's city. What do you think, Marie?

Marie: I went skiing once, back in the 80s. We went to Northern Italy on a school skiing trip. It was great.

Gang: Wow, your school took you skiing in Europe? What kind of school did you go to?

Marie: Just a normal secondary school. School trips abroad were more common then; nowadays it's easier for families to travel abroad. In fact all holidays were really different before; I mean, my parents used to go to holiday camps and stay in caravans near the beach back in the 60s. They would never have thought of going abroad. Then in the 1970s, when air travel became cheaper, my cousins had their first package tour to Spain. There was a real boom in package holidays then.

Greg: I took a gap year before I went to university. I got a round-the-world ticket and went to India, Thailand and South-East Asia, Australia and South America. It was absolutely fantastic. I'll never forget it as long as I live. I went to Spain — to Ibiza — back in 1992. That was when the rave scene was really big. It was fantastic — the nightclubs, the beach parties — the whole thing was just amazing.

Marie: Hehe — come on, Greg, you haven't mentioned the Ecstasy!

Gang: What's that?

Marie: Never mind — you don't want to know. Anyway, me and Greg[3] went to New York in the early 90s, didn't we, love? It was lovely. Really cool. Flights to the US got a lot cheaper during the 90s. They're still pretty cheap. In fact, one of the things that environmentalists complain about is the damaging effect that cheap air travel is having on the climate — you know — global warming caused by emissions from jet engines. It's a major problem.

Greg: Yes, well I think it's important to watch your carbon footprint. I think our next holiday should be a trip through Europe by rail.

Gang: You know? I was thinking of going back to China by train.

Marie: What? Through Russia? The Trans-Siberian?

Gang: No. Through Europe, Turkey, Iran and Central Asia, then into Western China from Kazakhstan to Xinjiang. it's possible to travel all the way from London to Beijing by train. Most Chinese wouldn't like to do that, though. We prefer package tours and groups.

---

3. Me and Greg. The correct grammatical form is "X and I," but many people say "me and X" in idiomatic speech.

谈 旅 行

王刚：嗨，格雷，我在看到奥地利滑雪的旅游册子，你觉得奥地利好玩吗？

格雷：噢，我从来没有滑过雪，我去过维也纳，不过我觉得那儿没有大家说的那么好。萨尔斯堡很不错，那是莫扎特的故乡。玛丽，你觉得呢？

玛丽：我在 80 年代滑过一次雪，当时我参加了学校组织的意大利北部滑雪之旅。好玩极了。

王刚：哇，你们学校带你到欧洲去滑雪？你上的是什么学校啊？

玛丽：我上的只是普通中学，我那个年代学校组织国外旅行比较普遍，现在一般家庭到国外旅游变得很容易了。事实上以前的假期跟现在很不一样。在上世纪 60 年代，我父母会开着旅行房车去海边的度假营，他们做梦也不会想到要出国度假。到了 70 年代，航空旅游便宜了，我的表兄弟们第一次跟了一个旅游团去了西班牙。那时候团队旅游急速发展。

格雷：我上大学前花了一年时间到处旅行。我买了一张环游世界机票，去了印度、泰国、东南亚、澳大利亚及南美洲。那真是太棒了，我将永生难忘。1992 年我去了西班牙的伊比萨，当时正盛行歌舞派对。那真是热闹极了，有很多的夜总会和沙滩派对让你玩个够。

玛丽：呵呵，格雷，你还没提到迷幻药呢。

王刚：那是什么？

玛丽：别提了，你不会想知道的。总而言之，我和格雷[3]在 90 年代初去了纽约，对吧，亲爱的？那真的很棒，非常酷。在 90 年代到美国的机票便宜多了，到现在还是很便宜。事实上，环保人士的抱怨之一就是廉价飞行对气候的破坏，你要知道飞机排放的废气会造成全球变暖。这是个大问题。

格雷：对啊，我觉得留心自己的二氧化碳产生量是很重要的。我想我们下一次度假应该是坐火车游欧洲。

王刚：知道吗？我刚才在想坐火车回中国呢。

玛丽：什么？坐火车经过俄罗斯？西伯利亚铁路？

王刚：不，是穿过欧洲、土耳其、伊朗及中亚，然后从哈萨克斯坦到达中国的西部新疆。从伦敦坐火车到北京是可行的，可是大部分中国人不喜欢这种方式，我们喜欢参加旅行团。

---

3. Me and Greg，正确的语法应为 "X and I"，但是在会话中许多人会说成 "me and X"。

Chapter 48

The British Seaside

英 国 海 滨

In these days of budget airlines and cool international holiday destinations where British people can escape the humdrum confines of their cold, rainy island, you might be surprised to know that thousands of ordinary British families love to head for the seaside to spend their bank-holiday weekends and longer summer holidays. The seaside? In Britain?

Seaside holidays first became popular when George III started travelled to resorts on the south coast to 'take the waters'. During the 19th century the residents of the newly industrialised cities flocked to the seaside towns like Brighton, Margate, Blackpool and Scarborough, and a whole seaside culture developed which is still with us today — things like fish and chips, ice cream, candy floss, rock, seaside fairgrounds, amusement arcades and the famous piers.

During the twentieth century the phenomenon of the holiday camp developed. Butlin's and Pontin's set up camp-style resorts where working-class families would go and stay in seaside huts for a couple of weeks at a time. The camps contained everything that the visitors needed from restaurants and canteens to shops, pubs, nightclubs and theatres. Holiday camps declined in popularity when foreign travel became cheaper during the 1970s, but have recently undergone an upsurge in popularity. Most people who stay at the seaside would stay in a small family-run guest house or B&B.

Nowadays, thousands of city dwellers head for seaside resorts to go swimming and indulge in water sports like windsurfing, sailing and jetskiing, or simply to go sunbathing and playing on the beach. These days, some places like Cornwall in the south-west of England are considered trendier than some others like Scarborough or Margate. Brighton, of course, will always have its own special allure for Londoners, while Blackpool has strong resonance for working class Northerners.

你也许会感到惊讶，在现今廉价机票及新奇有趣的国际度假景点充斥的年代，英国人本可以选择逃离寒冷多雨的单调环境，但还是有很多普通英国家庭喜欢到海边去度过法定假日、周末，或是较长的暑假。海边？在英国？

海滨度假兴起于乔治三世时期，这位国王旅行到英国南海岸的度假中心"玩水"。19世纪时，新兴工业城市的居民开始大规模地拥入海滨城镇如布赖顿、马盖特、布莱克普及史卡保罗度假，进而产生了延续至今的海滨文化，以炸鱼薯条、冰淇淋、棉花糖、彩色硬棒糖、海滨游乐场及著名的码头为代表。

度假营是在20世纪开发的。巴特林及庞堤设立了营地式的度假村，工人阶级家庭可以在那里的海滨小屋度过数周。区内拥有游客所需的各种设施，从餐厅到商店、酒吧、夜总会及剧院。这种度假方式在上世纪70年代后因国外旅游降价而受到影响，但是近年来又逐渐升温。大多数到海边度假的人会选择家庭经营的客房或那种含早餐的便宜小旅馆。

现在，数以千计的城市居民会到海滨浴场去游泳，或纵情水上活动，比如风帆冲浪、驾船航行、水上摩托艇，或只是在沙滩上做日光浴、玩耍。近来，有些地方例如英格兰西南方的康沃尔比起史卡保罗、马盖特要更受欢迎。布赖顿对伦敦人而言永远都有独特的吸引力，而对北方的工人阶级来说，布莱克普则与他们有相当的共鸣。

Arriving at the Seaside

Marie: Right! We're here at last. Where's the B&B?

Greg: Take the next right and it should be down at the end of the street on the left near the beach.

Gang: I've never stayed in a B&B before. What's it like?

Marie: You'll see. Don't worry.

Lei Lei: Wow, I can smell the sea. I'm dead excited.

* * *

In the afternoon

Greg: Wow that fairground was fantastic. I loved the rollercoaster and the helter-skelter was just great. Here, shall we go and get some candy floss and rock?

Marie: No let's just go down to the beach and just chill out after all that excitement.

Gang: What do you mean?

Marie: Let's just go and lie on the beach. I mean, we've got a rug. We don't have to change into our swimming costumes — we can just take our shoes and socks off and paddle in the water, or lie on the rug and watch the people jet skiing and windsurfing.

Greg: OK. Let's go down there.

Marie: Lei Lei you've got all your clothes on and you're still wearing your hat!

Lei Lei: I know. I don't want my skin to turn black!

Marie: Black? It's hardly likely to turn black! Ha ha you might get a bit of a tan; that'll be good for you. It's healthy.

Gang: Not for Chinese girls, it isn't! They all want to keep their skin as pale as possible. You know, in China, having a tan has connotations of being poor — like you have to work in the fields for a living. That's why the women who clean the streets in China cover their heads and arms when they're in the sun.

Greg: Well here it's traditionally been a sign of wealth to have a tan. It means that you have the money and time just to lie around in the sun; you don't need to work. Also of course, it shows that you are fit and healthy. People with really pale skin look ill, we think. You know — like junkies!

Marie: Yes, but it is changing a bit. They're advising people to use sun tan lotion and sunscreen and not to stay in the sun for too long. Skin cancer and melanomas, you know.

到达海边

玛丽：太好了！我们终于到了。B&B 在哪里？

格雷：下一个路口右转，应该就在街底的左边，靠近沙滩的地方。

王刚：我从来都没有住过 B&B，是什么样子啊？

玛丽：不用担心，你一会儿就能看到了。

蕾蕾：哇，我闻到海的味道了。我太激动了！

* * *

下午

格雷：哇，那个游乐场真棒！我爱死那
个云霄飞车了，还有那个赛车游戏。我
们去买棉花糖和棒糖好吗？

玛丽：不要，玩了那么多刺激的游戏，
我们到沙滩去透口气吧。

王刚：什么意思？

玛丽：去躺在海滩上休息一下。我们带

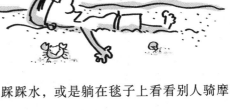

了毯子，不用换泳衣，只要把鞋袜脱掉然后踩踩水，或是躺在毯子上看看别人骑摩
托艇、冲浪。

格雷：好，我们去沙滩。

玛丽：蕾蕾，你怎么穿那么多衣服，还戴上帽子！

蕾蕾：我知道，可是我不想晒黑！

玛丽：晒黑？不太可能晒黑的！哈哈，你也许会有点麦色，那不是很好吗？那样比
较健康。

王刚：对中国女孩子来说不好。她们都喜欢把皮肤保养得白白净净的。你知道，在
中国皮肤黑是贫穷的象征，就像是你得在田里劳动似的。所以中国有许多女清洁工
在太阳底下扫街时会把头和手都包起来。

格雷：嗯，在这里，将皮肤晒黑是一种财富的象征。这表示你有钱和时间，不用工
作，可以尽情地去做日光浴。当然也是因为看起来比较健康。我们认为皮肤太苍白
的人看起来像是生了病，就像吸毒者一样。

玛丽：对啊，但是现在也有一些改变。专家们建议大家要用防晒霜等用品，而且不
要待在太阳下太久，你知道的，要预防皮肤癌和黑瘤。

Chapter 49

A Day at the Races

赛 马 场 的 一 日

The British are keen gamblers, and many people like to 'have a flutter'. This can be a bet on anything you like — The National Lottery, scratch cards, the football pools, dog racing, bingo, card games in casinos and slot machines (or one-armed bandits) in fun fairs and pubs. It is illegal to play cards, darts and dominoes for money in pubs, but these games are very popular.

Although it is known as the Sport of Kings, horse racing is phenomenally popular among all classes and provides one of the most enjoyable and exciting days out. So, if you want to do something different for a day out in Britain, you could do worse than a day at the races. A day out at the Grand National at Aintree or Ladies' Day (where ladies compete to show off the best hat) at Cheltenham are highlights in the national sporting calendar, and thousands of spectators converge on these events to have a drink and a flutter.

The sport is inextricably linked with gambling, and every high street in the country has at least one bookmaker's shop where people can go to place a bet on a horse. The breeding of thoroughbred racehorses is an economic activity in itself, and some of the richest people in the world are racehorse owners. Horse racing is covered in detail on many TV sports programmes.

Horse racing in Britain is generally divided into two types — national hunt, where the horse and jockey have to jump fences, and flat racing, where there are no fences.

There is a lobby in Britain which opposes gambling on moral and ethical grounds, and they argue that the National Lottery, for example, is a method of transferring money from the poorest sections of society to rich elites. They argue that the 'good causes' that the National Lottery raises money for are things like opera houses and country estates — not working men's clubs or snooker clubs.

英国人热衷于赌博，很多人都会下一点赌注。他们有很多地方可以下赌注，如乐透彩票、刮刮卡、足球彩票、赛狗、排五点、赌场的牌局、游乐场及酒吧的老虎机。在酒吧里玩牌、飞镖和骨牌非常受欢迎，但要小心，赌钱是非法的。

虽然被称为"国王的运动"，赛马在各阶级里都备受欢迎，它提供了最刺激有趣的赛事。所以如果你想在英国过一天不一样的户外活动，参加赛马会绝对是个不错的选择。不论安特里的全国马赛还是切尔滕纳姆的女士日（女士们会竞相炫耀她们的帽子）都是国家运动日历里重要的节日。届时会有数以千计的观赛者参与盛事，享用美酒并下注。

体育活动与赌博密不可分。在英国所有比较热闹的大街上至少都有一家博彩店接受下注。而饲养纯种赛马已成为一项经济活动，许多世界顶级富豪都养赛马。在电视上可以看到很多赛马的转播。

在英国，赛马一般可分为两类，一种是障碍赛，马与训马师必须跳跃障碍；另一种是平地赛，不设置任何障碍。

在英国，有一个院外活动集团基于道德和伦理的原因反对赌博。他们认为像乐透这类活动是将钱由穷人的手中转移至富有精英手中的工具。他们指出，乐透募钱要做的"善事"不过是修葺歌剧院及乡村宅院，而非修建工人阶级的俱乐部或是台球场等。

Down the Bookie's

Gang: Greg. I haven't got a clue how to place a bet here. I don't even know how to work out the odds.

Greg: OK. Let me show you. See the screen there on the wall? That shows you the list of runners — the horses that are running and their riders, owners and finally the odds that the bookmakers are giving.

Gang: Which one do you think is the best bet? Can you give me a tip?

Greg: Well, *Naughty Boy* is odds-on favourite. So for every two pounds you bet, you get a pound more if the horse wins. Then there's *Blue Man* which is evens — that means you'd just get your money back. So they're not actually very good bets if you want to take a risk. I mean, look at the others — there's *Red Prince* at three to one. If he won, you'd get three pounds for every pound you put on it. Then there's the ten-to-one outsider, *Green Hat*. If he won, you'd get ten pounds for every pound you bet.

Gang: Well, I actually want to play it safe and hedge my bets. What should I do?

Greg: Well, I think you should go for an each-way on *Red Prince*. That means that half of your bet will be on whether the horse wins and half of it will be on whether it finishes in the first five. The odds on the second part of that will be shorter, of course. I'm feeling lucky — so I'm going to go for *Green Hat*. I've checked the form in the newspaper, and it's pretty good.

Greg: Right, can we have a tenner each-way on *Red Prince*, and a tenner on *Green Hat* in the 3.35 at Lingfield?

Bookmaker: All right. Here you are. Don't lose the betting slip.

TV Commentator: And they're off! Twenty five runners here at Lingfield, and *Naughty Boy* has taken an early lead, followed by *Truth or Dare*, *Bluebeard*, *Lawrence of Arabia*... He's ahead of the rest by a length and it's *Green Hat* coming up on the outside, followed by *Red Prince* and *Green Hat* is coming up now it's *Green Hat*. pulling away from the rest now it's *Green Hat*. *Green Hat* wins by a furlong, followed by *Red Prince*!

Greg: Yipee! That's thirty quid for me. *Red Prince* came second, so you should get a little bit for that. Let's go to the window and see.

* * *

Bookmaker: Right, your winnings are...

Gang: Thanks. Where to now, Greg?

Greg: Down the pub to spend our winnings, I think.

在博彩店

王刚：格雷，我对如何下注一点头绪也没有，我甚至搞不清楚胜算如何。

格雷：好，我来教你。看到墙上的屏幕了吗？上面列出了所有的赛马、他们的骑师及赛马的主人，最后列出了博彩店给出的赔率。

王刚：你觉得哪一个最有胜算？可以给我一点提示吗？

格雷：噢，"调皮男孩"是胜算最大的。你每下注2镑，如果马赢了，你就可拿回3镑。"蓝人"胜算平平，所以如果"蓝人"赢了，你只是不赔不赚。如果你想冒一下险，这两个都不是很好的选择。看看其他的马，"红王子"3赔1，如果它赢了，你每下的1镑可赢回3镑。还有"绿帽子"，10赔1没有胜算的马，但是如果它赢了，你每赌的1镑就可赢回10镑。

王刚：噢，我想玩得安全一点，避免损失，该怎么做呢？

格雷：噢，我想你可以赌两面在"红王子"。就是说，你可以用一半的赌金赌"红王子"赢，另一半赌金赌它跑在前五名。当然，赌它跑在前5名的彩金会比较少。我今天觉得手气不错，所以我要赌"绿帽子"。我在报上查了它最近的表现，看起来它表现不错。

格雷：好了，我们下10镑在"红王子"，赌两面，还要下10镑在"绿帽子"，林菲尔德3点35分的马赛。

博彩店：好，这是你的彩券。小心别丢了。

电视评论员：开跑了！25匹马在林菲尔德，"调皮男孩"暂时领先，后面跟着"真心话大冒险"，"蓝胡子"，"阿拉伯的劳伦斯"……"调皮男孩"现在大幅领先其他的马……，"绿帽子"从外侧切入，后面紧跟着"红王子"……，"绿帽子"迎头赶上，"绿帽子"与其他赛马的距离越拉越大……"绿帽子"超前1/8英里获得第1名，后面紧跟着"红王子"！

格雷：耶！我赚了30镑。"红王子"得了第2名，你应该可以赚一点。我们去柜台那儿看看。

* * *

博彩店：好，你赢了……

王刚：谢谢。格雷，现在我们去哪儿？

格雷：我想我们应该去酒吧把钱花光。

Chapter 50

Getting Down to Business

谈 生 意

Britain is generally acknowledged as the first modern Capitalist nation, yet money is in many ways a dirty word in Britain, and the taboo on talking about money and the general squeamishness that British people feel around it makes it quite difficult for foreigners to do business face-to-face here. Even high-powered bankers and stockbrokers who work in The City find it difficult to talk about money on a personal level; the excuse that they use about their work is that "it's not real money." Foreign businessmen who come from cultures that are up front about money — for example Americans — find this habit extremely frustrating and often say that it is much easier to talk about money in faxes and emails rather than directly.

Of course, as with everything in Britain, class plays a part here. Originally working class people might start out uninhibited with money talk but, as they progress up the social scale, they will adopt an air of embarrassment and discomfort around the subject. Part of this is to do with the historical disdain for trade among the aristocracy in Britain who lived off rents and income from their lands. In the grand public schools of Victorian Britain, boys whose parents were engaged in trade were looked down on as new rich so, as they progressed through the class system, they perpetuated this prejudice.

Remember also, that showing off, bragging and boasting about one's wealth are seen as vulgar by British people. Self-effacing modesty is often the key when discussing business in Britain, so negotiators will be quite happy to talk about responsibilities, capacity, strategies, objectives sizes and measurements. However, when it comes down to the nitty gritty of cash, costs, payment, fees and price they will suddenly clam up and start hesitating, hedging and fretting. Sometimes they will become over-polite, apologetic and defensive. Young guns who work in financial institutions and pride themselves on a bullish approach will perhaps become aggressive and brash because they are not quite comfortable in themselves.

There is an exception to this rule; northern (particularly Yorkshire) businessmen who are perhaps self-made men will pride themselves on plain talking, and will have no qualms about talking about money without a hint of irony or self-consciousness.

■ ■ ■ ■ ■ ■ ■ ■ ■ ■ ■ ■ ■ ■ ■ ■

英国通常被认为是现代第一个资本主义国家，但是"钱"这个字对英国人来说像是个脏话，很多人将讨论钱视为禁忌，而英国人谈到钱时的拘谨态度也让外国人很难与英国人面对面地做生意。即使是在伦敦金融区工作的高级银行家和股票经纪人也发现很难与人讨论个人的金钱问题，他们对于自己干这份工作的借口是"那不是真的钱"。对金钱观比较开放的外国商人，例如美国人，对英国人的这种态度非常有挫折感，觉得以传真及电邮方式与英国人讨论金钱比面对面地谈容易多了。

当然，和所有在英国的事一样，等级在金钱方面也扮演了特有的角色。工人阶级原本对讨论金钱这件事不怎么受限制，但是当他们爬上社会等级的阶梯后，他们便会受到影响而对此感到窘迫不安。有一部分原因是与过去的英国贵族对商业鄙视的态度有关，这些贵族们靠着从土地得来的租金和收入过日子。在维多利亚时代的公学里，如果有学生的家里从事商业，他们会被取笑为暴发户。所以，当他们进入社会体制后，也沿续了这种偏见。

记住，英国人也将炫耀财富的行为视为庸俗。当讨论商业事宜时，英国人喜欢表现得十分谦虚，所以谈判者喜欢谈论责任、能力、策略、目标数量及衡量标准。但是，当谈论到钱、成本、付款方式、费用及价格时，他们会突然安静下来，开始变得踌躇不前、模棱两可。有时他们会变得异常客气并提高防卫性。在金融机构工作的、以积极工作态度为自豪的年轻人，自傲于积极的工作态度，也许会变得莽撞且带侵略性，因为他们对自己讨论金钱的作为还是觉得不自在。

然而也有例外，北边的商人（特别是约克郡人）通常是靠着个人努力而成功。他们为自己直来直去的个性而骄傲，说起钱来没有丝毫的不安，也不会自嘲或显得难为情。

Selling a Car

Neighbour: Greg, this car you're selling. How much do you want for it?

Greg: Oh. I don't know. How much do you want to offer?

Neighbour: Well, how much did you pay for it? £25,000?

Greg: No it was second-hand. It cost me £12,000. The mileage is quite low on it and it's in good condition. Fully taxed and MOTd.

Neighbour: So come on, then, how much do you want?

Greg: Erm ten grand? Or do you think that's too much? I can knock a bit off, if you think it's too much.

Neighbour: Hmm. That's a bit more than I was thinking of paying, actually.

Greg: So, how much can you pay, then?

Neighbour: Well, I dunno. I mean, it's a nice car and all, but I think it's gonna be quite expensive to run. Probably drinks quite a lot of petrol. Eight grand?

Greg: Hmm. I dunno, mate. I was hoping for a bit more than that. I'd really be losing out if I sold it for that. I might as well keep it in the garage for that.

Neighbour: Well, I suppose I could stretch to eight and a half. But I'm really going out on a limb there — the missus'll kill me. She told me that we can't afford more than eight.

Greg: Look let's say £8,250.

Neighbour: All right. Done. Shake on it. How do you want paying?

Greg: Could you give me cash? Or, I mean it's ok, like if you erm.

Neighbour: Can I give you a cheque?

Greg: Hmm... well... erm, I trust you and all, like, but... you know...

* * *

Gang: Greg. Why did you get so embarrassed talking about money there?

Greg: You know, Gang. I have absolutely no idea. I always get like that; I just can't discuss money.

Gang: I've noticed that. British people hate saying how much money they earn, or how much their houses and cars cost. You'd never think they spread Capitalism around the world.

Greg: I know. The thing is, though, that there's this contradiction in British culture; we feel really uncomfortable around money, yet the government goes on about the free market and stuff all the time.

Gang: Well, it's a little bit like that in China, I suppose. Our former premier *Deng Xiao Ping* said "to get rich is glorious", when he went on his famous Southern Tour back in the early 1980s, but I suppose there is a section of society that just feels uncomfortable around the issue of money and dealing with it. You need to be quite hard-faced to discuss it.

卖 车

邻居：格雷，你的那辆车，打算卖多少？

格雷：哦，我不知道。你想要付多少？

邻居：噢，你买的时候花了多少钱？25,000 英镑？

格雷：不是……我买的是二手车，只花了 12,000 镑。它的里程数还挺低的，而且车况很好。车子缴过税，也通过了车检。

邻居：那说说吧，你想要多少钱？

格雷：嗯，10,000 镑？太贵了吗？如果你觉得太贵，我可以降一点。

邻居：嗯，事实上，是比我想要付的贵了点。

格雷：那么，你能付多少呢？

邻居：噢，我不知道。我是说，这辆车是不错，不过我想这车要花很多钱来维护。而且耗油量可能也很大，8000 镑如何？

格雷：嗯，老兄，我不确定。我希望可以卖得更高一些。如果是这个价，我会赔钱的。还不如把车子停在车库里。

邻居：噢，我想我可以提高一点，8500 镑。但是我可是冒了很大的险，我老婆一定会杀了我。她跟我说我们不能出价超过 8000 镑。

格雷：那么，就 8250 镑吧。

邻居：好吧，成交，握手。那你要我用什么方式付钱呢？

格雷：你可以给我现金吗？或是，我是说……都可以啦……如果你……嗯。

邻居：我可以给你支票吗？

格雷：噢，嗯……我可以相信你，但是……你是知道的……

* * *

王刚：格雷。你刚才谈到钱时为什么那么不好意思？

格雷：王刚，你是知道的。我也不知道为什么，我只要谈到钱就会变成那样。

王刚：我注意到，英国人不喜欢谈论他们赚了多少钱，或他们的房屋、车子值多少钱。你不会想到是英国人将资本主义散播到全球的。

格雷：我明白你的意思。英国文化里存在着一种矛盾，我们对于金钱这件事非常的不自在，但是政府却老是在谈论自由市场及关于钱的事。

王刚：嗯，我想这跟中国有点像。我们的前总理邓小平于上世纪 80 年代南巡时提倡"致富光荣"，但是我想社会上还是有人可能对谈论金钱感到不自在。你必须脸皮很厚才能谈论这件事。

Expression Organizer

每课重点句型

Chapter 1

◆ So, does that mean that...? 所以，那是说

◆ Well, he likes to think... 他喜欢认为他是

◆ Come on! You know that's just... 别这么说嘛，你知道那只是……

◆ People are people. 人就是人（每个人都是不一样的）

◆ What do you mean? 你那样说是什么意思？

◆ Well, I mean... 噢，我是说……

◆ But, if you look at it... 但是如果你仔细研究……

◆ Oh, come on! 喔，别这么说嘛！

◆ You do...你真的……

◆ What do you mean by that? 你那样说是什么意思？

◆ Rubbish! 胡扯！

◆ I don't mean... I mean... 我不是指……我指的是……

◆ I mean, they think... Well, there you go! 我是指，他们认为……噢，你看吧！

◆ That just proves my point! 这证明了我的想法！

◆ I/we/they wouldn't even... 我/我们/他们不会……吧。

◆ Gosh! It looks like... 天啊，看来是……

Chapter 2

◆ I was round at... 我去……

◆ Well, yes and no. 噢，可以说是与不是。

◆ That's just so... ……就这样

◆ You've got a chip on your shoulder! 你有点愤世嫉俗！

◆ Don't get above yourself! 不要逾越自己的等级！

◆ Well, you know what I mean. 噢，你知道我的意思。

◆ It's not like that at all! 不是那样的！

◆ I'm not saying... 我不是说……

◆ It's just that... 只是……

◆ It's all a bit like... 这好像是……

◆ Well, surely it's... 噢，想要有这些应该是一件好事。

◆ It's hard to say. 这很难说。

◆ We live in a different world now. 我们现在生活在不同的世界了。

◆ That... is gone now. 那些……已经消失了。

◆ He/ they would never have... that 他/他们是永远也没办法……

Chapter 3

◆ Having said that, however... 话虽如此，但是……

◆ Don't worry about making/ doing... 别担心你会……

◆ Well that's what worries/ bothers/ annoys me. 噢，这个就是我担心/烦扰/烦恼的。

◆ It's funny you should say that. 你正好提到。

◆ They were saying that... 他们说……

◆ There's nothing worse/ better/ nicer than... 没有比……更糟/好/吸引人的

◆ What about saying/ asking/ going...? 还有该怎么说/问/做……?

◆ Well that's a difficult one. 噢，那是个难题。

◆ The thing is that... 但事情是……

◆ As a general rule, you should... 一般的规则是，你应该……

Chapter 4

◆ Why can't they just say what they mean? 为什么不直接把想说的话表达出来呢?

◆ Mustn't grumble. 不要抱怨了。

◆ Oh, you know... 哦，你是知道的……

◆ He's his usual... self... 他还是一副老样子。

◆ The sooner, the better. 越快越好。

◆ If I have anything to do with it. 如果由我决定的话。

◆ Let me introduce... 让我介绍……

◆ That's all right. 没关系。

◆ You know what happened...? 你知道发生了什么事?

◆ So, you wouldn't recommend/ go to this place again, then?
  所以你不推荐/再去这家餐厅啰?

◆ Well, it wasn't very nice/ pleasant/ good/ comfortable. 噢，感觉很不好/愉快/棒/舒适。

◆ Gosh! That's amazing! 天呐! 那真有意思!

◆ You must be really smart/ bright/ happy! 你一定很聪明/机灵/快乐!

◆ I'm not... at all. 我一点也不……

◆ There's a difference between being smart and looking smart!
  看起来很聪明跟实际上很聪明是有很大的差异!

◆ Saving the world/ the starving children, are we? 我们在拯救世界/饥饿的小孩吗?

◆ I have such a social conscience/ big head, don't I?
  我真的很有社会良知/自以为是，不是吗?

Chapter 5

◆ I'm so sorry about the weather! 真抱歉，天气这么差。

◆ That's me. 是我

◆ Brrr... cold, isn't it? 嗯，天气很冷，不是吗?

◆ Really? Do you think so? 真的吗? 你觉得吗?

◆ I tend to find/ notice/ feel... 我总觉得/注意/感受到……

◆ You should go to... 你应该去……

◆ Now, that's really/ dead cold/ hot/ wet! 喂，那里真的很冷/热/湿!

◆ It feels quite warm/ cold/ humid to me. 我觉得有点暖和/冷/潮湿。

◆ Yes, well at least it's not raining/ snowing/ blowing a gale.

噢，对啊，至少没有下雨/下雪/刮大风。

◆ It really gets me going. 让我可以开始活动。

◆ It's a bit hot, isn't it? 有点热，不是吗?

◆ It's not as hot/ cold/ wet as... 不像……那么热/冷/潮湿

◆ I don't think I could stand that. 我觉得我没有办法忍受。

◆ This global warming/ greenhouse effect/ summer rain is getting ridiculous/ too much.

全球变暖/温室效应/夏天的雨变得越来越离谱/严重。

Chapter 6

◆ Oi! I was next! 喂! 我排下一个。

◆ What do you think you're doing? 你以为你在做什么?

◆ Well, you should have come sooner/ thought about that before. 那你应该早一点来/想到。

◆ This is outrageous! 这真的是太过分了!

◆ Don't they have queues/ the word 'please' in your country?

你们国家的人都不排队/不说"请"的吗?

◆ Get to the back of the queue! 到后面排队!

◆ Who do you think you are? 你以为你是谁啊?

◆ Don't you dare do that/ tell me to queue! 你敢那样做/叫我排队!

◆ What a rude man! 真是个没礼貌的人!

◆ You'll never believe what happened... 你绝对不会相信发生了什么事。

◆ This guy tried to... 有个家伙试着要……

◆ You'd be surprised how angry/ upset/ annoyed that makes me.

你会很讶异这件事会让我觉得有多生气/难过/惹恼。

◆ It's as if... 这就像是……

◆ I guess that's what we need to do. 我猜我们应该那么做。

◆ That would totally/ completely confuse people. 那就可以把人完全搞混了。

Chapter 7

◆ So, have you come far? 你从很远的地方来吗?

◆ The traffic/ weather/ road was awful/ a nightmare. 交通/天气/道路一塌糊涂/像个噩梦。

◆ It took me... to get here. 到这儿花了我……

◆ So, you're a doctor/ teacher/ engineer, then? 所以你是个医生/老师/工程师啰?

◆ Well, actually, I'm in business/ unemployed. 事实上，我从商/失业中。

◆ Oh really? How fascinating/ interesting. 哦，真的吗? 多有趣/有意思啊!

◆ So, do you live far/ nearby/ in town, then? 所以，你住很远/在附近/城里啰?

◆ I live just round the corner/ up the road/ down the street/ across the square/ upstairs.

我就住在转角/街头/街尾/对面/楼上。

◆ What do they say...? 他们怎么说的?

◆ I thought she was a bit... 我觉得她有一点……

◆ Good job I didn't say anything/ kept my mouth shut. 还好我没说什么/没说话。

◆ Smart new car/ nice jacket/ cool sunglasses you've got there.
你有一部漂亮的新车/一件新外套/一副超酷的太阳眼镜。

◆ It must have cost a fortune/ a pretty penny/a mint. 一定花了很多钱。

◆ Get away! 去你的

◆ Pull the other one! 别糊弄我!

Chapter 8

◆ Huh! Typical! 哼! 老毛病!

◆ You're missing the point! 你忽略了重点!

◆ For god's sake! 看在上帝的分上!

◆ I'm terribly sorry to be such a pain. 很抱歉给你找麻烦。

◆ Oh! I'm sorry, sir. 哦! 先生,很抱歉。

◆ Let me take/ change/ replace your dish/ drink. 让我帮你拿走/更换/换一盘菜/一杯饮料。

◆ He must have made a mistake. 他一定是弄错了。

◆ I'm awfully sorry. 我真的很抱歉。

◆ See! Easy, wasn't it? 你看! 很简单不是吗?

◆ Here you are, sir. 先生, 这是您的……

◆ With the compliments of the house/ On the house. 本店免费赠送。

◆ Sorry. 抱歉。

◆ Excuse me. 对不起。

◆ I'm really sorry to bother you, but... 对不请, 很抱歉打扰你, 但是……

◆ Do you think you could... 你可不可以……

◆ Sorry, mate. 对不起, 哥们儿。

◆ Turn that music down/ switch that TV off, will you?
你把音乐关小声一点/把电视关掉行吗?

◆ I can't stand this. 我没办法忍受了

◆ If you don't... I'll have to... 如果你们不……, 我就要……

◆ Why don't you... 你为什么不……

◆ Don't be so boring. 不要这么扫兴嘛。

Chapter 9

◆ Don't speak with your mouth full! 不要一边吃东西一边讲话!

◆ Elbows off the table! 不要把手肘靠在桌上!

◆ It sounds complicated. 听起来好复杂。

◆ Actually. It doesn't matter too much. 事实上, 不用担心那么多。

◆ As long as you are polite/ don't shout... 只要你有礼貌/不要高声喊叫……

◆ I hear that/ I heard that/ I've heard that... 我听说在/我听过/我曾听过……

◆ That's not really true. 那不是真的。

◆ By the way... 对了……

Chapter 10

◆ It looks great/ You look great. 真的很好看/你看起来很好。

◆ I wish I had hair/ legs/ cheeks like yours. 我真希望我的头发/腿形/脸型像你的一样。

◆ Oh no! My legs/ cheeks/ eyes are so... 哦，不，我的腿/脸颊/眼睛很……

◆ I love your shoes/ glasses. They're lovely. 我喜欢你的鞋子/眼镜，真好看。

◆ I just got them down the market/ at the supermarket/ in the sales.

我刚在市场上/大卖场/大甩卖时买的。

◆ I'm going to have to... 我必须得……

◆ Guess what? 你猜怎么了？

◆ Go on! Tell me! 赶快说！

◆ You know what I heard? 你知道我听到什么？

◆ Well you have to promise not to tell anyone. 噢，你得保证你不会跟别人说。

◆ No! Really? 不会吧！真的吗？

◆ Oh my god! 我的天啊！

◆ It's all right/ pretty cool , isn't it? 那很棒/很酷，不是吗？

◆ Know what I mean? 你懂我在说什么吗？

Chapter 11

◆ There's something I don't understand about... 我对……并不是很清楚

◆ It's a democracy/ republic/ independent state, right?

……是民主政治/共和政体/独立国家，对吧？

◆ How come you have a Queen/ president/ political prisoners?

那你们为什么有女王/总统/政治囚犯呢？

◆ I'm only kidding! 我只是开玩笑！

◆ Despite all this talk of democracy/ freedom/ peace.

虽然大家都在谈论民主政治/自由/和平。

◆ Why isn't he called... 为什么不叫他……

Chapter 12

◆ Naah! They're all the same, aren't they! 没有。那些人不是一丘之貉吗！

◆ Of course they aren't! 当然他们才不一样的！

◆ Well, of course there are going to be problems, but... 噢，当然会有些问题，但是……

◆ Of course they wouldn't! 他们当然不会！

◆ Does everyone get this worked up/ excited/ angry?

大家在选举日都这么积极/兴奋/生气吗？

◆ I suppose they call each other comrade/ brother/ Mr/ sir.

我想他们称呼对方为"同志"/兄弟/先生/阁下。

◆ I'll tell you later. 我以后再跟你说。

Chapter 13

◆ What do we have in common? 我们有什么共同点吗？

◆ It/ he is often criticised for being/ doing... 他经常被批评……

◆ What do you/ they think of... 你/他们怎么看……

◆ It depends on who you're talking to. 那是因人而异。

◆ Well, it's not really like that. 噢，事情不是像你想的那样。

◆ I suppose you're right. 你说得对。

◆ You could say the same for... as well. ……也是这样

◆ That's like a completely Chinese city. 那里简直像是一个中国城市了。

Chapter 14

◆ Uugh, I'm ill. I feel terrible. 啊，我生病了，觉得糟透了。

◆ This is serious. 这很严重。

◆ Come on, ... it can't be that bad. 别这么说，没那么糟吧。

◆ That's mad! 疯了啊！

◆ What a bunch of hypochondriacs! 大家都得了疑病症啊！

◆ What am I supposed to do? 那我要怎么办呢？

◆ A cold lasts for a week with treatment and seven days without.

感冒治疗持续7天，不治疗也持续7天。

◆ Open your mouth/ bend over and let me see inside/ look. 嘴巴张开/弯下去让我看一下。

◆ How long have you been here? 你来这儿多久了？

◆ All you can do is... 你能做的就是……

Chapter 15

◆ It was set up by Royal Charter/ special edict. 依据皇家特许令/特别法令所设立

◆ Having said that, ... 虽说如此……

◆ Back from the shops/ the pub/ work? 刚逛街/从酒吧/下班回来吗？

◆ Where do you fancy going/ eating tonight? 你今天晚上想到哪去/去哪吃饭呢？

◆ I can't face going out/ eating there/ speaking to him.

我不想再走出去/去那里吃饭/跟他说话。

◆ Why don't we... 我们为什么不……

◆ Sounds good. 听起来不错噢。

◆ What's on? 晚上有什么节目呢？

◆ Dunno. 不知道耶。

◆ Let's have a look. 我们来看一下

◆ You've spoiled it now! 你破坏我的兴致了！

◆ We'll just have to... 我们只好……

◆ I think I'm going to be sick. 我想我快要吐了。

◆ Are we going to make up our minds, then? 我们到底要不要决定一下呢？

◆ Make up your mind! 下定决心！

◆ All right! Keep your hair on! 好啦，你冷静一点。

Chapter 16

◆ It's The Sun Wot Won It! 《太阳报》赢了！

◆ Well, they claim that/ he claims that... 噢，他们/他宣称……

◆ Of course, its critics say/ the other side argues...

当然，他的反对者批评/他的对手争议……

◆ Oh yes. I've heard of him. 对哦，我听说过他。

◆ Well, if you want to call it that. 噢，如果你要这样说。

◆ I think it's better than having/ reading/ watching... 我觉得这比让/读/看……要好

◆ Come on! They can't be that stupid/ people aren't that silly!
别这么说嘛！他们不会那么笨吧/人们不会那么傻吧！
◆ Wanna bet? 要赌吗？

Chapter 17

◆ You know, I'm really worried about... 你知道吗，我很担心。
◆ That's a bit racist/ naughty/ rude, isn't it? 你这有点种族歧视/顽皮/无礼，不是吗？
◆ What's wrong with that? 那有什么问题吗？
◆ I know it sounds awful/ bad/ terrible, but... 我知道，这听起来有点糟/坏/可怕，但是……
◆ Well, if it wasn't/ weren't for... we wouldn't have this problem.
噢，如果不是……，我们就不会有这个问题。
◆ That way, we can/ we'll be able to... 那样，我们就可以……
◆ I am so! 我是！
◆ You don't even believe in god/ like Chinese food/ speak French!
你一点也不相信上帝/喜欢中国菜/会讲法文！
◆ I do believe in something. 我是相信一些事情。
◆ I do think there's something out there. 我相信世上有一些事情存在的。

Chapter 18

◆ We need to get down to/ get up to/ get over to... by... 我们需要坐……到……去
◆ That gives us... 我们只有……
◆ Go to... and type in... in the... 到……在……输入
◆ Gosh! That's typical! 天啊！真是典型！
◆ Why is it only foreigners/ me/ my mother who understands...?
为什么只有外国人/我/我妈妈才知道……？
◆ Click on..., then type in... 按一下……，然后再输入……
◆ People are always moaning/ complaining, but they never seem to do anything about it.
大家常常在抱怨/发牢骚，可是他们从来都没有采取任何举动。
◆ Sounds like stating the obvious, to me. 对我来说这听起来很明显。
◆ We can have them sent out/ have our hair cut/ have the car washed.
我想我们可以请他们寄来/帮我们剪头发/帮我们洗车。
◆ Now all we need to worry about is getting/ going/ finding...
现在我们只需担心如何到/去/找……

Chapter 19

◆ An Englishman's home is his castle! 英国人的家就是他的城堡！
◆ Safe as houses, mate! 像房屋那样安稳，哥们儿！
◆ How much is this worth? 值多少钱？
◆ The point is that... 重点是……
◆ You get all these guys/ people/ speculators buying/ coming/ invading...
很多人/投机客买下/来/侵略……
◆ I certainly couldn't afford to buy a house/ get married/ go back to university.
我绝对负担不起买房屋/结婚/上大学。

◆ I'd have to... 我得……

◆ At least it means that you can move into the house now. 至少现在你可以搬进房屋了。

◆ As long as you keep working/ paying/ going, you'll...

只要你一直有工作/付款/去，你将会……

◆ That's the whole point. 那就是问题所在。

Chapter 20

◆ This is a really nice house. 这房屋真的很漂亮。

◆ We picked this place/ it/ the thing up for... 我们以……买这房屋/这东西。

◆ I don't know how youngsters/ old people/ the unemployed manage these days.

我真不知道现在的年轻人/老年人/失业者要怎么过活。

◆ Well I think your house/ it/ she is beautiful, anyway. 噢，我认为你的房屋真的很漂亮。

◆ You must be really pleased/ happy/ satisfied with it.

你一定很满意/高兴/满足拥有这样的房屋。

◆ The estate agent/ boss/ salesman was a complete idiot!

那个房屋中介商/老板/售货员真是一个白痴！

◆ Well, what do you expect?! 噢，你还能期待什么?!

◆ Thick as two short planks! 笨得跟猪一样！

◆ You're telling me! 还要你说啊！

◆ It's not what we/ I would have chosen. 这不是我们/我想要的房屋。

◆ I suppose we'll/ I'll just have to live with it for now.

不过我想我们现在得凑合着住一段时间了。

◆ It/ he/ the house does have potential. 这个东西/他/这房屋很有潜力。

◆ Be careful. 小心点儿。

Chapter 21

◆ Religion is the opium of the masses! 宗教是大众的鸦片！

◆ Some people/ the police/ a salesman came to the door. 今天早上有人/警察/业务员来拜访。

◆ Jesus loves you! 耶稣爱你！

◆ Nobody believes in that mumbo jumbo/ nonsense/ rubbish any more.

没人再相信那些胡言乱语/胡扯/废话了。

◆ If you want that, you can... 如果你想要……，你应该……

◆ I'm going to see what it's all about. 我想去看看究竟。

◆ Don't do it, Gang! Don't let them brainwash/ persuade you!

王刚，别去！不要被他们洗脑/说服你！

◆ You can't tell me there's a God/ justice/ democracy when the world is...

当这个世界这么……时你怎么能告诉我有神/正义/民主的存在呢？

◆ Who am I to say that there's a God/ they are right/ he's wrong or not?

我凭什么决定有没有神的存在/他们是对的/他是对是错呢？

◆ Hallelujah! Praise the Lord! 哈利路亚！赞美神！

Chapter 22

◆ Watch out! I'm the seventh son of a seventh son!

小心！我是第 7 个儿子所生的第 7 个儿子！

◆ I'm not so sure about that. 我不是很确定。

◆ Yes. I know that one. 噢，我知道那部片子。

◆ Do you have any local myths and legends here? 你知道有哪些当地的神怪故事或传说吗？

◆ Well, there's the story about... 噢，有个故事是说……

◆ One of the most classical/ oldest/ most interesting sources/ stories/ legends is...
有个最经典/古老/有趣的消息/故事/传说……

◆ It's a bit like... 有点像是……

Chapter 23

◆ Sorry for your trouble. 为你的麻烦感到难过。

◆ He'll/ she'll be sadly missed. 我们会悲伤地怀念逝者。

◆ Dearly beloved. We are gathered here today... to join...
亲爱的朋友们，我们今天聚在这里共同见证……

◆ Do you take this man to be your lawfully wedded husband?
你愿意接纳这个男人为你的丈夫？

◆ For better, for worse, for richer for poorer, in sickness and in health, till death do you/ us
part. 无论生活好坏、贫穷富裕、生病或健康，屏除一切对他忠诚，永远爱护并珍惜他，直
到死亡将你们分开？

◆ With this ring, I thee wed. With my body, I the worship, and with all my worldly goods I
thee endow. 我给你这枚戒指象征我的爱与忠诚。当我将戒指为你戴上时，我将我的心及灵
魂委托于你。

◆ In the Name of the Father, and of the Son and of the Holy Spirit, Amen.
以圣父、圣子、圣灵之名，阿门。

◆ You may now kiss the bride. 你可以亲吻新娘了。

◆ Doesn't she look beautiful/ he look hand-some? 哇。新娘看起来真美/他看起来真帅！

◆ I think I'm going to cry. 我想我快要哭了。

◆ He'd/ you'd better take care of her! 他得好好照顾她！

◆ I was honoured when Jim/ Mr Smith/ Mrs Jones asked me to...
当吉姆/史密斯先生/琼斯太太邀请我……觉得非常荣幸。

◆ Please join me in a toast to the bride and groom/ the father of the bride/ the happy couple!
请你们起立举杯与我一起敬贺新郎及新娘/新娘的父亲/快乐的夫妻！

◆ We would never do that here! 我们这里绝对不会这么做！

◆ Nobody would ever do that here! 在这里绝对没有人会这么做。

Chapter 24

◆ An interesting point about... is that... 有趣的是……

◆ Chinese, Koreans and Japanese would be referred to...
而中国人、日本人及韩国人则被称为……

◆ Some people consider the latter/ former/ second term condescending/ patronising/ racist.
有些人认为后者/前者/第二种称呼屈尊/傲慢的/有种族歧视的意味。

◆ It seems to me, though, that... 但是在我来看……

◆ In China, we have fifty six ethnic 在中国我们有 56 个民族。

◆ Does the government treat them differently between them? 政府对不同种族的待遇不同吗?

◆ That's difficult to say. 那很难说。

Chapter 25

◆ Right. We're here. This is where... 噢，我们到了，这里就是……

◆ I thought it looked familiar/ memorable. 我就觉得有点眼熟/有点记忆。

◆ I never knew about all of this. 我从来都不知道这些。

◆ Let's have a walk/ drive/ run around... 我们到……走一走/开车绕一绕/跑一跑吧。

◆ Do you have any ancient sites/ historical buildings/ tourist attractions like this in...?
你们在……有像这样的古老城镇/历史建筑/观光景点吗?

◆ Of course. There's the... 当然有。我们有……

◆ Well, it's true that... That's because... 噢，那是真的……那是因为……

◆ It's the actual site/ building/ person that's more important/ interesting/ useful.
我们觉得遗址/建筑/人比较重要/有趣/有用。

◆ We believe that...; that's why we... 我们认为……，那是为什么我们……

◆ The thing is, though, that... 然而重要的是……

Chapter 26

◆ Apart from the obvious fact that..., it is also... 除了很明显的事实……另一个……

◆ Do you think he/ she would make a good wife/ husband/ student/ secretary?
你觉得他/她会是个好老婆/好老公/好学生/好秘书吗?

◆ I wanted to ask your advice. 我想先听你的意见。

◆ It would have been a nightmare trying to reconcile/ match/ combine...
那会是个噩梦去排解/配合/结合……

◆ You need to be absolutely certain before you... 在……之前，你一定要十分确定你想结婚。

◆ How about that? 怎么说?

◆ I don't know if that would go down well/ be popular/ be acceptable in... 我不知道在……行
不行的通/受不受欢迎/能不能被接受

◆ The neighbours would talk! 邻居们一定会在背后讲闲话。

◆ Everyone likes/ loves/ adores a bit of tittle-tattle/ gossip/ scandal.
每个人都喜欢说长道短。

Chapter 27

◆ Over the last ten years/ the last decade there has been... 在过去十年……

◆ Go into any... and you will find... 到任何一家……你会发现……

◆ There is plenty of room for negotiation/ bargaining/ haggling.
有很大的协商/议价/讨价还价的空间。

◆ As with everything in Britain/ China/ the world, ... features in people's behaviour.
跟所有在英国/中国/世界上的事情一样，……是人们的特点。

◆ How much is this vase/ poster/ hat, here? 这个花瓶/海报/帽子多少钱?

◆ That's a bit much. 这太贵了点。

◆ I was sure it was genuine Ming/ porcelain/ gold. 我确定这是真的明代花瓶/瓷器/金子。

◆ It's been in my family for years. 这花瓶在我们家很久了。

◆ I knew it! 我就知道!

◆ I'll/ I can let you have it for... How about that? 我就卖你……，如何?

◆ Could you go a bit lower? 可以卖便宜一点吗?

◆ I'll give you a fiver/ £ 10/ three quid. 我出 5 镑/10 镑/3 镑。

◆ Here you are. 给你。

◆ You're robbing me blind! 你们真是会抢钱!

◆ I've got to make a living. 我还得过日子。

◆ We Chinese/ English/ British find them/ it/ this a bit tacky/ embarrassing.
我们中国人/英国人会觉得那些商品有点俗气/难为情。

◆ If we can't... we'll have to... 如果我们不能……我们就只好……

Chapter 28

◆ Tea/ beer is to Britain what coffee/ red wine is to America/ France.
茶/啤酒之于英国人就像红酒之于法国人，咖啡之于美国人。

◆ Sorry. Who's next? 对不起，谁是下一位?

◆ What are you having? 你想要什么?

◆ What do they have? 他们有些什么?

◆ I'll have/ Can I get/ Could I possibly have a..., please? 请给我/可以给我/我可以要……

◆ A pint of lager/ A half of Guinness, please. 请给我一品脱的淡啤酒/半品脱的黑啤酒。

◆ I like the look of that. 我喜欢那个看起来的样子。

◆ I fancy something a bit lighter/ heavier/ spicier.
我喜欢清淡一点的/口味重一点的/辣一点的。

◆ That's sounds nice/ lovely/ interesting. 听起来不错/很可爱/很有趣。

◆ I don't like the sound of that. 听起来不怎么喜欢。

◆ I think I'll have/ I'm going to have... 我想我要……

Chapter 29

◆ There's no such thing! 没那种事!

◆ How can... possibly compare with...? ……怎么能跟……比呢?

◆ You'd be surprised/ shocked/ pleasantly surprised. 会让你意外/震惊的。

◆ What were you eating/ doing/ watching? 你吃了/做了/看了什么?

◆ It sounds disgusting/ horrible/ weird! 听起来有点恶心/恐怖/怪异!

◆ Basically, you can eat/ do/ say whatever you want/ like/ feel like there.
基本上你可以吃/做/说任何你要/喜欢/想的事。

◆ Etiquette/ rules/ the law isn't as strict/ rigid/ conservative as it was.
礼仪/规则/法律已经不向几年前那么严格/保守了。

◆ Is that a class/ gender/ race thing? 这跟阶级/性别/种族有关吗?

◆ That... doesn't really exist any more. ……已经不存在了。

Chapter 30

◆ So, what does it consist of? 所以这到底包含了什么呢?

◆ My head/ back/ neck is killing me! 我的头/背/脖子快痛死了。

◆ You won't be wanting/ looking for…, then? 那你不想/不要……啰?

◆ OK. A fry up it is. 好吧，油炸早餐就是了。

◆ Let's see what we've got. 我来看有什么材料。

◆ What a rigmarole/ fuss/ nightmare! 真是麻烦/大惊小怪/一个噩梦!

◆ What are you doing putting orange juice on corn flakes/ eating beans with spaghetti/ drinking beer with coke?
你怎么把果汁倒到玉米片里/把青豆跟意大利面一起吃/把啤酒跟可乐一起喝?

◆ Let him/ me eat (them/ it) the way he wants/ I want. 让他/我用他/我的方式吃。

Chapter 31

◆ Fast food/ Electronic dictionaries is/are the bane of many a(n) nutritionist's/ English teacher's life. 快餐/电子字典，通常是营养师/英语老师眼中的有害食品/物品之一。

◆ Some of this can be blamed on/ has been caused by… 其中一部分可归咎于/是因为……

◆ I'm starving! 我快饿死了!

◆ I could murder a Chinese/ an Indian/ a Pizza! 我想吃中国菜/印度菜/比萨饼!

◆ What do you fancy? I really fancy… 你想吃什么? 我真的很想吃……

◆ I've never heard of it. 我从来都没听过。

◆ I couldn't eat/ drink/ stand that. 我没有办法吃/喝/忍受那个。

Chapter 32

◆ One of the first things you will notice about Britain/ China/ Europe is…
到英国/中国/欧洲你第一个会发现……

◆ It's hard to say. 这很难说。

◆ Are there any real British cars/ restaurants/ gentlemen?
所以哪几种车是真的英国车/餐厅/绅士啊?

◆ You're partly right. 你只对了一半。

◆ What I can't understand is why… 我实在不懂为什么……

◆ You're right to an extent. 某种程度上你是对的。

◆ Other governments protected their industries/ people/ resources — ours just abandoned them.
当其它国家的政府，对他们的工业进行保护政策时，我们的政府则是遗弃了自己的工业

◆ Will you stop?! 你可以闭嘴吗?!

◆ Get down off your high horse! 别一副高高在上的样子。

Chapter 33

◆ Being a taxi driver/ doctor/ lawyer is a job that requires a lot of training.
要成为出租车司机/医生/律师需要经过很多的训练。

◆ Isn't it terrible — that news about the earthquake/ the hurricane/ the plane crash there?
有关于大地震/飓风/坠机的消息，真是可怕啊!

◆ I'm so sorry. 我很抱歉。

◆ Yes. It's bad news. 是啊，真是个不幸的消息。

◆ I must say, it's very impressive/ interesting/ curious, the way they…
我必须说……他们去……的方式令人印象深刻/真有趣/令人觉得好奇。

◆ Years ago/ In the past/ Not long ago, they would never have broadcast/ done/ said that.
要是几年前/过去/不久前，他们是不会播报这种新闻的/这么做的/这么说的。

◆ China has been opening up ever since the open-door policy/ the early 1980s.
自从对外开放政策实施/20 世纪 80 年代后，中国真的开始对外开放了。

◆ You Westerners/ British/ Europeans are always going on/ complaining/ talking about that!
你们西方人/英国人/欧洲人老是危言耸听/抱怨/老生常谈。

Chapter 34

◆ Although he is not..., he is certainly not .... 虽然他也许没有……，但是他并不……

◆ Do you need a hand? 你需要帮忙吗？

◆ Hello, there. 你好。

◆ (Are) you Chinese/ Russian/ American, then? 那你是中国人/俄国人/美国人？

◆ Good choice, mate. 选得好，哥们儿。

◆ I've got no time for... 我不会花时间在……

◆ (Do you) know what I mean? 你懂我的意思吗？

◆ I'm not being funny, but... 我不是在开玩笑，但是……

◆ No offence, mate. 别介意，哥们儿。

◆ I don't mean you, of course. 我当然不是指你。

◆ Mind you, you've got to hand it to them. 说实在的，你不得不佩服这些人。

◆ Well they/ we/ he/ I would... if it wasn't for...
噢，要不是……，他们/我们/他/我会想要……

Chapter 35

◆ Imagine a country where they've never heard of The Beatles/ the Internet/ Big Macs!
想象一个从来都没有听过披头士/因特网/巨无霸的国家！

◆ Walk around any street in London/ Beijing/ Edinburgh these days, and you will see...
走在伦敦/北京/爱丁堡的任何街道上，你可以看到……

◆ Have you seen this in the paper? It says... 你看到报上写的吗？报上说……

◆ Don't listen to her. She's just jealous/ envious/ angry because...
别听她说。她只是很忌妒/美慕/生气，因为她……

◆ Shut up, you! 你给我闭嘴！

◆ What else does it say? 报上还写些什么？

◆ Well, more fool them/ you! Don't they/ you know that...?
噢，她们/你真是白痴！难道他们/你不知道……

◆ I think Chinese 'fat' / 'cute' / 'radical' is different to British 'fat' / 'cute' /
'radical', isn't it?
我觉得中国人说的胖/可爱/极端跟英国人认为的胖/可爱/极端是不一样的，不是吗？

◆ But that's just an impossible ideal. The vast majority of women/ students/ people can never
be like that. 可是那是很理想化的观念。大多数的女生/学生/人没办法成为那样的。

Chapter 36

◆ When you look at... you might be forgiven for thinking that...
……当你观赏……你也许会很自然地认为……

◆ You will find people like... adapting/ changing/ trying... while mixing... at the same time.
你会发现一人像是……配合/改变/试着……同时混合……

◆ Despite complaints/ protests/ opposition from... youth cultures are actually...
尽管……抱怨/抗议/反对，年轻人的文化事实上……

◆ He's trying to show how cool/ modern/ hip he is. 他是要显示出他有多酷/摩登/流行。

◆ You know those kids/ lads/ guys who...? 你知道那些小孩/小伙子/男人……

◆ Well the things they wear/ carry/ use are called...
噢，事情是他们身上穿着/带着/用着，称为……

◆ I suppose we dressed/ behaved/ talked a bit weird（ly）when we were...
我觉得我们……的打扮/行为/说话也有一点标新立异。

◆ Please don't remind me. I'd rather forget that, if you don't mind.
请你不要再提醒我了！如果你不介意我宁可忘了那些事。

◆ Your parents/ family/ friends and mine would probably never have mixed.
我是说你的父母亲/家人/朋友就绝对不会混在一起。

Chapter 37

◆ Most directors/ foreigners/ people are unable to distinguish between American and British English. 很多主任/外国人/人无法分辨美式英语及英式英语。

◆ Reverence/ respect for RP has absolutely nothing to do with linguistic rules/ features, but （and）everything to do with social/ class factors.
对标准口音的尊崇/尊重并无任何语言学上的相关性，但是却与社会因素相关。

◆ Is that why you can't understand him? 你是不是因为这样而听不懂他说的话？

◆ The fact is, though, that you won't hear a real Cockney accent in London/ British people speak in a whole variety of accents.
事实上你在伦敦东区是听不到真正的伦敦佬口音了，英国人讲的是不同的口音。

◆ It's what posh/ young/ white people speak when they want to sound cool/ fashionable/ edgy. 那是赶时髦的人想让自己说起话来更酷，更时髦。

Chapter 38

◆ The reality is that... 事实是……

◆ Festivals/ theatre/ cinema have/has been undergoing/ experiencing a revival/ renaissance/ resurgence over the last... 音乐节/戏剧在过去……又慢慢的流行/复兴/复苏起来。

◆ They are now so popular that... 他们现在非常受欢迎……

◆ Glastonbury/ Reading is famous not only for... but also for...
格拉斯顿伯里及雷丁之所以闻名于世并非只是……还因为……

◆ We're thinking of going to... 我们想要去……

◆ What was it like? 那是像什么？

◆ If the music isn't what the crowd wants, they'll pelt the band with bottles and cans until...
如果观众们不喜欢台上的表演，他们会向乐队丢酒瓶、罐头直到……

◆ That's the whole point. 这就是重点。

◆ I'm all peace and love, man! 我个性平和心眼好，老兄！

Chapter 39

◆ If you read/ watch... you might think/believe that...

如果你读/看……你可能会认为/相信……

◆ For instance, British men will / might avoid/ resist paying... for fear of appearing...
例如，英国男人为了怕表现……而避免/拒绝赞美……

◆ You might wonder how... 你也许会怀疑……

◆ I just don't understand the way British kids flirt/ court/ chat each other up.
我真的搞不懂英国年轻人怎么调情/求爱/与人搭讪的。

◆ Look who's talking! 看是谁在说话！

◆ Do you really think anyone/ I would fancy you? 你真的觉得有人/我会喜欢你？

◆ What makes you think anyone'd/ I'd fancy you, anyway? 你凭什么认为有人/我会喜欢你？

◆ You're so right. 你说的真对。

◆ See you around. 下次再见。

◆ Sounds about right. 听起来是这样。

Chapter 40

◆ He/ They once dismissed the British/ French as a nation of shopkeepers/ a bunch of peasants. 他/他们曾说英国/法国只是个小店主之国/一群农夫。

◆ He/ she/ I got a (n) response/ answer he/ she/ I wasn't expecting. 他/她/我得到了一个意外的响应/答案是他/她/我没有预料到的。

◆ There is still some truth in what he/ she/ I said. 他/她/我所说的似乎还有一点真实性。

◆ They are blamed for causing the decline of the high street/ the financial crisis/ the problem. 他们被批评是造成市中心商业街业绩下滑/金融危机/问题的原因。

◆ They are divided into different areas/ departments/ countries.
他们被分成不同的地区/部门/国家。

◆ This is a card/ battery... you slot it in like this.
这是一张卡/一个电池……把它像这样插入……

◆ This is a memory stick... you plug it in like this. 这是记忆卡……把它像这样插入……

◆ This is a disk/ cassette... you slide it in like this. 这是磁盘/卡匣……把它像这样滑入……

Chapter 41

◆ Turn on the TV/ Watch any news programme and you'll come across...
打开电视/观看任何新闻性节目你就会看到……

◆ For every one of these stories, you'll find alternatives/ two others/ many other ones.
在阅读这些新闻的同时你也会发现其它/另外的/很多其它的新闻。

◆ I'm really going to have to... 我真的得要……

◆ I just can't seem to... 我就是没办法……

◆ How many units a week are you drinking? / hours a day are you studying? / words a day are you writing?
你一个星期喝多少单位的酒/一天学习多少个小时/一天写多少字？

◆ I haven't done anything/ seen him/ spoken Chinese for years.
我很多年都没做什么/看到他/说中文了。

◆ You'd be surprised the kind of people who take drugs/ break the law.
你会很讶异什么样的人会沉迷于这些毒品/犯法。

Chapter 42

◆ Despite the rise of the internet, British publishing has never been more profitable/ vibrant.

尽管互联网的兴起，英国的出版业界的高获利/活跃却是前所未有的，

◆ This shows that English language is not the property of the English themselves, but has been adopted/ taken over/ embraced by...

这展现出英文不是英国人的特有财产，英文已被……接受/接收/接纳。

◆ How can I know which are/ is the best/ most interesting/ most useful...?

我怎么知道哪些是最好的/最有趣的/最有用的……？

◆ You should never judge a book by its cover. 大家都说买书不能只凭封面。

◆ If you like... it's probably a good idea to... 如果你喜欢……，最好的方法是……

◆ What? Writers like...? 什么啊？作家像……

◆ He's/ she's influenced by... 他/她受到……的影响。

◆ His novels have been translated into English. 她的小说也曾被翻译成英文。

Chapter 43

◆ The Proms/ Olympics/ Commonwealth Games have often been criticised for being/ harking back/ concentrating on...

逍遥音乐节/奥运会/英联邦运动会经常被批评想/回到/专注于……

◆ Whatever side you come down on/ support/ prefer, it cannot be denied that...

不管你赞成/支持/喜欢那一种说法，不可否认的……

◆ Hark at you! 听你说的！

◆ Who do you think you are? 你以为你是谁？

◆ It's just... That's all. 那只是……而已。

◆ It depends what you mean by... 那要看你指的是……

◆ We have what's called/ known as... 我们有所谓的/称之……

◆ You've probably heard of/ seen/ witnessed... 你大概有听过/看过/目睹过……

Chapter 44

◆ You will arrive at... 你会抵达……

◆ Coming out of the station, you will see/ find/ come across... on the right/ to the left/ across the road. 一出车站，在右手边/左手边/隔着马路可以看到/找到/遇到……

◆ If you look up/ across the..., you will find/ encounter/ see the...

如果你抬头看/走过/……则可找到/遇到/看到……

◆ Walk up/ along/ down... past the... and you will experience/ feel/ see...

沿着……而上/而下经过……你可以经历到/感到/看到……

◆ Have you got a programme, please? 请问你有节目表吗？

◆ What's it about? 内容是什么啊？

◆ It's about... 是关于……

◆ Why don't you try this? 你们为什么不试试看这个？

◆ If you want to get seats/ see it/ buy tickets, you'll need to...

如果你想要有位子/看这个/买票，你得……

◆ All that... was an English/ a Chinese/ an American invention, anyway!

所有的……不过是英格兰人/中国人/美国人的发明罢了!

Chapter 45

◆ This is the longest running soap, having started in 1952.

这部肥皂剧自 1952 开播,是播放时间最长的电视节目。

◆ It takes place/ comes from/is based on/ is set in Manchester.

其内容发生在/来自/是以曼彻斯特索尔福德区为主

◆ British soaps are down-to-earth, whereas/ while American ones are more glitzy and glamorous.

与腐化虚饰的美国肥皂剧相比,英国肥皂剧以一般大众日常生活所遇到的问题为主。

◆ Some of the main criticisms are... 有些人批评……

◆ How can all of these things happen to one person?

怎么可能所有的祸事都发生在同一个人的身上?

◆ Like real operas, they are emotional and over-the-top, but ...

像其它剧情片虽然内容过于激情夸张,但还是……

◆ I didn't see much of that during... 我在……都没看到

◆ They watch the DVD, thinking it's a Hollywood film.

他们观赏他买的光盘,还以为是好莱坞电影。

◆ Pretty cool, huh? 很酷吧?

◆ I bet that got high viewer ratings! 我打赌这一集一定有很高的收视率!

◆ I don't think that's be allowed. I'm sure Chinese people would love Eastenders.

我不觉得这会被允许。我确定中国人会喜欢看像《伦敦东区》这样的节目。

Chapter 46

◆ The British are said to be passionate about sport/ tradition/ pubs...

英国人可以说对参与运动/传统/酒吧非常疯狂……

◆ Not only do... but there are... 不仅是……连也……

◆ I went to bed at midnight. 我半夜去睡觉。

◆ I don't want you waking the baby up/ coming in drunk/ making a noise!

我不要你把小孩吵醒/喝醉回来/制造噪音!

◆ I want to prove to myself that I can do it. 我想要证明我可以做到。

◆ Sounds like masochism/ nonsense/ rubbish to me!

我听起来像是在做自我虐待/胡说八道/鬼扯。

◆ No pain, no gain! 没有付出就没有收获!

◆ I'm going to get a team/ my friends together. 我想组成一队/找朋友一起参加。

◆ Will you sponsor/ help/ support me? As long as you sponsor/ help/ support me.

你会资助/帮/支持我吗?只要你也资助/帮/支持我。

◆ Doesn't that mean we cancel each other out? 我们这样不是相互抵消了吗?

◆ We might as well just not go. 我们不如就不要去了。

◆ It's going round the houses a bit, isn't it? 这有一点像是再绕圈子,不是吗?

Chapter 47

◆ That's another story. 那又说来话长了。

◆ Visits by British people to the USA increased by 6% to 4.2 million between 2001 and 2005.
从 2001 年到 2005 年到美国旅行的英国人约有 420 万人次，增长了 6%。

◆ There were nearly 14 million visits to Spain by British people in 2005.
在 2005 年到西班牙旅行的英国人约有 1400 万人次。

◆ The number of visits abroad has tripled to 66 million since 1985.
从 1985 年至今到海外的人次已增长了 3 倍，约有 6600 万人次

◆ The figure has risen tenfold. 这个数字约增长了 10 倍。

◆ Seventy five percent of these trips were holidays. 这里面大约有 75% 的人出国度假。

◆ Forty three million trips were made by air. 有 4300 万人次是搭飞机出国。

◆ Six million were made using the Channel Tunnel. 有 600 万人次使用英法海底隧道。

◆ I think it's overrated. 我认为是它是被高估了。

◆ They would never have thought of/ dreamed of/ imagined going abroad.
他们从来也不会想到/梦到/想象到要到国外。

◆ I was thinking of going back by rail/ air/ sea. 我才在想坐火车/搭飞机/坐船回去。

◆ I think it sounds like a great adventure. 我想这听起来像是大冒险。

Chapter 48

◆ In these days of cheap flights/ budget airlines/ easy travel.
在现今便宜机票/廉价航空/旅游便利。

◆ Brighton/ she/ that film will always have its/ her own special allure for me.
布赖顿/她/那部电影/对我而言永远都有它/她独特的吸引力。

◆ We're here at last. 我们终于到了。

◆ Take the next right. 下一个路口右转。

◆ It should be down the end of the street on the left near the beach.
应该就在街底的左手边靠近沙滩的地方。

◆ I'm dead excited/ hungry/ tired. 我好兴奋/饿/累喔。

◆ It's hardly likely to turn black/ do that/ be a problem! 不太可能晒黑的/那么做/出问题！

◆ Yes, but it's changing a bit. 但是现在也有一些改变。

Chapter 49

◆ You can have a flutter on anything you like. 你可以下一点赌注在任何你喜欢的东西上。

◆ You could do worse than a day at the races/ a night at the opera/ an afternoon at the
match. 参加赛马会/去看歌剧/去看足球赛绝对会是不错的选择。

◆ The breeding of horses/ the rearing of animals/ the writing of books is an economic activity
in itself. 饲养纯种赛马/出书本身已成为一种经济活动。

◆ I haven't got a clue how to do this. 我对如何处理这件事一点头绪也没有。

◆ Let me show you. 我来教你。

◆ Can you give me a tip? 可以给我一点提示好吗？

◆ For every two pounds you bet, you get a pound more. 你每下注 2 镑，就可拿回 3 镑。

◆ There's Red Prince at three-to-one/ two-to-one/ ten-to-one.
如果红王子赢了，你每下的 1 镑可赢回 3 镑/每赌 1 镑赢回 2 镑/每赌 1 镑赢回 10 镑。

◆ If he won, you'd get ten pounds for every pound you bet.

如果他赢了，你每赌 1 镑可以赢回 10 镑。

◆ Half will be on whether it wins and half will be on whether it finishes in the first five.
一半的赌金赌它赢，另一半赌金赌它跑在前 5 名。

◆ And they're off! 它们开跑了！

◆ Where to now? 现在我们到哪去呢？

◆ Down the pub to spend our winnings/ have a pint/ have a drink.
到酒吧去把赢来的钱花光/喝一品脱/喝一杯。

Chapter 50

◆ Britain is acknowledged as/ to be the first Capitalist nation.
英国被认为是第一个资本主义国家。

◆ Of course, as with everything, class/ race/ money plays a part here.
当然在金钱方面，跟所有英国的事一样，等级也扮演了重要的角色。

◆ I have no qualms about talking about money/ personal issues/ politics.
我对讨论与金钱有关的事物/个人私事/政治一点也不会内疚的。

◆ When it comes down to talk of money/ cash/ details, they will suddenly…
当谈论到钱/现金/细节时，他们会突然……

◆ This car/ house/ computer you're selling. How much do you want for it?
你的那部车/房屋/电子计算机，你要卖多少钱？

◆ How much do you want to offer? 你想要付多少钱？

◆ How much did you pay for it? 你买多少钱？

◆ Do you think that's too much? 你觉得太贵了吗？

◆ That's a bit more than I was thinking of paying, actually. 事实上，是比我想要付的贵了点。

◆ How much can you pay, then? 所以，你能付多少呢？

◆ It's a nice car, and all, but… 这辆车是不错，不过……

◆ I was hoping for a bit more than that. 我希望可以卖得比那高一点。

◆ I might as well keep it in the garage/ at home. 我还不如把车子停在车库里/在家里。

◆ I suppose I could stretch to…, but I'm going out on a limb, there.
我想我可以提高一点到……但是我可是冒很大的险。

◆ The missus/ my wife/ the girlfriend'll kill me. 老婆/我老婆/女朋友一定会杀了我。

◆ How do you want paying? 你要我用什么方式付钱呢？

◆ Well, erm… I trust you and all, like, but… you know…
噢，嗯……我可以相信你，但是……你是知道的……

◆ I have absolutely no idea. 我也不知道为什么。

◆ To get rich is glorious. 致富光荣。

Glossary

词 汇 表

Chapter 1

stereotype 刻板印象
tweed-clad 猎装
aristocrat 贵族
Grenadier Guards 近卫步兵团
Household Cavalry 豪斯霍德骑兵团
prime minister 英国首相
New Labour 新工党
hip 赶时髦的
ethnic group 民族
dynamic 高效率
excess 暴力
get short shrift 得到冷漠的对待
pejorative 轻蔑的
aye (yes). 对，英国北方、苏格兰及古老的方言
straight-forward 直率
posh 时髦
refined 高尚的
Geordie 纽卡斯尔人
keep up with the Joneses 与邻居们攀比
Home Counties 大伦敦地区
whining 牢骚
self-pitying 自怨自艾
Scouser 利物浦人

Chapter 2

class-ridden 被等级差别所支配
elite 贵族的，精英的
inheritance 世袭
enterprise culture 创业文化
sheer 纯粹的
newly-privatised industry 刚刚私有化的新的国有民营化的企业
marker 指标

modified 修改后的，改良的
assert 断言
barrier 藩篱
social researcher 社会学者
idealised 理想化
myth 神话
City of London (The City) 伦敦金融中心
core 核心
aristocracy 贵族
globalised financial elite 全球化财富精英
oil tycoon 石油大亨
indicator 指标
medical consultant 医疗顾问
connotations 言外之意
hypocrisy 虚伪
pretentiousness 矫揉造作
social climbing 跻身上流社会
four-by-four 四轮驱动
trap 绑着
pension 退休金
organic food 有机食品
state-owned factory 国营工厂
management buyout 参与资方买断

Chapter 3

hangover 遗物
Victorian times 维多利亚时代
etiquette 礼仪
formalised 郑重其事
cultural commentator 文化评论家
unsavoury 令人不快的
lager lout 喝酒闹事的人
hoodie 小混混
football hooligan 足球流氓

bowler hat 高帽
disaffected 不满
insular 偏狭
self-important 自负
stuck-up 骄傲自大
irritating 令人生厌
obsessed 着迷，崇拜
celebrity 知名人士，名星，社会名流
beer-swilling 狂饮啤酒
overweight telly addict 超重电视迷
caricature 漫画
reserve 拘谨
punctuality 准时
self-deprecation 自我贬低
ill-at-ease 手足无措
fail-safe 避免出错
prying 探问隐私
burp 打嗝
hacking 干咳
lubricant 润滑剂
conventional norm 传统的规范
universal 完全的
mess up 搞砸
faux pas 失态
wet fish 柔软无力的握手
trustworthy 诚实可靠
glide 滑过
brush lips 碰到嘴唇
bump noses 擦撞了鼻子
air kiss 飞吻
status 身份
take the lead 主动
vous 您
be funny 故意卖弄（带讽刺意味）

Chapter 4

understatement 轻描淡写
irony 反讽
razor-sharp wit 锋利的机智
pervade 充斥
naive 天真
back to front 前后颠倒
teasing 戏弄
banter 取笑
mockery 挖苦
default mode 先天设定
gushing 过分的热情
pompous 夸大
wear one's heart on one's sleeve
流露情感
clichéd platitudes 陈腔滥调
cringe with embarrassment 觉
得难为情
smugly amused 很可笑
sentimental 多愁善感
over-the-top earnestness 过分
的热情
stubborn 固执
cynicism 愤世嫉俗
satire 讽刺
restrained 严谨
bewildering 让人不知所措
infuriating 令人生气
be on the lookout for 时时注意
dry (humour) 冷漠型的幽默
deadpan 毫无表情
indifference 不在乎
convoluted 复杂难解
game of bluff 虚张声势
grumble 报怨
attentive 体贴
foul mood 心情不好
overrated 估计过高
pissed off with 很生气（人或事）
overcooked 煮过头了
leathery 食物煮得太硬
soggy 食物煮得过烂
go on and on 一直唠叨

creep out 偷偷离开
barrister 能出席高级法庭的律师
brainy 聪明
swot 临时抱佛脚
nosey 喜欢探人隐私的
workaholic 工作狂
Fairtrade 公平贸易
social conscience 社会良知
guilt-ridden 内疚的

Chapter 5

sonorous 响亮的
religious mantra 诵经
soothing 冷静的
moderate 温和的
measured 谨慎
phenomenally 非常的
annoying 厌烦
unpredictable 无法预测
hurricane 台风
cyclone 旋风
blizzard 暴风雪
drought 干旱
eccentricity 怪癖
ritual 仪式
choreographed 设计好的
contradict 反驳
apologetic 抱歉的
registered letter 挂号信
miserable 沮丧
invigorating 提神
air con 冷气
ridiculous 离谱

Chapter 6

unsportsmanlike 非运动家精神
unethical 不道德
cricket 板球
upstanding 正直
cheat 作弊
act in bad faith 不诚实的行为
push into 挤入
ungentlemanly 非绅士的
commitment 承诺

cooperation 合作
acknowledgement 承认
social convention 社会习俗
opponent 对手
poor attitude 不好的态度
queue-jumping 插队
welfare 福利
social services 社会福利
abuse 滥用
council housing 廉租房
waiting list 等待名单
deeply offensive 严重违反的
demeaning 贬低
underhand 台面下的小动作
laughable 笑话
dodgy deal 见不得人的交易
hypocrisy 伪善
outrageous 太过分
kick off 开始…事
violate 侵犯
shudder 打颤
tense up 紧绷
inconsiderate 不会为别人着想
en masse 大量
subvert 颠覆

Chapter 7

odd 奇怪
social function 社交场合
gifted 天赋的
chit-chat 聊天
imaginative 有想象力
Manchester United 曼联队
Chelsea 切尔西队
vulgar 平民百姓
therapy 治疗
gross violation 严重的侵犯
taboo 禁忌
physical appearance 长相
marital status 婚姻状况
clue-dropping 找线索
deflect the compliment 转移称赞
jokey 开玩笑
downplay 看轻

play by ear 听别人怎么说

test the water 测试一下水温

controversial issues 争议性的话题

take one's cue 接受暗示

GP 全科医生，非专科医生

dedicated 认真

hard-working 辛苦工作

turn up 出席

get promoted 升职

NHS（National Health Service）全民医疗服务

round the corner 转角

bridesmaid 伴娘

pregnant 怀孕

watch out 小心

a pretty penny 很多钱

second hand 二手货

cost a fortune 花很多钱

Chapter 8

notoriously 出了名的

bottle up 憋在心里

inappropriate 不适当的

outpouring 迸发

candid camera 偷拍的视频

put up with 忍受

draw attention 吸引别人的眼光

Tube 地铁

wearily 疲倦地

resigned 怨恨

irate 激动的

riot 暴动

burn down 烧了

Metro 地铁

in-your-face 直接

miss the point 忽略重点

create a scene 闹出动静

roast potato 烤马铃薯

complements 配料

On the house 免费

turn down 关小声

keep up 吵得睡不着

Chapter 9

precise 精确的

fussy 过度讲究

cultery 餐具

tilt 倾斜

queasy 使人作呕

slurp 咕噜咕噜地喝

state banquet 国宴

index finger 食指

transfer 送到

turn one's stomach 令人作恶

greedy 贪心

elaborate 详细的

bottoms up 干杯

honoured guest 贵宾

shot 一杯

in turn 轮流

propose a toast 敬酒

macho 有胆量的

generous 大方

mean 小气

chips 炸薯条

switch off 关掉

Chapter 10

facilitate 促进

bonding 关系

naughty 没规矩

dress sth up as 把…包装成

analytical 分析的

highbrow 卖弄学问的

stage whisper 交头接耳

scandalous 诽谤的，中伤的

sly 狡诈的

vindictive 报复的

embellish 装饰

observation 观察

swear words 脏话

elation 兴高采烈

denial 拒绝接受

self-critical remark 自我批评

put oneself down 贬低自己

arrogant 自傲

mock 嘲弄

earnest 认真

manly 男性化

mousy 缺乏活力的

frizzy 鬈

cheekbones 颧骨

acne 粉刺

pock marks 疤痕

self-control 克制力

affair 婚外情

cost an arm and a leg 花很多钱

gallon 加仑

Chapter 11

constitutional monarchy 君主立宪

Head of State 国家元首

General Election 大选

Labour 工党

Conservative 保守党

Liberal Democrats 自由民主党

SNP（Scottish National Party）苏格兰民主党

Plaid Cymru（Welsh Party）威尔士民主党

member of parliament 下议院

House of Commons 国会大厦

House of Lords 上议院

appointed 指派

hereditary 世袭

peer 贵族

vigorous 强烈的

constitutional settlement 宪政协议

democratic 民主的

Bill of Rights 权利法案

legal 合法的

Establishment 体制

ceremonial 仪式的

vote 投票

monarchist 保王派，君主主义者

Windsor 温莎

royal family 王室家族

succession 继承

abolish 废除

Nationalist 民族主义者

overthrow 推翻

republic 共和国
be stuck in the past 沉缅于过去

Chapter 12

The Civil War 内战
The Great Reform Act 改革法案
constituency 选区
cabinet 内阁
The Opposition 反对党
The Shadow Cabinet 影子内阁
ruling party 执政党
bill 法案
left-wing 左派
right-wing 右派
middle-of-the-road 中间派
division 区隔
allegiance 忠诚
intellectual 知识分子
public-sector 政府机关
professional 专业人士
overturn 打破
Socialist 社会主义者
intervention 干预
Capitalist 资本主义者
low taxes 低税率
public spending 公共支出
moderate 稳健的，温和的
alternative 可选择之物
polling station 投票处
fulfil 履行
compulsory 强制性的
mayoral 市长
electorate 选民
that lot 那一票人
nursery provision 育婴福利
tackle 解决
inflation 通货膨胀
asylum seeker 政治难民
knock-on effect 连锁效应
mortgage market 抵押市场
out-of-touch 不了解
thrive on 获益
apathy 冷漠
worked up 冲动的
laid back 闲散的、懒惰的

cadre 干部
representative 代表
Great Hall of the People 人民大会堂
People's Assembly 人民代表
the honourable gentleman 可敬的

Chapter 13

sovereign state 独立自主的国家
declaration 声明
promotion 促进
individual liberty 个人自由
good governance 善治
multilateralism 多边主义
egalitarianism 平等主义
symbolic figurehead 名义元首
Head of State 领导人
secretary general 秘书长
talking shop 谈话会
prestigious 有威信的
expel 开除
Apartheid 种族隔离政策
suspend 中止
scholarship 奖学金
The Commonwealth Games 英联邦运动会
controversial 有争议性
love-hate relationship 爱恨交加
outgrow 超越
colony 殖民地
independent grouping 独立的组织
neutral 中立的
emigrate 移民

Chapter 14

publicly-funded 公费提供
healthcare system 医疗体系
peace dividend 和平红利
cradle-to-grave 从出生到死亡
welfare services 福利设施
charitable 慈善
resident 居民
local family practitioner 家庭医生
the first port of call 第一站，优先选择

A&E department 急诊室
persistently 不断
bureaucratic 官僚
inefficient 效率低
sponger 好吃懒做者
malingerer 装病者
prescription 药方
dental care 看牙
public opinion 民意
post-code lottery 邮政编码乐透
ancillary staff 助手
grind to a halt 无法运作
crash out 躺着
antibiotics 消炎药
virus 病毒
IV drip 滴注
hypochondriacs 疑病症
threaten 威胁
appointment 预约
surgery 诊所
walk-in centre 门诊中心
take one's temperature 量体温
pop 放进
resistance 抵抗力
asprin 阿司匹灵
paracetomol 镇痛剂
abuse 滥用

Chapter 15

Royal Charter 皇家许可证
broadcasting 广播
quasi-autonomous public corpo-ration 准自主的公营机构
legal status 法律地位
state-owned 国营
viewer 观众
licence fee 执照费
politically-motivated 有政治动机的
subversives 颠覆分子
newscaster 新闻播报员
highbrow （自以为）有学问的
mission 使命

inform 告知

entertain 娱乐

motto 座右铭

inception 开始

mischievous 恶意

dumbing down 肤浅的，讨巧的

knackered 精疲力竭的

crash out 躺着

National Lottery Draws 乐透抽奖

lottery ticket 乐透奖券

ITV（Independent Television）独立台（独立电视频道）

British Museum 大英博物馆

digital channels 数字频道

Chapter 16

rush hour 高峰时间

indulge 满足

broadsheet 宽页报纸

The Times 泰晤士报

The Guardian 卫报

The Daily Telegraph 每日电讯

tabloid 八卦小报

red top 红色报头

The Sun 太阳报

The Daily Mirror 镜报

in-between 介于两者之间

The Daily Mail 每日邮报

The Daily Express 每日快讯

The Independent 独立报

stance 立场

editorial 社论

mayoral election 市长选举

colour supplements 彩色加页

periodical 期刊

model railways 火车模型

train spotting 搜集火车机车的号码

lads' mags 小伙子杂志

reporting 报导

wishy-washy liberal 软弱的自由派

in-your-face 直接

simplistic 简单

tacky 粗俗

trivial 浅薄

cheeky 无耻

irreverent 无礼

puns 俏皮话

double-entendre 双关语

rabidly 狂热的

agenda 议题

brainwash 洗脑

News International 国际新闻社

magnate 大亨

Star TV 卫视电视台

New York Post 纽约邮报

court 奉承

censor 审查

baron 富商

shallow 肤浅

Chapter 17

peculiar 特有的

public school 公学

state schools 国立学校

disproportionate 不平均

Oxbridge 牛津及剑桥大学

old school tie network 老校友关系网

prep（preparatory school）预科学校

overbearing interference 过度的干扰

pupil-teacher ratio 师生比例

bastion 大本营

perpetuate 持续

fudge and muddle 模棱两可

voluntary-aided 自愿捐助

regardless of 不论

city academy 城市学院

faith school 信仰学校

over-subscribed 超收

catchment area 学区

vicious circle 恶性循环

ensue 接着而来

OFSTED inspection report 小学的检测报告

racist 种族歧视

mass 弥撒

baptise 受洗

priest 神父

religious 虔诚的

Chapter 18

late-running 误点

punctuality 准时

make a fuss 小题大作

Tory 托利党，英国保守党的代称

deteriorate 恶化

few-and-far-between 零星

political will 政治意愿

astronomical 庞大的

coach 大巴

subsidise 补贴

outward date 出发日期

duration 搭乘时间

click on 按下

type in 输入

Young Person's Railcard 青年卡

Saver Return 便宜的来回票

One-Day Travelcard 一日票

off-peak 非高峰时段

itinerary 行程表

engineering work 工程检修

post out 寄出

permitted route 许可路线

terms and conditions 权利及条件

special delivery 限时快递

same-day delivery 当天快捷邮件

shopping basket 购物车

insurance 保险

Chapter 19

government agent 政府官员

metaphorical 比喻的

downright 彻底的

pokey 极小的房子

crash 猛撞，破产

to the contrary 相反的

Britons 英国人

prolific 肥沃的，多产的

social sector 公有部分
estate agent 房屋中介
two-up-two-down 楼上楼下各两间
spiral 攀升
restrictions 限制
speculators 投机客
club together 集资
stressful 压力
spend ages 花很多时间
overlap 重复
take into account 考虑
deposit 保证金
credit check 信用调查
creditworthy 有信誉的
pay slip 薪水单
secure income 固定收入
in principle 原则
vendor 卖方
solicitor 律师
conveyancing 不动产转让手续
draw up 草拟
liaise 联系
structural survey 房屋结构勘查
valuation 估价
in debt 负债

Chapter 20
builders 建筑商
deregulated 缺少管制的
political consensus 政治意见一致
dodginess 偷鸡摸狗行为
DIY 自己动手做
low-end 低阶层
cater to 供应给
home improvements 家庭装潢
shabby 破旧
frayed 磨损
handed down 历代流传
ridicule 嘲笑
nouveaux riches 新富
wide-screen 宽屏电视
focal point 焦点

floral chintz 印花棉布
tasteful 有品味的
floorboards 地板
shabby-chic 新怀旧风
renovate 重新装潢
vulgar 庸俗
pick up 买
reasonable 合理
rip off 剥削
sly 狡猾
incompetent 无用
used-car salesman 卖二手车的人
thick 笨
take forever 耗费时日
potential 潜力
rip out 拆掉
feature 特色
conservatory 温室
skip hire 垃圾箱出租

Chapter 21
opium 鸦片
Church service 教堂礼拜
ambivalent 矛盾
weird 怪异的
leave office 卸任
Christ 基督
Jesus 耶稣
Christian 基督教
branch 分支
Catholic 天主教
Protestant 新教
Orthodox 东正教
subdivide 细分
sect 派别
Pope 教宗
Roman Catholic Church 罗马天主教
Middle Ages 中世纪
Church of England 英国国教
Anglican 英国国教，圣公会
consolidate 巩固
quintessentially 典型的

fudge 谎言，欺骗
compromise 妥协
cathedral 主教座堂，大教堂
moderate 温和的
persecuted minority 受到迫害的少数
Muslim 穆斯林
Somalia 索马里
mosque 清真寺
Sikh 锡克教
Hindu 印度教
Jewish 犹太人
leaflet 传单
eternal life 永生
nuts 怪胎
Bible 圣经
spread the Word 散播福音
saviour 救世主
mumbo jumbo 胡言乱语
weirdos 怪胎
maniacs 狂热份子
crutch 精神支柱
genuine 真诚
spirituality 精神上的
brainwash 洗脑
vulnerable 脆弱
rationality 理性
evolution 进化
supernatural 超自然的
famines 饥荒
Hallelujah! 哈利路亚!
Amen. 阿门!

Chapter 22
griffin 鹫头飞狮
folklore 民间传说
spine-tingling 毛骨悚然
legends 传说
witness 目击者
pirates 海盗
monks 修道士
chant 诵经
monastery 修道院

pixies 精灵
fairy 仙女
elf（elves）小矮人
goblins 妖魔
phenomenon 现象
supernatural 超自然
condemn 谴责
witches 女巫
devil 恶魔
saints 圣者
pray 祈祷
black sheep 败类，害群之马
toss and turn 翻来覆去
hearse 灵车
crack a whip 挥动着马鞭
breaking point 极点
fantasy 神幻
pact 约定
witty 机智
spiked armour 盔甲

Chapter 23
lavish 豪华
ceremonies 仪式
clumsy 笨手笨脚
engagement 订婚
stilted 不自然
shuffle 手足无措
denomination 国度
copious 大量
stiff-upper-lipped 拘谨的
best man 伴郎
drunken speech 演讲时胡言乱语
sprinkle 洒
minister 新教牧师
godparents 教父母
bridesmaid 伴娘
frock 长裙
register office 户籍登记处
procession 仪式
groom 新郎
vows 誓言
altar 法坛

bless 祝福
bereavement 居丧
matrimony 婚姻
discreetly 深思熟虑地
solemnly 庄重地
hold one's peace 保持沉默
cherish 珍惜
forsake 屏除
thee 你
endow 授与
radiant 散发出光芒
red envelope 红包
ledger 账簿
flaunt 招摇
wedding list 结婚礼品清单

Chapter 24
ethnicities 种族
diversity 多样
stir fry 炒菜
melting pot 熔炉
Afro-Caribbean 非裔加勒比人
integrate 融入
assimilate 同化
misguided 误导
political correctness 政治正确性
isolated 孤立
Indian sub-continent 印度次大陆
Oriental 东方人
condescending 屈尊的
old-fashioned 老旧
next-door neighbour 隔壁邻居
subscribe to 同意，赞成
tolerance 宽容
decline 衰落
radicalised 激进的
heritage 遗产

Chapter 25
continuity 延续
patriotism 爱国主义
nationalism 国家主义
listed buildings 登记有案的古迹
charge with 使承担责任

charitable organisation 慈善机构
subscriptions 认捐
entrance fees 门票
legacies 遗赠
coastal defences 海防
typify 代表着
strand 一个组成部分
hark back to 回复
glorious 光荣的
Norman Conquest 诺曼征服
battlefields 战场
abbeys 修道院
Hadrian's Wall 哈德良长城
coast-to-coast 沿海岸
moors 沼地
reverence 尊敬
geomancers 风水师
flow 流动

Chapter 26
care home 养老院
factors 原因
nuclear family 核心家庭
reconstitute 重新组成
household 家庭
breakdown 瓦解
abandon 遗弃
civil partnership 民事伴侣
alternative 选择
gay couples 同性恋伴侣
inherit 继承
take the leap 下决定
concentrate 集中
ex-partner 之前的伴侣
go down well 行得通
tittle-tattle 说长道短

Chapter 27
eccentricity 怪僻
car-boot sale 汽车跳蚤市场
charity shop 慈善商店
garden fete 慈善清仓大拍卖
charitable causes 慈善工作
Oxfam 乐施会

The Salvation Army 救世军
donate 捐赠
market-led 市场化的
well-to-do 高档
up-market retailers 高级零售店
rummage 东翻西找
bargain 交易
brand-name 名牌
overt 明显的
trestle table 折叠式的桌子
class anxiety 等级焦虑
embarrassed 难为情
chipped 有缺损
genuine antique 真的古董
blue glaze 蓝釉
a fiver 5 镑
pitch 摊位
a tenner 10 镑
rob someone blind 抢钱
flea markets 跳蚤市场
stuff 东西
bric-a-brac 纪念品
fake 假的
posters 海报
tacky 俗气
churn out 制造出
policemen's helmets 警帽
flog（sell）卖

Chapter 28

major draw 最能吸引
public house 酒吧
alcoholic beverages 含酒精的饮料
pastime 休闲
clientele 顾客
cosy 舒适
wooden panelling 木板墙
bookshelves 书柜
functional 功能化
benches 板凳
futuristict 未来主义的
metallic décOor 金属制的装潢
pub grub 酒吧提供的食物
gingerly 战战兢兢

work one's way around 了解
draught 生啤酒
rounds 帮朋友们买酒的习俗
pint 一品脱
half 半品脱
spirits 烈酒
regulars 常客
counter 柜台
barmaid 酒保
lager 淡啤酒
bitter 苦味啤酒
Guinness 黑啤酒
cider 苹果酒
bottled 罐装
chiller cabinet 冰柜
alcopops 含酒精的果汁饮料
fizzy 气泡式
gin and tonic 金汤尼
dry white wine 干白葡萄酒
breezer 百加得冰锐
steak and kidney pie 牛排腰子派
chef's salad 主厨沙拉
breaded scampi 面包屑海螯虾
breadcrumbs 面包屑
debit card 现金卡
pop in（to）插入
tap in 输入
PIN 密码
mate（gen me）哥们

Chapter 29

bland 平淡
delightful 讨人喜欢
variety 多变
spiciness 充满香料
sophistication 精致的
courses 几道菜
starter 前菜
dessert 甜点
staple diet 主菜
meat and two veg 一种肉加上
两种蔬菜
ingrain 深植于
psyche 心理

incongruous combinations 不协
调的组合
canteen 餐厅
carbohydrate 淀粉类
exotic 异国
processed foods 加工食品
renaissance 复兴时期
celebrity chef 知名的大厨
game 野味
puddings 布丁
snigger 暗自窃笑
protein 蛋白质
cabbage 甘蓝菜
carrots 胡萝卜
gravy 卤汁
rhubarb crumble 大黄派
custard 蛋奶沙司
easy-going 随和，简单
chew 嚼食
working patterns 工作模式

Chapter 30

B&B（Bed & Breakfast）提供
床与早餐的小旅馆
put off 吓到
greasy 油腻腻
all-day breakfast 全天早餐
bacon 培根
cereal 麦片
sausages 腊肠
hash browns 薯饼
scramble 炒
poach 煮
toast 烤土司
greasy spoon 卖油炸早餐的实
惠小店
traffic warden 停车管理员
omelettes 煎蛋饼
croissants 羊角面包
yoghurt 酸奶
muesli 燕麦片
fry up 油炸早餐
soak up 吸收

turn on 打开
grill 烤
kettle 烧水壶
toaster 烤面包机
frying pan 炒锅
crack 打蛋
butter 涂黄油
teabags 茶包
pour 倒入
rigmarole 麻烦
corn flakes 玉米片
pickles 泡菜
peanuts 花生米
congee 粥
gruel 糊状
soya milk 豆浆
dumplings 煎饺
fritters 馅饼

Chapter 31
bane 有害之物
nutritionist 营养师
obesity 肥胖
epidemic 流行传染病
Fish and Chips 炸鱼和薯条
inextricably 密不可分的
Cantonese 广东
appealing 有吸引力的
equate 使相等
authentic 真正的
curry 咖喱菜
adapt to 适应
ubiquitous 无所不在的
kebabs 烤肉
post-modern 后现代
Special Fried Rice 招牌炒饭
Doner Kebab 多纳卡巴
Chicken Tikka Masala 马沙拉鸡
Sweet and Sour Pork 糖醋排骨
Egg Fried Rice 蛋炒饭
Chicken and Sweet Corn Soup
玉米鸡茸汤
Chicken Chow mein 鸡肉炒面

Chicken Chop Suey 鸡肉杂烩
shortage 缺乏
roast 烤
bake 炖
clay pot 陶锅
meat-filled dumplings 水饺
Szchuan Spicy Chicken 四川辣
鸡（宫保鸡丁）
chillies 辣椒
Singapore Noodles 新加坡炒面
prawn crackers 虾片
Peking Duck 北京烤鸭
pancakes 饼
call up 打电话
deliver 外送

Chapter 32
steering wheel 方向盘
quirk 奇特
perplex 困扰
left-hand side 左手边
feudal 封建体制的
switch 转变
reorganisation 改革
left-handed 左撇子
sever ties 脱离关系
doomed 黯淡
reliable 可靠
billions 亿
motor manufacturing industry
汽车制造业
collapse 崩溃
high-end 高级
notorious 声名狼藉
industrial relations 劳资关系
reliable 可靠
abandon 遗弃

Chapter 33
icon 象征
imposing 显眼的，壮丽的
dependable 可靠的
exude 流露出
dinky 小巧的，精致的

turning circle 转弯幅度
U-turn 回转
reverse 倒车
cabbie 出租车司机
landmarks 路标
council 行政机关
hop in 跳上
discourse 高谈阔论
politically reactionary 政治保守
立场
hard-line 强硬
satirical 讽刺性
mock 嘲笑
well-paid 待遇相当高
saloon car 轿车
hail 叫车
moonlight 晚上兼差
on-stream 在生产
mobilise 调派
decisive 果断
cyclone 旋风
geological disaster 地质上的大
灾难
secretive 隐密的

Chapter 34
company lettering 公司名称
self-employed 不受雇于别人的
manual work 劳动工作
carpenter 木匠
plumber 水电工
removals man 搬运工人
have no qualms 不内疚
work ethic 工作伦理
fervently 强烈的
averse 避讳
sexist 性别歧视的
soft on crime 对罪犯手软
caff 早餐店
ambitious 有野心的
upwardly-mobile 积极向上的
private pension 私人退休金
bare midriff 平坦的腹部

bling 金光闪闪的手饰
straight-talking 心直口快的
mince words 装腔作势
have no time for 不喜欢，看不上
Sociology 社会学
Media Studies 传媒
free ride 不劳而获
claim asylum 申请庇护
DSS 社会福利中心
dole 失业救济
housing benefit 住宿福利金
take someone for a ride 耍人
you have to hand it to sb. 崇拜某人
work one's way up 一路往上爬
same-sex couples 同性伴侣

Chapter 35
dramatically 极大地
haute couture 高级女装
cutting-edge 尖端
swinging sixties 摇摆的 60 年代
Punk 朋克
trough 低谷，凹处
resurgent 复兴的
pick up on 捕捉到
in 最流行的风格
reflector 反射镜
multifarious 五花八门的
vibrant 活泼的
bloated impose 强调
conformity 顺从，一致
multi-faceted 多面性
ban 禁止
catwalk 走秀
platform 舞台
fashion show 服装表演
skinny 皮包骨
anorexia 厌食症
bulimia 易饥症
eating disorder 饮食失调症
waif-like 超瘦
off-putting 倒胃口

willowy 瘦瘦高高
chubby 圆乎乎
wax 除毛

Chapter 36
be forgiven for thinking 很自然地就会想到
disaffected 不满的
rebellious 叛逆
sinister 恐怖的
lipstick and eyeliner 嘴膏及眼线
Soul 灵魂乐
The Blues 蓝调
Rock "n" Roll 摇滚乐
Hip-Hop 嘻哈音乐
R&B 节奏蓝调
Techno 强劲摇头
Trance 狂飙电音
metal 金属音乐
Death Metal 重金属音乐
hard-core fans 死忠粉丝
mainstream 主流
conform 依照
rigidity 僵硬的
eccentricity 古怪
mix and match 混合搭配
hence 因此
hoodie 穿着连帽衫的年轻人
feral 野蛮
rock band 乐团
skinhead 剃光头的
shaggy 蓬乱的
braces 背带
hooligan 流氓
mellow 成熟
hippy 嬉皮

Chapter 37
distinguish 分辨
prestigious 享有民望的
linguist 语言学家
colonial administration 殖民地的行政单位
airwaves 广播

authority 威信
charming 迷人的
artificial 人造的
reverence 尊崇
postman 邮差
grocer 杂货商
postie 邮差
bloke 家伙
nasal 鼻音
whining 讨厌的，抱怨的
caricature 讽刺画
impenetrable 无法理解
Cockney 伦敦佬口音
inclusive 包含的，包括的
modified 修饰过的

Chapter 38
hedonism 享乐主义
passé 陈旧的
folk festivals 乡村音乐节
undergo 经历
revival 流行
camping 露营
boybands 男子乐团
divas 天后
quagmire 泥沼
scorching 炎热
indie 独立音乐
alternative 替代
hairy 可怕的，危险的
demanding 要求
bottle off 轰下台

Chapter 39
antics 古怪行为
up-front 直接
courtship 求爱
tongue-tied 口齿不清
self-conscious 思前想后的，心神不宁的
complement 赞美
rejection 拒绝
subtle hints 精心设计的暗示
manoeuvre 花招

arrogant 自傲

aloof 冷淡

chat up 搭讪

springboard 跳板

keep up the pretence 假装一点都不知情

spin round 回头

for a bet 打赌

acne cream 去痘药膏

sad geek 可怜的怪胎

mating ritual 求爱仪式

wink 眨眼

convoluted 旋绕的

fiddle with 玩

Chapter 40

shopaholic 购物狂

browse 浏览

window shopping 逛大街

shopkeeper 小店主

retailer 零售商

hardware 五金行

greengrocer 蔬果商

conglomerate 大型集团

in-bulk 大量批发

convenient 便利

check out 收银台

trunk road 大型道路

aisle 信道

white goods 家电用品

lorry 卡车

loyalty card 积分卡

high street 市中心商店街

ready-made 熟食

disabled bay 残障区

wheelchair 轮椅

boot 后车厢

slide across 滑过

trainers 球鞋

wireless adaptor 无线网卡

stick 棒状

slot in 插入

compatible 兼容

operating system 操作系统

Chapter 41

binge drinking 酗酒

stagger 蹒跚地走

shoot up 滥打

chatter classes 喋喋不休的阶段（尤指喜欢批判当前文化的城市中产自由主义者）

clubber 夜店客

ecstasy 摇头丸

lager 啤酒

dysfunctional 不健康

pub-licensing laws 酒吧管理法令

rite-of-passage 成年典礼

fit 健康

sedentary 懒得动

jogging 慢跑

cycling 骑自行车

recreational drugs 毒品

cannabis 大麻

coke（cocaine）古柯碱

scales 秤

clinically obese 临床上的肥胖

low-carbohydrate 低淀粉质

low-sodium 低盐

Chapter 42

sculpture 雕塑

eclectic 折中精神

short-list 入围名单

prestigious 有威信的

vitality 活力

fiction 小说

non-fiction 非小说

critics 书评家

publications 出版的书籍

blurb 新书推荐广告

recommendations 推荐

book review 书评

blur 模糊

classify 界定

politically-correct 政治正确的

detective 侦探

bestselling 最畅销

Chapter 43

orchestral 管弦乐

chamber concert 室内音乐

patriotic 爱国

composer 作曲家

conductor 指挥

deliberately 有意地

undemanding 要求不高的

overtly 显然的

exclusive 排外的

sell like hot cakes 热卖

anniversary 周年

evocative 唤起

Cello Concerto 大提琴协奏曲

climax 高潮

culminate 压轴

national anthem 国歌

cynic 愤世嫉俗的人

co-opt 同化，吸收

woodwind 木管乐器

percussion 打击乐器

bowed string 弦乐器

pluck 拨响

Chapter 44

rival 竞争对手

thoroughfare 大街

outgrow 超越

showcase 陈列

performing arts 表演类艺术

avant garde 舞台剧

troupe 剧团

magnet 磁石

animosity 嫌隙

in tandem 以纵列，协作

objective 客观的

testing ground 测试场所

programme 节目表

direct 执导

courtroom drama 法庭剧

role 角色

jury 陪审团

guilty 有罪
impromptu 即兴
flyer 传单
Military Tattoo 军乐表演
pipes 管乐器
drums 打击乐器
military bands 军乐队
kilt 苏格兰裙
bagpipes 风笛
tartan 苏格兰方格呢

Chapter 45

peak viewing times 收视率高峰
Eastenders 伦敦东区的人物
fund 出资
glitzy 虚饰的，光亮的
glamorous 亮丽
sentimental 多愁善感
downside 低潮
mawkishness 无味
over-the-top 过于感性夸张
life-affirming 激励人生的
storyline 剧情
gripping 扣人心弦的
banal 陈腐的
appeal to 投入所好
base 卑鄙的
superficial 肤浅
constant 持续
envious 猜忌
petty 心胸狭隘
mean-spirited 坏心眼儿
vengeful 报复心重的
spiteful 怨恨
domestic violence 家庭暴力
fiancée 未婚妻
blockbuster 电影大片
ratings 收视率
moral message 道德意识

Chapter 46

pay-to-view 付费电视台
dedicated to 专门
marathon 马拉松

fun run 趣味赛跑
fulfil 达到
corporate 企业
Royal Box 王家包厢
stadium 体育场
estimate 估计
participants 参加人数
pantomime 童话剧
butler 管家
deep-sea diver 深海潜水者
first and foremost 首先，第一
buzz 感觉
out-of-this-world 腾云驾雾
knackering 很累
training run 练习跑
camaraderie 友谊
sponsor 资助
cancel out 抵消
donation 赞助
cop-out 逃避，妥协
go round the houses 绕圈子
six-pack 一盒6瓶的

Chapter 47

resort 度假胜地
further afield 遥远
culture vulture 文化饥渴者
Grand Tour 大旅行
far-flung 偏远的
palm-fringed 种满棕榈树的
scuba diving 潜水
Great Barrier Reef 大堡礁
safari（东非）徒步考察
grab 订
package tour 套装旅游
gap year 年轻人在上大学前会
花一年的时间一边打工一边环
游世界
lump 将……混在一起
go backpacking 背着背包旅行
budget airline 廉价飞行
triple 三倍的
tenfold 十倍的

skiing break 滑雪假期
city break 城市旅行
overrated 被高估的
holiday camp 度假营
caravan 旅居车
boom 急速发展
round-the-world ticket 环游世
界机票
environmentalists 环境人士
jet engine 飞机引擎
carbon footprint 二氧化碳产生量
Trans-Siberian 横穿西伯利亚
Central Asia 中亚

Chapter 48

humdrum 无聊
confines 疆界，境界
bank-holiday weekend 国定假
日周末
take the waters 玩水
candy floss 棉花糖
rock 硬棒糖
amusement arcade 游乐场
pier 码头
upsurge 回升
family-run 家庭经营
guest house 客房
indulge in 纵情
windsurfing 风帆冲浪
sailing 航行
jetskiing 水上摩托艇
sunbathing 日光浴
trendy 时髦
allure 吸引
resonance 共鸣
rollercoaster 环滑车
helter-skelter 赛车游戏
rug 毯子
swimming costume 泳衣
paddle 踩水
tan 晒成棕褐色
junkie 吸毒者
sun tan lotion 防晒乳液

melanoma 黑瘤

Chapter 49
have a flutter 下一点赌注
scratch card 刮刮卡
dog racing 赛狗
bingo 排五点
casino 赌场
one-armed bandit 老虎机
illegal 非法
darts 飞镖
dominoes 骨牌
inextricably 纠缠的
bookmaker 博彩店
place a bet 下注
breed 饲养
thoroughbred racehorse 纯种
赛马
national hunt 障碍赛
jockey 训马师
jump fence 跳跃障碍
flat racing 平地赛马

lobby（议会的）院外活动集团
good causes 善事
snooker club 撞球场
have a clue 头绪
odds 胜算
rider 骑师
give a tip 给一点提示
odds-on favourite 胜算最大
evens 胜算平平

Chapter 50
acknowledge 认为
a dirty word 脏话
squeamishness 过于拘谨的
uninhibited 不受抑制的
disdain 鄙视
live off 以…为生
look down on 鄙视
prejudice 偏见
show off 炫耀
brag 自夸
boast 夸耀

negotiator 谈判者
strategy 策略
objective 目标
clam up 安静下来
fret 模棱两可
young gun 年轻人
brash 莽撞
self-made men 靠自己努力成功
的人
plain talking 直来直往
qualms 不安
mileage 里程数
MOT 车检
Grand 千
knock off 降价
gonna〔美俚〕= going to 即将
drink 喝，这里指消耗
petrol 汽油
dunno = don't know 不知道
out on a limb 冒很大的险
missus 老婆